Oh, God!
My Skeptical Journey
Through the Bible

James E. Clark

In Loving Memory of Dad, a Giant in Real Life

TABLE OF CONTENTS

INTRODUCTION

According to William Faulkner, "The past is never dead. It's not even past." When it comes to the Bible, this is certainly true. The Bible has played a formative role in the development of Judaism, Christianity, and Islam—major world religions followed by billions, each recognizing, in its own way, the text's historical and sacred importance. Today, it continues to shape the lives, values, and spiritual practices of countless believers around the world.

Sixty-five percent of Americans still identify as Christian, a decline from 90% in the 1980s, but nevertheless a significant majority. And this majority is politically ascendant, with some megachurch pastors amassing vast wealth, religious schools pushing for access to public funds, and a fundamentalist vision of human sexuality gaining influence. For many believers, faith and politics have merged into a combustible stew of nostalgia, cultural identity, and grievance, bound together by a longing for a version of American greatness that never actually existed.

This landscape, for all its complexity and contradictions, is why engaging seriously with the Bible matters. If America can adopt a less strident version of faith, one more open to difference and less absolute, we will all be better able to exercise our freedom of and from religion. Religious people should, of course, engage with modern science and ethics, but it is equally important for secularists to understand their Bible-believing neighbors. That understanding begins with cracking open the Bible.

This book began as a Substack experiment, born of curiosity and the urge to explore the Bible as a critical reader rather than a devout one. I tried to publish a daily reflection on the text, usually tackling three or four chapters at a time, though occasionally powering through genealogies and priestly instructions with greater speed. Much of this book is a refined version of those posts, edited for clarity and conciseness. The

1

observations I offer are my own, developed through deliberate and attentive reading, bolstered by research into the history of biblical books and the political conditions of ancient Palestine. At times I consulted both sympathetic scholars and critical voices to weigh competing interpretations.

My approach was both skeptical and empathetic. I did not presume divine inspiration, but neither did I dismiss the text as entirely bankrupt or outdated. My hope is that readers, both secular and faithful, will find something valuable in this exploration. Several religious readers have told me that my reflections helped them reconnect with their "old friend," even if it highlighted some uncomfortable shortcomings.

The Bible is an extraordinarily complex document: composed over centuries, in multiple languages, by dozens of authors, most of them anonymous. The Old Testament was written almost entirely in ancient Hebrew, while the New Testament was written in ancient Greek. Many New Testament writers relied on the Septuagint, a Greek translation of the Hebrew Scriptures, rather than the original Hebrew texts—likely because their audiences spoke Greek and because they themselves were more fluent in Greek than in Hebrew or Aramaic, the language of Jesus. This means the version of "the Bible" we know today is already layers removed from its original voices.

Unsurprisingly, the text contains hundreds of inconsistencies and contradictions, some trivial, others theologically significant. While most Gospels describe Jesus riding a donkey into Jerusalem, the Gospel of Matthew has him riding two animals simultaneously. More consequentially, the Gospel accounts disagree over who first witnessed the resurrection, the details of Jesus' birth narrative, and the timeline of his ministry.

There are also barriers to understanding even when the text is internally consistent. Chief among these is the affinity for the King James Version, which I used here primarily because it's free from modern copyright constraints. Despite its majestic prose, the KJV is often archaic and inaccurate. For instance,

Isaiah 7:14 in the KJV proclaims that a virgin shall conceive, while more accurate modern translations say a young woman has conceived—a significant distinction. Many superior translations such as the New Revised Standard Version and the Jewish Study Bible now exist, but tradition clings stubbornly to the familiar.

Another major issue is authorship. Despite longstanding tradition, it is now widely understood that Moses did not write the Bible's first five books (the Pentateuch), nor did Matthew write the Gospel of Matthew, nor Paul all the letters attributed to him. Still, we lean on convenient shorthand: "Paul says..." or "Mark writes..."—even when we know better.

Our understanding of the Bible continues to evolve thanks to major archaeological discoveries. The Dead Sea Scrolls, discovered in caves near Qumran (in the West Bank), between 1946 and 1956, contain some of the oldest known manuscripts of the Hebrew Bible, along with apocalyptic, legal, and sectarian texts. They offer crucial insight into the religious diversity of Second Temple Judaism—the world in which Jesus lived.

The Gnostic Gospels, a collection of early Christian writings with mystical and unorthodox themes, were discovered in 1945 near Nag Hammadi, Egypt. These include texts like the *Gospel of Thomas*, which presents Jesus as a wisdom teacher rather than a divine redeemer. A separate text, the *Gospel of Judas*, emerged decades later and was published in 2006. In that version, Judas is not the infamous traitor but Jesus' most trusted disciple. These texts were rejected by early church authorities but reveal how varied and contested early Christianity actually was.

Despite its contradictions, confusion, and some truly disturbing passages—the command to kill a man for gathering wood on the Sabbath, the unsettling blood rituals, the exclusionary purity laws—the Bible remains a source of deep meaning for many. Its calls to love the stranger, care for the poor, and to forgive one's enemies still resonate. At its best, Scripture offers a poetic vision of justice, mercy, and grace. And yet, too often, this vision is eclipsed. The Jesus of the

3

Gospels cared for the poor, challenged the powerful, and warned against storing up earthly treasure, values now dismissed as "woke" by many present-day believers. One suspects they'd have jeered at the Sermon on the Mount, too.

Of course, in America, everyone has the right to believe, or not, as they choose. But we also have the right—really, the responsibility—to challenge the weaponization of faith, especially when it threatens the values that have helped our nation grow more inclusive, just, and free.

Jesus once told a parable about a Sower scattering seed. Not every seed took root, but some did, and bore fruit. Perhaps we too can scatter new seeds: honest engagement, curiosity, and respectful challenge. We don't need to convert believers into atheists, but we can meet them in their own text and raise difficult questions. If we can help religious neighbors resist fear and paranoia and embrace nuance, we might just cultivate something closer to the compassionate ethic Jesus preached— one rooted in humility, justice, and care for the least among us.

And perhaps we might even rise to the apostle Paul's invitation to the Galatians: to act with love, joy, peace, forbearance, kindness, goodness, faithfulness, gentleness, and self-control.

Final notes: This commentary doesn't use traditional footnotes. Instead, I've listed key sources in the "For Further Reading" section and inserted brief attributions where useful. All timelines, historical notes, and theological summaries reflect my understanding of mainstream scholarship, drawn from historians, archaeologists, and biblical critics. I also use the term "God" to refer to the deity of the Israelites, even though the name "Yahweh" is now often used in scholarly and theological contexts.

Now, let's begin.

THE OLD TESTAMENT

"The Bible is not a book for children. It is a text full of
violence, obscenity, and cruelty, and should be approached
with the same critical spirit that we bring to other ancient
texts. To read it without reflection is to mistake mythology
for morality."
Karen Armstrong, *A History of God*

GENESIS

Genesis 1-5

Before there were stars, atoms, or MAGA hats, there was *Genesis*, the creation story where plants exist before sunlight, talking snakes are moral actors, and God needs a week to do what science says took billions of years. God takes on the project with the confidence of a contractor who's never read the manual but insists the work will get done ahead of schedule. And it starts with a bang.

Genesis 1:1-2: "In the beginning God created the heavens and the earth; And the earth was without form, and void; and darkness was upon the face of the deep. And the Spirit of God moved upon the face of the waters."

Genesis continues to outline the divine to-do list in a majestic, if sometimes baffling, sequence:

- **Day 1:** Light is created. Not from the sun, just light.
- **Day 2:** God adds the "firmament" (essentially a dome) to divide the waters above from the waters below.

- **Day 3:** Dry land, grass, herbs, and fruit trees appear.
- **Day 4:** Now, the sun and stars are created, after the light they produce and the plants that need it to live and reproduce. Without the sun, what does a "day" even mean?
- **Day 5:** Sea creatures and birds emerge, including "great whales."
- **Day 6:** God creates land animals and finally humankind, saying: "Let us make man in our image."
- **Day 7:** God rests, presumably exhausted, although the necessity of PTO days for an all-powerful being remains unclear.

It's no surprise that the imagery of Genesis has captivated generations. You can practically feel the salt mist as God hovers over the chaotic waters. This is the God of thunder, rock and roll, and cosmic authority.

But why does God need six days, anyway? Couldn't He have snapped His fingers and been done? Or taken millions of years, aligning things with geological and evolutionary evidence? Also, what about that plural, "Let us make man in our image"? Who's "us"? Is this a hint of the Trinity, a holdover from earlier polytheism, or just a grammatical glitch?

And then there's what is conspicuously absent: no volcanoes, tectonic plates, undersea rift zones, or bacteria. God's creation list seems to include only things recognizable to the average Bronze Age herdsman. The omission of microbes alone should give pause to anyone hoping to square Genesis with modern science.

If taken as a metaphor, Genesis 1 paints a vivid picture. But if you insist it's a scientific explanation of the universe's origins...good luck with that.

Genesis 2:7 reboots the creation account, saying God "formed man of the dust of the ground, and breathed into his nostrils the breath of life." Then He plants a garden, throws in the Tree of Life and the Tree of Knowledge of Good and Evil, and sets Adam loose. Animals come next—formed after Adam this time—and finally, a woman, constructed from Adam's rib while he sleeps. No name yet, though.

This version directly contradicts Genesis 1, where animals came first and male and female were created together. But the ancient authors didn't appear to mind. They weren't writing scientific chronology; they were spinning an origin myth. The contradiction between "Let us make man in our image" (Gen. 1:26) and "formed man from dust" (Gen. 2:7) is often brushed aside by claiming the second chapter explains the first. That connection isn't made by the text itself, however.

Then there's the infamous fruit incident. Still unnamed, the woman chats with a snake about whether she should eat from the Tree of Knowledge. The snake, which is not identified as the devil, just a talking snake, says yes. She eats first, then Adam does too. Suddenly they realize they're naked, grab fig leaves for cover, and try to hide. God goes looking for them, apparently unaware of their location, and asks Adam, "Where art thou?" This must have been a super embarrassing question for God to ask. After all, he had just created the universe but then found himself unable to find its only male inhabitant.

When confronted, Adam could have taken responsibility; but instead, he blames Eve: "The woman whom thou gavest to be with me, she gave me of the tree, and I did eat" (Gen. 3:12). That's a two-for-one deflection: Adam blames Eve and implies it's God's fault for giving her to him in the first place. And God, instead of challenging this cowardly evasion, goes along with it. He directs his punishment first at the snake, then at Eve—telling her she'll suffer painful childbirth and be ruled over by her husband—before finally turning to Adam.

So now we've got a divine hierarchy of blame: Snake tempts → Woman eats → Man follows → Woman gets cursed → Man gets a warning. God may be all-knowing, but in this moment, he's surprisingly quick to side with the guy who just threw everyone else under the bus. Finally, He names Eve and gives them animal-skin clothing (a curious gesture of compassion from someone who just damned the species).

And here's the kicker: God says, "The man is become as one of us, to know good and evil," and promptly boots them from Eden, stationing Cherubim and a flaming sword to keep them out. Again, with the "us." By this point, God has already made several questionable choices. He created beings without knowledge of good and evil, placed a forbidden tree within reach, and allowed a smooth-talking serpent to wander (slither) around. Then He bailed, returned to find His creation predictably disobedient, and punished them forever. He should have known better.

Post-Eden, Adam and Eve produce two sons: Cain the farmer and Abel the shepherd. Both bring offerings to God who prefers Abel's lamb to Cain's crops. Stung by rejection, Cain kills his brother. When God asks where Abel is, Cain replies with the famously misused line, "Am I my brother's keeper?," not as a noble call to compassion, but as a sarcastic dodge from a guilty man. Far from a model of empathy, it's a murderer wriggling out of accountability.

God punishes Cain by cursing the ground so it will no longer yield crops for him and condemning him to be "a fugitive and a vagabond." Cain protests that this is more than he can bear and God responds by placing a mark on him—an ancient version of diplomatic immunity—and promising to avenge him sevenfold if anyone harms him. Then Cain somehow finds a wife (from where, exactly?) and starts a family.

Genesis 5 offers a genealogy of Adam's descendants. It's the chapter of "begats." Adam begat Seth, Seth begat Enos, Enos begat Cainan, and on it goes. The lifespans are absurd. Seth lives 912 years, Methuselah clocks in at 969, and even the short-lived Enoch makes it to 365. Kids don't show up until these patriarchs are over a hundred, because biblical biology is on its own calendar.

It was this list that 17th-century Archbishop James Ussher used to date the creation of the world to exactly 4004 BCE, putting the earth at about 5,650 years old. A disturbingly large number of people still believe this. That would make Earth younger than Stonehenge, the walls of Jericho, and thousands of other objects dug up all over the world: pottery, reed baskets, woven textiles, carved figurines, jewelry, tools, weapons, and even early written tablets. Meanwhile, scientists estimate the earth is 4.5 billion years old. But for the biblical literalists, fossils are just elaborate tricks planted by Satan to test your faith.

At this point, God is 0 for 4 with humans: Adam is weak, Eve is naïve, Cain is a murderer, and Abel is dead. And the Bible doesn't even blink at the question of where Cain's wife came from. But fear not, when we pick things up in Genesis 6-8, God unveils His next plan to save humanity: drown almost everyone and start over with a 600-year-old man, a floating zoo, and a highly suspect marine engineering project.

Genesis 6-8

Genesis 6:4 casually drops a bombshell: "There were giants in the earth in those days; and also after that, when the sons of God came in unto the daughters of men, and they bare children to them, the same became mighty men which were of old, men of renown." Giants? Divine-human hybrids? This sounds more like Greek mythology than Hebrew theology, but the text offers no elaboration. The writers just tossed out a line about demigods and moved on. No wonder this passage has fueled everything from *Book of Enoch* speculation to David Koresh's apocalyptic visions of "mighty men."

God is displeased with humanity's unspecified wickedness and decides to wipe the slate clean. But He has a soft spot for Noah, "a just man and perfect in his generations" (Gen. 6:9). God commands him to build an ark, giving him detailed specs and clear instructions: two of every sort of bird, cattle, and creeping thing—male and female, just to be clear. In case Noah wasn't familiar with basic reproductive biology, God reiterates several times the importance of pairing.

Then God throws in a curveball: actually, take seven pairs of every clean animal and just one pair of the unclean. No definitions are offered; presumably Bronze Age readers just knew which animals made the cut.

So Noah, 600 years old, gathers his family, consisting of his unnamed wife, sons Shem, Ham, and Japheth, and their unnamed wives, and loads the ark. Then the rains come: 40 days and 40 nights of deluge, followed by 150 days of global flooding. Eventually, the ark comes to rest on Mount Ararat (modern eastern Turkey). Noah sends out a dove, which returns with an olive leaf in a sign of hope that is one of the Bible's most enduring symbols.

When the floodwaters recede, Noah emerges, builds an altar, and makes a burnt offering to God. In response, Genesis 8:21 tells us: "The Lord smelled a sweet savor, and the Lord said in his heart, I will not again curse the ground any more for man's sake; for the imagination of man's heart is evil from his youth..." That's a mixed message if ever there was one: humanity is inherently wicked, but God won't wipe us out again, perhaps out of resignation more than mercy.

The story's imagery is undeniably powerful: a planet drowning, a creaking ark full of anxious animals, a dove with an olive branch. It's no wonder this narrative echoes through literature and art. Henri Barbusse, in *Le Feu*, likened the horrors of trench warfare to those of Noah's flood. Russell Crowe starred in a Hollywood epic version. John Cusack navigated an apocalypse in *2012* aboard a high-tech ark. Even Peter Gabriel—of the band Genesis, no less—sang a haunting track imagining future cataclysm (*The Flood*).

But the logistical absurdities pile up fast. Are we to believe a geriatric man and a few relatives collected every species of animal on Earth? Did penguins march from Antarctica? Did pandas bring their own bamboo? Were African and Asian elephants both included, or did post-Flood evolution just sort that out? Were there dinosaurs on the ark? And how did the lions resist eating the gazelles for months?

11

Theologically, it's just as troubling. God creates the world, gives humans free will, then is shocked—*shocked!*—when they misbehave. His solution? A global extinction-level event, followed by a vow not to do it again, even though nothing fundamental had changed. The whole thing feels more like a divine tantrum than a moral lesson.

And let's spare a thought for the animals who survived the flood, only to be immediately sacrificed by Noah as a burnt offering. After enduring chaos and captivity, their reward was the "sweet savor" of their own demise. If they'd known what was coming, they might have preferred the rain.

Genesis 9-15

We begin Genesis 9 with God commanding Noah and his sons to be fruitful, multiply, and replenish the earth. Who are they to be fruitful with? Everyone just drowned in the flood, right? Most of the rest of Genesis 9 discusses God's covenant with Noah, "everlasting between God and every living creature of all flesh that is upon the earth" (Gen 9:16). We then move on to the post-ark Noah, who drinks too much wine and passes out. Son Ham "sees his father's nakedness," and his brothers Shem and Japheth cover their father. Noah is furious with Ham, cursing him and promising that God would enlarge the importance of his brothers. Then Noah dies at age 950.

Noah seems to make too much of a perceived transgression from his son. Ham didn't cause Noah to drink to excess and alerted his brothers to Dad's condition. So, I'm not sure what the sin was.

Genesis 10 provides an exhaustive and painful-to-read genealogy and then moves on to the Tower of Babel. The descendants of Noah journeyed east to Shinar and stumbled into a major construction project already underway—a tower meant to reach the heavens. At this point, the whole world spoke a single language, which should have made coordination easy. But God sees this unity as a threat and in Genesis 11:7 says, "Let us" (there's that plural again) "go down, and there confound their language, that they may not understand one another's speech." What's never explained is *why* God would object to a unified human language. Wouldn't effective communication have helped people understand His will? Instead, God deliberately introduces confusion—sabotaging clarity and scattering the people—just when it seemed they were finally able to work together. It's an odd move for a deity supposedly intent on spreading a universal message.

Another lengthy ancestry lesson follows before we reach Abram: Shem begat Arphaxad, who begat Salah, and so on. Life expectancy appears to have decreased, with most of Shem's ancestors only living to the age of 200 or so. There is no word on why people's lifespan has declined from 900 years to mere hundreds, which you would think might merit some discussion.

Abram travels with Lot (his brother's son) and wife Sarai to Canaan, when God promises in Genesis 12-13 to bless Abram and make his name great, to bless those who bless Abram and curse those who curse him. Abram hightails it to Egypt to escape the famine, but realizing that Sarai is a hottie, he makes her promise to say that she is his sister. Pharaoh, unaware that Sarai is in an LTR, takes a fancy to her and has her move into the palace. God sends plagues to Egypt as retribution for Sarai giving herself to Pharaoh, who complains that Abram never told him Sarai was already married. With this mix-up sorted, Abram and Sarai flee Egypt, likely leaving a confused Pharaoh in their wake.

In Genesis 13, Abram returns to Canaan, and a conflict over grazing rights leads him and Lot to part ways. Lot settles near Sodom, while Abram is promised all of Canaan by the Lord, along with descendants as numerous as the dust of the earth. In Genesis 14, a war breaks out between four eastern kings and five Canaanite kings, during which Lot is taken prisoner. Abram mounts a swift rescue, freeing Lot and recovering the plunder, and they return to Sodom as heroes.

In Genesis 15, God reasserts His covenant with Abram, promising to give him control over the River Euphrates, the

Kenites, Kenizzites, Kadmonites, Hittites, Perizzites, and Rephaim. In Gen. 15:9–10, God instructs Abram to construct an offering of a heifer, a she goat, a ram, a turtledove, and a young pigeon. If a modern evangelical were asked to make a sacrificial offering like that, they would probably denounce it as sorcery.

Genesis 16-25

In Genesis 16, we learn that although Abram and Sarai cannot conceive, the prospects for a child would improve if Abram hooked up with their Egyptian handmaid, Hagar. Abram obliges—was this plural marriage or just sanctioned infidelity? Either way, Hagar becomes pregnant, which upsets Sarai, who clearly hadn't thought things through. The situation deteriorates so badly that Hagar flees into the desert, where she's approached by an angel who in Genesis 16:9, tells her to "return to thy mistress, and submit thyself under her hands." The angel clearly missed the workshop on empathy, informing Hagar that her son will be a "wild man; his hand will be against every man, and every man's hand against him." Hagar nonetheless returns and bears a son, Ishmael, when Abram is 86 years old (four score and six).

In Genesis 17, God makes a formal covenant with Abram, promising that he will be "a father of many nations." To seal the deal, God introduces circumcision as the official mark of the covenant, because when it comes to divine contracts, body modification is in. God also changes Abram's name to Abraham and Sarai's to Sarah and assures Abraham that Sarah, at 90, will bear a child. Abraham, 99 at the time, understandably finds this laughable. But God insists, hands him a blue pill, and says, "Trust me, this'll do the trick."

Then comes a divine side plot: God and Abraham discuss the impending destruction of Sodom and Gomorrah, where "the sin is very grievous." Abraham, worried about collateral damage, negotiates with God: "Wilt thou also destroy the righteous with the wicked?" he asks in Gen. 18:23. God says he'll spare the cities if even ten righteous people are found there. Spoiler: they're not.

Genesis 19 spells out the nature of the sin, and it's not genocide, incest, or enslaving people. Rather, when two angels arrive at Lot's house in Sodom, a local mob demands that the visitors be brought out to be gang raped. Lot blanches at this request, but he has Plan B in mind and offers his virgin daughters to the crowd: "Do ye to them as is good in your eyes." I am not making this up. Fortunately, the angels step in, pull Lot back inside, blind the mob, and then hustle Lot and his family out of the city with a warning: don't look back. Lot's wife glances back and is turned into a pillar of salt—no explanation given, no second chances.

Afterward, Lot and his two daughters take shelter in a cave. Convinced they're the last people on Earth (?), the daughters get Lot drunk and sleep with him on successive nights. The result: two sons, Moab and Ben-Ammi. These scenes alone are probably why the Bible gets flagged in middle school libraries.

Let's pause for a moment on Sodom. Are we really meant to believe this city was overrun by gay rapist mobs lying in wait to assault every passerby? If true, that *would* be a problem.

So many questions, so much divine dysfunction. If God could make Sarah fertile at will, why the detour with Hagar? Was Ishmael just a narrative filler? Also, wasn't there already a covenant with Noah? Say what you will, though, God was right about one thing: Abraham did end up being the foundation for several major religions.

Genesis 20 finds Abraham and Sarah back on the road, this time in Gerar. They meet King Abimelech, and Abraham, reprising his greatest hit from Gen. 12, tells him Sarah is his sister. Again. The king takes Sarah into his house, but God appears to Abimelech in a dream and warns him off. The king, more righteous than the patriarch, apologizes, compensates Abraham generously, and restores Sarah. Meanwhile, God lifts a divine embargo on childbirth He had imposed on the women of the region.

In Genesis 21, Sarah conceives and bears Isaac, sparking a celebration. But Sarah still holds a grudge against Hagar—despite having created the whole mess—and demands that Abraham send her and Ishmael away. Abraham spinelessly complies and hands them a single bottle of water before exiling them to the desert. Hagar, expecting death, lays Ishmael under a bush and walks away weeping: "Let me not see the death of the child." God intervenes, conjures a well, and saves them both.

Oddly, Ishmael isn't even named in this sad tale: He's just "the lad" or "the child," as if the writers couldn't bring themselves to fully acknowledge Abraham's cruelty. One suspects they knew how bad this looked.

I don't wish to be indelicate…but given Sarah's hookups with Pharaoh and Abimelech, how confident are we about Isaac's paternity? Still, hats off to the 90-year-old Sarah, who is still so stunning that kings can't resist her. She's aging like Helen Mirren on a fine wine tour.

Later, there's a dispute between Abraham and Abimelech over a well. Unlike so much else in Genesis, it ends peacefully, and they plant a tree to mark the occasion. Abimelech was probably just glad Abraham didn't try to pawn off Sarah as his sister again.

Then comes Genesis 22: the infamous command to sacrifice Isaac. God tells Abraham to take his only son (what about Ishmael?) and offer him as a burnt offering. Abraham, without protest, takes Isaac and some servants, builds a pyre, and ties Isaac to it. Isaac, no dummy, asks, "Where is the lamb for the burnt offering?" Abraham replies, "God will provide." Just as Abraham raises the knife, an angel calls out to stop him. A ram appears, and Isaac gets swapped out, followed by a really tense ride back to camp for father and son.

Whether this is a story of devotion or abuse, it's not exactly an uplifting parenting moment. For believers, it's a tale of faith. For skeptics, it's a cautionary story about blind obedience. Either way, it leaves an aftertaste as bitter as Lot's wife's pillar-of-salt finale.

The comparison to Greek mythology is also apt. In the story of Iphigenia, Artemis swaps in a deer to spare the girl from sacrifice: same basic plot structure, different pantheon. It's a familiar dramatic device, though hardly one that improves God's character arc.

Genesis 23 records Sarah's death at age 127. Abraham, now 137, buys a cave and buries her near Hebron. But he's not done matchmaking or procreating. In Genesis 24, he sends a servant to find a wife for Isaac. Rebekah agrees to marry Isaac sight unseen after being lavishly adorned with jewelry. In Gen. 25, Abraham marries Keturah, covertly gets God to provide some more Doc Yahweh's Little Performance Poppers, and fathers six more children. The man was a machine.

Rebekah, like Sarah before her, can't conceive until God steps in. She ends up with twins. God tells her in Gen. 25:23: "Two nations are in thy womb…and the elder shall serve the younger." Spoiler: sibling rivalry incoming.

Genesis 26-31

Rebekah delivers twins, first Esau, who comes out red and hairy like a "garment" (Gen. 25:25), and then Jacob, who's clinging to his brother's heel like an annoying younger sibling. Esau grows up to be a rugged hunter and the favorite of his father, Isaac. Jacob, a homebody, is favored by his mother. One day, Esau comes home famished and trades away his birthright to Jacob for a bowl of lentil soup. Good trade?

Then a famine hits. God instructs Isaac and Rebekah to go to Egypt, but they never make it. Instead, they stop in Gerar and encounter King Abimelech. Yes, him again. Isaac copies his dad Abraham's favorite move and claims Rebekah is his sister. But Abimelech sees through it and promises to kill anyone who touches her.

The rationale seems to be that jealous locals might kill Isaac to steal his wife but would leave him alone if she were just his sister. Really? If the locals were that murderous, would a marital technicality matter? And let's be honest: this isn't about preserving Rebekah's honor, it's about protecting Isaac's neck.

Despite the drama, Isaac thrives, planting crops and digging wells. Abimelech, threatened by his growing influence, tells him to leave and take his "sister" with him. Isaac settles in a nearby valley, finds more water, and names the city Shibah (Beersheba). Meanwhile, Esau, now forty, marries two Hittite women, Judith and Bashemath, much to the displeasure of his parents, who clearly wanted him avoid alliances with the local Canaanite tribes. But the stage is now set for a family meltdown and a tale of trickery worthy of *Gilligan's Island*, beginning in Genesis 27.

Isaac, now blind and near death, tells Esau in Gen. 27:4: "Make me savory meat such as I love and bring it to me, that I may eat; that my soul may bless thee before I die." Esau grabs his bow and heads out, but Rebekah overhears the plan. She springs into action, calling Jacob and preparing a goat-based imitation meal. She even covers Jacob in goatskins, so he feels like his hairy brother.

Jacob presents himself to Isaac, claiming to be Esau. Isaac is skeptical—he questions how the meal came so quickly and asks to feel his son's skin. Still, he's fooled and delivers the blessing in Gen. 27:29: "Let people serve thee, and nations bow down to thee; be lord over thy brethren…"

Just then, Esau returns. He's devastated to learn his blessing has been stolen. He begs Isaac for another, but Isaac replies in Gen. 27:40: "By thy sword shalt thou live…and thou shalt serve thy brother…" Furious, Esau mutters, "When my father dies, I'll kill Jacob." Rebekah hears and sends Jacob packing to Haran until Esau cools down.

This whole mix-up over birthrights and blessings serves as a plot device to get Jacob on the road. But why does Isaac honor a blessing obtained through deception? Can't he just void it? Apparently not, as Isaac insists there's no going back.

This story parallels that of Cain and Abel. In both, the younger brother wrongs the older (Cain kills Abel; Jacob steals from Esau), and both perpetrators are shielded (Cain by God's mark, Jacob by Isaac's passivity and Rebekah's scheming). Genesis 25:23 is fulfilled: "the elder shall serve the younger."

Esau, still livid, marries a Canaanite woman out of spite. Meanwhile, Jacob heads toward Haran. One night, he rests with a rock as a pillow and dreams of a ladder stretching to heaven, with angels ascending and descending (Gen. 28:12). He wakes up, probably with a sore neck, and names the site Bethel. He promises that if God brings him back safely, he'll give a tenth of all he gains.

Finally, Jacob reaches Haran and chats with some shepherds about watering sheep. Riveting stuff. Then Rachel appears, Laban's hot younger daughter. She leads Jacob to her father's house, where he also meets Leah, her less hot older sister.

Jacob falls for Rachel, and Laban strikes a deal: work seven years, and Rachel is his. The years pass, and a wedding is held—but surprise! Laban sneaks Leah into the marital bed. In the morning, Jacob realizes he's been duped and protests in Gen. 29:25: "What is this thou hast done unto me? Did I not serve thee for Rachel?" Laban shrugs: it's local custom to marry off the eldest first. But if Jacob still wants Rachel, he can marry her too so long as he signs up for another seven years of labor.

Leah gets a fast start in the baby race, producing four sons in a row: Reuben, Simeon, Levi, and Judah. Rachel, still childless and fuming, hands over her maid Bilhah to Jacob, who obligingly sires Dan and Naphtali. Leah, not to be outdone, gives him her maid Zilpah, who turns out Gad and Asher. Then Leah's eldest, Reuben, brings home some mandrakes (mmm…mandrakes), and Leah trades them to Rachel for more quality time with Jacob. Result: two more sons, Issachar and Zebulun, plus a daughter, Dinah. Finally, Rachel herself has a son, Joseph. Much later, she dies giving birth to the twelfth and final one, Benjamin.

Summary of Jacob's Twelve Sons:
- With Leah: Reuben, Simeon, Levi, Judah, Issachar, Zebulun (plus Dinah)

19

- With Bilhah (Rachel's maid): Dan, Naphtali
- With Zilpah (Leah's maid): Gad, Asher
- With Rachel: Joseph, Benjamin

Eventually, Jacob tells Laban it's time to return to Canaan. Laban agrees and offers all the speckled goats as Jacob's wages, then promptly removes them from the flock to shortchange him. But Jacob has a trick: he peels striped patterns into sticks and puts them in front of the goats while they are mating. The result? Speckled offspring. Genesis 30:37 lays it out—striped wood equals speckled goats. Who says the Bible isn't a science textbook?

Jacob's dream of the ladder implies a divine travel system, though we've seen angels appear anywhere without much explanation. Also, Jacob's promise to tithe raises questions. Shouldn't God dictate the terms? And how exactly does one deliver payment to God? This only makes sense if you're a priest looking for a divine excuse to collect dues. Also, did ancient people really use rocks for pillows?

As for Laban and Jacob, poetic justice is served, with Jacob, the deceiver, getting deceived. But Laban's schemes entangle Leah, Rachel, and their handmaids in a patriarchal mess. Did Jacob not notice he was sleeping with the wrong sister? He comes off as either dim or someone with a serious kink. He's manipulated by both wives and lets himself be a pawn in their feud.

Eventually, Jacob sees Laban's attitude darken (Gen. 31:2), and an angelic dream tells him it's time to go. Jacob gathers his family and slips away—but not before Rachel swipes some household idols. Three days later, Laban catches up at Mount Gilead. God warns him in Gen. 31:24 to "speak not to Jacob either good or bad," a lukewarm divine directive. We are then given a useful time check: Jacob has been with Laban for twenty years (Gen. 31:38).

But Laban ignores the warning and confronts Jacob, fuming about the missing figurines. Jacob, unaware of Rachel's theft, invites Laban to search the camp. Rachel claims she's menstruating and hides the idols in her saddlebag. The two men eventually agree to a truce, sealing it with a pile of stones as witness. With that, Jacob journeys on toward a fateful reunion with the brother he betrayed.

Genesis 32-36

Jacob anticipates trouble and sends an advance party, which reports that Esau is on his way with 400 men. Is this a welcoming party or a warband? In Gen. 32:11, Jacob prays to God to be delivered "from the hand of my brother, from the hand of Esau, for I fear him..." That night, near the ford at Jabbok, Jacob wrestles with a mysterious stranger and throws out his hip in the process. When Jacob demands a name, the stranger offers only a cryptic reply and declares that Jacob shall now be called Israel, meaning "he who struggles with God." Jacob believes he has seen God face-to-face and survived. The story is ambiguous—is this God, an angel, or some symbolic struggle? The text never says, which gives the episode a mythic, dreamlike quality. Sometimes, less is more.

In the morning, Jacob divides his caravan into two groups so that if one is attacked, the other might escape. But it turns out to be unnecessary. Esau sees his long-lost brother and races to embrace him. Still, some tension lingers. When Esau offers to assign some of his men to accompany Jacob's caravan, Jacob declines—thanks, but no thanks.

Trouble soon returns. Dinah, Jacob's daughter with Leah, is raped by Shechem, son of the local chieftain Hamor. Hamor, trying to clean up the mess, approaches Jacob and his sons, saying (Gen. 34:8): "The soul of my son Shechem longeth for your daughter: I pray you to give her him to wife." Jacob says little, but his sons, Simeon and Levi, plot revenge. They agree to the marriage on one condition: every male in Hamor's tribe must be circumcised. Believing this will cement an alliance and give rapist Shechem a get out-of-jail-free card, the men agree. But while they're still recovering—circumcision for adult males being, shall we say, no small thing—Simeon and Levi attack, killing the men and looting the city.

Jacob is furious, not over the violence per se, but because it might provoke retaliation from nearby tribes. His sons fire back: "Should he deal with our sister as with a harlot?" For once in Genesis, someone stands up for a woman's honor, although it's not the father, but the brothers. Good for them. Still, it's fair to ask: did every man in the town deserve to die?

The journey continues. At Beth-el, the site of Jacob's "stairway to heaven" vision, he orders a spiritual housecleaning by purging the camp of foreign gods and idols. The "terror of God" keeps neighboring towns from interfering. God reiterates Jacob's new identity: Israel. Along the way, Deborah, Rachel's nurse, dies, and then Rachel herself dies giving birth to her second son. In her final breath, she names him Ben-Oni ("son of my sorrow"), but Jacob overrules her and renames him Benjamin. In a final act of control, he refuses her last request and claims the naming rights for himself.

More family drama follows. Jacob's father, Isaac, dies at 180. His oldest son Reuben, not content with waiting his turn, sleeps with his father's concubine Bilhah, a definite no-no (she is, after all, his stepmother). This power move will later cost Reuben his birthright. Genesis 36 follows with one of those long genealogy lists, this one covering the descendants of Esau, the Edomites, who become persistent rivals of Jacob's tribe.

Backing up slightly, Jacob's earlier flight from Laban in Gen. 31 contains themes that will echo in the next major saga—that of Joseph. Like Jacob, Joseph will have dreams. Like Rachel, Joseph will use trickery (framing Benjamin for theft). Jacob's story ends not with his tail between his legs, as when he fled Esau, but with wealth, a large family, divine approval, and a new name.

The groundwork is now laid for one of the most vivid narratives in the Old Testament, a story of dreams, betrayal, fake deaths, and political intrigue. Joseph, the favored son with the technicolor coat, is about to take center stage.

Genesis 37-50

In Genesis 37, we are introduced to Israel's favorite son, Joseph (he and Benjamin were fathered with the love of Israel's life, Rachel). Israel gives Joseph a "coat of many colors," triggering his brothers' intense jealousy and resentment. Joseph, unable to read the room, makes matters worse by telling everyone about his dreams: in one, his brothers' sheaves of corn bow to his; in another, eleven stars bow down to him. (It's unclear how stars bow, but the symbolism wasn't lost on his family.)

When the brothers are out in the fields, they first throw Joseph into a pit, but then, seeing a caravan of Ishmaelites, decide to sell him into slavery instead. They bring back his blood-smeared coat to convince their father that a wild beast has devoured his favorite son.

Back in Canaan, the present was tough. Judah, one of Israel's sons, instructs his son Onan to impregnate Tamar, the widow of his deceased son Er. Onan is not keen on the arrangement and famously "spilled his seed on the ground," prompting God to strike him dead. Tamar, in turn, disguises herself as a prostitute and seduces Judah himself. When Judah finds out that his daughter-in-law is pregnant, he orders her to be burned alive—until he realizes the child is his, at which point he backs off. Tamar bears twins: Pharez and Zarah. Now that this awkward interlude is behind us, the story shifts back to the somehow more coherent tale of Joseph.

Joseph has been sold to Potiphar, captain of Pharaoh's guard, whose randy wife tries to seduce him. Joseph refuses her advances, but she accuses him of assault, and he lands in prison. There, he meets a butler and a baker with troubling dreams. Joseph interprets the dreams: the butler will be restored to his position, but the baker will be executed. And sure enough, three days later, Pharaoh reinstates the butler and hangs the baker.

Two years later, Pharaoh dreams of seven fat cows devoured by seven ugly, lean ones, followed by seven full heads of grain swallowed up by seven withered ones. None of his advisors can interpret the dreams, but the butler finally remembers Joseph. Brought before Pharaoh, Joseph explains: seven years of abundance will be followed by seven years of famine. As Genesis 41:29–30 puts it: "Behold, there come seven years of great plenty throughout all the land of Egypt. And there shall arise after them seven years of famine, and all the plenty shall be forgotten in the land of Egypt, and the famine shall consume the land."

Impressed, Pharaoh appoints Joseph to oversee food storage and distribution. He becomes second-in-command and is given Asenath, the daughter of a high priest, as his wife. Thanks to Joseph's vision, Egypt stockpiles grain in preparation for the impending disaster.

Meanwhile, in Canaan, Israel's family is starving. He sends ten sons, except Benjamin and the "dead" Joseph, to Egypt to buy grain. They bow before Joseph (like the stars or sheaves of corn that Joseph saw in his dreams) but Joseph keeps his identity secret. Claiming to suspect them of spying, Joseph detains Simeon as a hostage and demands they return with Benjamin as proof of their honesty. He fills their bags with grain, secretly returns their payment, and sends them home.

Eventually, food runs out again (they seem oddly unbothered by Simeon's imprisonment), and the brothers return to Egypt with Benjamin. Joseph hosts them at a feast and sends them away with more grain, this time planting a silver cup in Benjamin's sack. When accused of theft, the brothers protest, and Judah pleads for mercy, confessing their earlier betrayal of Joseph. Moved, Joseph reveals his identity, and they have a heartfelt reunion.

The brothers return for Israel, who journeys triumphantly to Goshen, in Egypt, with 66 family members (see Genesis 46:8–27 for the headcount). Despite its betrayal and dysfunction, the story has a "feel-good" arc, familiar to many via Sunday school or *Joseph and the Amazing Technicolor Dreamcoat*. Most biblically literate folks probably think the tale ends here. Honestly, I wish it did.

But Genesis insists there's more. As Genesis 47:13 makes clear, "there was no bread in all the land...all the land of Egypt and of Canaan fainted by reason of the famine." When the money was gone, Joseph accepted livestock in exchange for food. When the animals ran out, he acquired land. Genesis 47:20 reports: "And Joseph bought all the land in Egypt for Pharaoh; for the Egyptians sold every man his field, because the famine prevailed over them: so the land became Pharaoh's."

Joseph and Pharaoh exploited famine to consolidate wealth and power. As a condition for continued survival, the people had to surrender a fifth of their harvest to Pharaoh. Unlike the vague ten percent Jacob once pledged to God, Pharaoh knew exactly what to do with land, labor, and grain.

Genesis ends with the death of Israel 17 years later, at age 147. He blesses his sons (symbolizing the twelve tribes) and insists on being buried in Canaan. Joseph dies a relative spring chicken at the age of 110 and is then embalmed and placed in a coffin in Egypt.

Joseph's saga spans 14 chapters, far more than any other Old Testament story. Creation? Two chapters. The Flood? Three. Sodom's destruction? Just one. Joseph's story is a page-turner, and the Webber-Rice musical tells it with great fidelity, but not without some revisions.

For one, the musical skips the *Series of Unfortunate Sperm Events* of Genesis 38 where Onan spilled his "seed" on the ground instead of into Tamar as ordered. This was probably a wise omission. The musical also compresses the repeated food-buying trips into a single encounter, a change that improves the narrative. But most glaringly, it omits Joseph's role in transforming an entire population into Pharaoh's serfs. It's no surprise this part got left out. But it's a shame that such a consequential aspect of the story is often whitewashed. Despite Joseph's admirable traits—vision, forgiveness, administrative skill—he ultimately served elite interests and secured his family's prosperity at the expense of the Egyptian people.

EXODUS

Exodus 1-4

We start the action after several centuries have passed. Joseph's clan has multiplied to the point that they are a nuisance to the Egyptian pharaoh, and the Israelites are put to work. Exodus 1:14: "And they made their lives bitter with hard bondage in mortar and in brick and in all manner of service in the field..."

Not content to work them to death, the pharaoh instructs a pair of midwives to kill any Hebrew boys while allowing the girls to live. Midwives Shiphrah and Puah are called to account by Pharaoh after not following through with this murderous order, but they demur by saying Hebrew women give birth so easily there is no time to kill them. Pharaoh is not amused and orders all his people to kill their baby boys and spare only the girls. He is specific that all boys, not just Hebrew boys, must be "cast into the river." How does this address the problem? If his order were followed, he would reduce the native Egyptian population; if it were flouted, he would risk rebellion. This makes no sense.

Anyway, we cut to the birth of a boy to a couple from the house of Levi. Ninety days after the birth, they cannot hide the child any longer and release the boy downstream in the Nile in a basket.

Pharaoh's daughter happens to be washing herself in the river at that exact moment (did Egyptian royalty really wash up in the river)? and has her housekeeper fish out the hapless boy, who she takes pity on and raises as her own. I see a parallel with the tale of Hagar, who could not bear to see her son die, hiding him in a bush. As with Ishmael, little Moses is surely going to die after being placed in the Nile with its birds of prey and crocodiles, but again, a higher power intervenes to save the child.

We now fast forward: Moses is an adult and witnesses an Egyptian abusing an Israelite. Moses then kills the Egyptian and hides the body in the sand. With a bounty on his head, Moses flees to Midian, where he impresses the local priest, Jethro, and is given Jethro's daughter, Zipporah, in marriage. She bears him a son, Gershom, and Moses reflects that he is "a stranger in a strange land," belonging neither to his past nor fully to his new life. Meanwhile, the pharaoh dies, and God suddenly remembers His earlier promises to the Israelites. He has "heard their groaning" and decides to act. But if God is omnipresent, why did it take Him so long to notice their suffering?

Moses is with his flock when he sees a burning bush and hears the voice of God, who orders him to lead the Israelites out of Egyptian bondage. Ex. 3:14: "And God said unto Moses, I AM THAT I AM: and he said, Thus shalt thou say unto the children of Israel..." God knows this is a really big ask, but he turns Moses' walking staff into a snake, and temporarily infects his hand with leprosy, saying he can use these miracles to convince others about his mandate. God also tells Moses that he can take along his more articulate brother, Aaron, to help deliver His message to the Israelites and to the new pharaoh. God also tells Moses that He will "harden" Pharaoh's heart to the message and that Moses must threaten Pharaoh with the death of his firstborn son.

Moses sets out on his journey with his wife, but things take a bizarre turn. God suddenly tries to kill Moses, but the threat is averted when Zipporah quickly circumcises their son and touches Moses' feet with the blood. I *think* it was Moses' feet that got the blood, but it might have been the infant's feet; the text isn't super clear. After this strange ritual, the danger passes, everyone breathes a sigh of relief, and they continue on their merry way.

Moses and Aaron then meet with the elders of Israel, deliver God's message, and win their support. But the real challenge lies ahead: Moses must now convince Pharaoh to let the Israelites go, an impossible task, since God has already declared that He will harden Pharaoh's heart against it.

I feel like there is a lot of narrative missing. We are to understand that Pharaoh's daughter brings back a baby and raises him in court. Was she pregnant when she went to the Nile to rinse off? If she was not pregnant, where did people think the baby came from? Why would the (unnamed) daughter of (unnamed) pharaoh not just tell the maturing Moses he was a native Egyptian, which would have surely made things easier for everyone? Maybe the infant had already been circumcised as a Hebrew, but the Bible does not say that. Hadn't Pharaoh given a death sentence for any newborns, or was that just a rule for his subjects?

We also skip Moses' entire upbringing in Pharaoh's court. We learn he was not skilled at speaking but that he had a temper and was capable of violence (he killed the Egyptian who was harassing an Israelite). The Bible missed a chance to give us useful information on how "Moses became Moses," or perhaps only the post-revelation Moses should be of interest.

I do not know what to make of Zipporah placating a potentially murderous God by rubbing circumcision blood on Moses' feet. Was this a customary practice, or is there symbolism I'm missing? Please tell me "feet" isn't a euphemism. If He had gone through with killing Moses, would Aaron have just been promoted on the spot? Is God's plan really that improvisational?

I am also struck that all the Hebrews have names (including two midwives), but the pharaoh and his daughter, well-known and powerful figures, do not. It is as if the writers did not know or care who the Egyptian protagonists were; when the Bible was printed, these names might have already been lost to the sands of time.

I don't want to turn this into a debate on ancient languages, but surely Moses would have spoken Egyptian, right? After all, he'd been brought up in the Egyptian court. The traditional religious understanding is that the exodus was circa 1500 BCE; however, Biblical Hebrew doesn't seem to have materialized as a language until the 900s BCE. So, are we to believe that Moses would have led his people out of Egypt in 1500 BCE, died circa 1400 BCE, and wrote the Pentateuch in 1000 BCE? Or did he write in Egyptian, which was later translated into Hebrew?

A final point: If there were only two midwives, that means the Israelite population was rather small, right?

Exodus 5-11

Moses tells Pharaoh in Exodus 5:1, "Let my people go, that they may hold a feast unto God in the wilderness." Pharaoh isn't having it. Instead of relenting, he keeps the brick production quota in place and cruelly tells the Israelites they'll have to gather their own straw. Naturally, the Israelite foremen are furious with Moses for making things worse. Moses, in turn, complains to God that his mission has only brought misery on his people.

It's worth pointing out that in *The Ten Commandments* (1956), the Charlton Heston epic directed by Cecil B. DeMille, the Israelites are shown as slaves hauling massive stone blocks and building the Egyptian pyramids. This is a Hollywood invention. By the time the biblical Moses story would be set (even in the earliest proposed dates, c. 15th century BCE), Egypt had not been building pyramids for centuries. The large-scale pyramid construction program that started c. 2700 BCE had largely ended by 1650 BCE, long before the New Kingdom period in which the Exodus is usually imagined.

Anyway, in addition to getting heat from his workers, Moses might have also be wondering if he and Aaron are simply too old for this task. He's 80 now, and Aaron is 83, but God is resolute. In Exodus 7:1, He says, "Thou shalt speak all that I command thee; and Aaron thy brother shall speak unto Pharaoh, that he send the children of Israel out of his land."

So Moses and Aaron go again before Pharaoh. Aaron throws down his staff, and it becomes a serpent. Pharaoh's magicians replicate the trick with their own staves, but Aaron's serpent eats theirs (a king cobra, perhaps?). Then follows the famous sequence of ten escalating plagues that God unleashes on Egypt to pressure Pharaoh into releasing the Israelites.

1. Water turns to blood, killing all the fish. Oddly, Exodus 7:22 says the Egyptian magicians also turn water into blood. That doesn't seem helpful.
2. Frogs swarm the land. Again, Pharaoh's magicians somehow replicate this (how? summoning more frogs?). Pharaoh promises to let the Israelites go, then breaks his word.
3. Lice or gnats, possibly mosquitoes. This time, the magicians give up—they can't replicate it (a relief?).
4. Flies invade, but the Israelite area of Goshen is spared.
5. All Egyptian livestock die. The Israelites' animals are untouched.
6. Boils afflict both people and animals.
7. Hail, heavy enough to kill any person or animal left outdoors. Goshen is again spared.
8. Locusts swarm "throughout the land of Egypt."
9. Three days of darkness, so thick it can be felt.
10. Finally, the death of all firstborn Egyptian sons, the most brutal plague of all.

In Exodus 12, God gives detailed instructions for what would become Passover. Each Israelite family is to slaughter a lamb and mark their doorposts with its blood: "And they shall take of the blood, and strike it on the two side posts and on the upper door post of the houses, wherein they shall eat it" (Ex. 12:7). This blood sign tells God which homes to spare. But if God is omniscient, why would He need such crude visual markers? And if the Israelites were slaves, would they really have lived in their own separate houses?

Nevertheless, God follows through. Exodus 12:30 reports, "And Pharaoh rose up in the night, he, and all his servants, and all the Egyptians; and there was a great cry in Egypt: for there was not a house where there was not one dead." At last, Pharaoh gives in. He tells Moses and Aaron to take their people and livestock and get lost. As they leave, the Israelites plunder the Egyptians, walking off with their silver and gold. Exodus 12:37–41 claims 600,000 men (plus women and children) left Egypt, ending 430 years of Israelite presence there.

Rivers of blood, frogs, lice, hail, and death...Exodus paints a bleak picture of divine vengeance. As with other memorable Bible stories, the imagery is vivid, and the text is sparse, leaving readers to imagine the trauma for themselves. There's even a kind of grim ecological logic to the sequence: blood-tainted water, displaced frogs, swarming insects, diseased animals, and human suffering—a cascade of environmental collapse. The final plague, death of the firstborn, is a chilling callback to Pharaoh's earlier decree to kill Israelite sons. You know what they say about payback.

Still, some plagues seem to overlap. Plague 5 kills all livestock. Then those animals get boils in Plague 6. Then they die again in Plague 7 from hail. Just how many times can the same animals be killed?

Pharaoh's stubbornness is striking. And it's not like he didn't have precedent: back in Genesis 12, an earlier pharaoh suffered plagues for taking Abram's wife, Sarai. That story lacks detail, but you'd think institutional memory might have helped this pharaoh avoid a repeat performance. Then again, the Bible insists that God Himself "hardened Pharaoh's heart," repeatedly preventing him from relenting—just so God could escalate the drama and display His power. So, was Pharaoh ever really free to make a different choice?

It's also noteworthy that Pharaoh's magicians were able to mimic some of the early plagues. This suggests that miraculous power, or at least stage magic, wasn't unique to the Hebrew God. But why would they replicate the plague of blood? Wouldn't that just make things worse for their own people?

And why does God always choose a single elderly male intermediary to do His bidding? If He can harden hearts, couldn't He also soften them? That would have saved Egypt a lot of misery. And if He wanted everyone to know His will, why not just appear directly before Pharaoh or the Israelites? Surely an all-powerful God could manage better messaging.

The figure of 600,000 Israelite men (likely 2–3 million people in total) is almost certainly inflated. Ancient texts routinely exaggerate numbers for dramatic effect. Plutarch claimed that Alexander the Great faced a Persian army of one million at Gaugamela, while most modern historians say it was a quarter of that, at most.

It's worth asking: did any of this happen? Some scholars point to the biblical text as evidence of historical enslavement, treating it as a starting point. But most historians begin with the evidence, and there's very little. Given how small the region was and how interconnected its peoples, it's likely that some Israelites lived in Egypt and vice versa. But a mass migration of millions would have left a major archaeological footprint.

We can trace Caesar's cavalry at Alesia (in Gaul) by the indentations their horses made in the earth. Yet we can't find a single trail, artifact, or site confirming an exodus of this scale. The obvious explanation is that the exodus didn't happen, at least on the scale the Bible reports.

Exodus 12-20

Pharaoh specifically authorized the Israelites to leave. In Exodus 12:32, he says, "Take your flocks and your herds… and be gone." But the Egyptians have short attention spans. According to Exodus 14:7, Pharaoh, whose heart had again hardened by God, sent 600 chariots to pursue the Israelites into the desert.

Moses, undeterred, brings along Joseph's bones as a sort of talisman. God, meanwhile, is still busy micromanaging dietary laws. To commemorate the Passover, Israelites are instructed to eat only unleavened bread for seven days, and the firstborn of every animal must have its neck broken, an oddly brutal flourish for a festival of liberation.

The Israelites continue "through the way of the wilderness of the Red Sea," guided by a pillar of cloud by day and a pillar of fire by night. At one point, God moves the cloud behind them to obscure the Israelite camp from Egyptian view. Then comes the big cinematic moment: Moses stretches out his hand over the sea, and the waters part. The Israelites pass through, and when the Egyptians follow, God makes their chariot wheels fall off. Moses raises his hand again, the waters return, and the Egyptian army is wiped out, a graphic demonstration of divine power. As Exodus 14:31 puts it: "The people feared the Lord, and believed the Lord, and his servant Moses."

In my Bible, the episode of the parting waters is titled *The Miraculous Crossing of the Red Sea*, but the text never explicitly identifies it as the Red Sea. Scholars suggest that "Red Sea" may be a mistranslation of "Yam Suph," more accurately rendered "Sea of Reeds," possibly a marshy area or lake. Indeed, the traditional exodus route starts in Goshen (near modern-day Tanis in northern Egypt), moves southeast into the Sinai Peninsula, and likely crosses near the Great Bitter Lake or a nearby swamp. One clue supporting this interpretation: the narrative says the Egyptians' chariot wheels were removed, suggesting they got stuck in mud, not washed away.

Like the image of the Israelites laboring at the pyramids, the grand spectacle of Moses parting the waters is also greatly influenced by the movie *The Ten Commandments*. Ironically, Charlton Heston's rendering of this scene, not the biblical text, has captured public imagination.

I'm also struck by how small Pharaoh's pursuing force was. Even with 600 chariots (and possibly cavalry), they were chasing 600,000 Israelite men "equipped for war" (Ex. 12:37). Chariots weren't suited for head-on engagements against mass infantry. They functioned more like mobile platforms for archers or shock troops against scattered opponents, so even if the Israelites had faced 600 chariots they probably wouldn't have been too impressed.

What follows in Exodus 15:1–18 is a lengthy victory song that recounts the episode in verse. But the good vibes don't last. After three days without water, the Israelites reach Marah, only to find the water there undrinkable. Moses consults God, who instructs him to throw a branch into the water to make it sweet.

God also promises to spare them from diseases if they obey. Soon, however, their food supply runs low, prompting another round of kvetching. In Exodus 16:3, the Israelites lament: "Would to God we had died by the hand of the Lord in Egypt, when we sat by the flesh pots, and ate bread to the full; for ye have brought us into this wilderness to kill this whole assembly with hunger."

In response, God provides a daily ration of bread (manna) in the morning and meat in the evening. On the sixth day, they're to gather a double portion so they can rest on the seventh. Still, some stubborn souls go out looking for food on the Sabbath, earning God's displeasure. Later, when thirst strikes again, Moses asks in exasperation, "What shall I do unto this people?" God tells him to strike a rock at Horeb, and water flows out.

Then come the Amalekites. In the ensuing battle, Moses raises his hands, and as long as they're raised, the Israelites prevail. But when he tires and lowers them, the tide turns. So

Aaron and Hur support his arms until the enemy is defeated. This odd battle tactic concludes with Exodus 17:16: "The Lord hath sworn that the Lord will have war with Amalek from generation to generation." That's quite a grudge.

By the third month after leaving Egypt, the Israelites reach the desert of Sinai. God tells Moses that He will descend upon the mountain in three days, and that no one else is to approach it under penalty of death. There, God reveals the Commandments to Moses, who then conveys them to the Israelites in Ex. 20:1–17).

1. I am the Lord thy God; thou shalt have no other gods before me.
2. Thou shalt not make graven images or bow down to them; for I am a jealous God.
3. Thou shalt not take the name of the Lord in vain.
4. Remember the Sabbath, to keep it holy.
5. Honor thy father and thy mother.
6. Thou shalt not kill.
7. Thou shalt not commit adultery.
8. Thou shalt not steal.
9. Thou shalt not bear false witness against thy neighbor.
10. Thou shalt not covet thy neighbor's house, wife, servant, ox, or donkey.

In the modern United States, some schools want to post the Ten Commandments in classrooms, treating them as foundational to moral law. Yet, in truth, they are a mixed bag. Some are overt orders to worship God, others milquetoast directives not to kill or steal, and one, not to covet, seems to convict thought crime.

- **Commandment 1:** "Have no other gods before me," seems oddly unnecessary given the series of miracles the Israelites had just witnessed. Why would they even want another god?

- **Commandment 2:** What counts? Walk through St. Peter's Square and you'll see statues of saints, Jesus, and popes for sale. Aren't these graven images?
- **Commandment 3:** Not taking the Lord's name in vain is a decent religious rule, but it's not a moral principle.
- **Commandment 4:** Observing the Sabbath raises practical concerns. If we all stopped working one day a week, what about hospitals, gas stations, or food services? Does "no work" include preparing meals or caring for children?
- **Commandment 5:** Honoring parents is not revolutionary but is broadly sensible.
- **Commandment 6:** "Thou shalt not kill," is ambiguous. Does this prohibit all killing? Or just murder? The Israelites had just drowned an army and slaughtered the Amalekites, so some forms of killing are fine.
- **Commandment 7:** This forbids adultery, but biblical patriarchs had multiple wives and concubines. Was Jacob an adulterer or just a family man with options?
- **Commandment 8:** Not stealing is foundational to any society.
- **Commandment 9:** The order not to bear false witness is perhaps the most modern of the bunch.
- **Commandment 10:** This prohibits coveting; not physical crime, just the thought. But coveting is part of the human condition. Doesn't ambition often start with wanting what someone else has? If no one coveted, would we have capitalism, innovation, or much of modern society?

Exodus 21-32

Exodus 21–23 presents an extensive list of laws covering slaves, property rights, sexuality, farming, and a surprising amount of concern about oxen. These chapters revisit material from the Ten Commandments but expand on it with new decrees, like the treatment of Hebrew slaves, who are to be freed after six years of service. The death penalty is prescribed not only for murder but also for hitting one's parents and for beating a servant to death (though there's no penalty if the servant survives a few days—Ex. 21:20–21).

Ex. 21:24 captures the tone of these ordinances: "Eye for eye, tooth for tooth, hand for hand, foot for foot." This principle appears to be borrowed directly from the Babylonian Code of Hammurabi, which predates Exodus by centuries. Hammurabi ruled southern Mesopotamia from 1792 to 1750 BCE, and his law code famously states that if a man destroys another man's eye, his own eye shall be destroyed in return. These laws would have been familiar to educated scribes in Moses' supposed time.

In Exodus 22, the death penalty is mandated for witchcraft, bestiality, and for sacrificing to any god but Yahweh. But amid these harsh penalties are some unexpectedly humane instructions. Ex. 22:21–22 states: "Thou shalt neither vex a stranger, nor oppress him: for ye were strangers in the land of Egypt. Ye shall not afflict any widow or fatherless child." Similarly, in Ex. 23:9: "Also thou shalt not oppress a stranger: for ye know the heart of a stranger, seeing ye were strangers in the land of Egypt." We also find early environmental law: fields must lie fallow every seventh year.

After this detour into legal code, the narrative returns to the wilderness journey and God's reaffirmation of the Ten Commandments. God sends an angel to lead the Israelites and again warns them not to worship foreign gods. He promises to drive out the Hivites, Canaanites, and Hittites. Moses alone is allowed to approach God and is summoned to Mount Sinai, where he remains for 40 days and nights.

By now, God has liberated the Israelites, drowned the Egyptian army in the Red Sea, rained bread from the sky, and made water spring from rocks. You'd think He could take a short miracle break without chaos erupting, but you'd be wrong. (More on that in Chapter 32.)

While on the mountain, Moses receives detailed instructions on transporting the commandments in an ornate ark, housing them in a portable tabernacle, and dressing the priests. God requests offerings: gold, silver, yarn, linen, ram skins, spices, and gemstones. The ark is to be 4 feet long, 2 feet wide, and 2 feet deep, made of acacia wood, covered in gold, topped with cherubim, and placed beside a golden lampstand.

Ex. 26:1–3: "Moreover thou shalt make the tabernacle with ten curtains of fine twined linen, and blue and purple and scarlet: with cherubims of cunning work shalt thou make them..." Priestly fashion is also a top priority. Ex. 28:31–33 lays out the wardrobe: "And thou shalt make the robe of the ephod all of blue...And beneath upon the hem of it thou shalt make pomegranates of blue, and of purple, and of scarlet, round about the hem thereof; and bells of gold between them..."

It reads less like a religious manual and more like wardrobe notes from Elton John's *Goodbye Yellow Brick Road* tour.

In Ex. 31:18, God hands Moses two tablets, "written with the finger of God." In Exodus 20, the list of commandments was verbal, now it's written down. But while Moses is away, the Israelites grow impatient. Aaron collects their gold and crafts a golden calf idol. God is enraged: "I have seen this people, and behold, it is a stiff-necked people...now let me alone, that my wrath may wax hot against them, and that I may consume them" (Ex. 32:9–10).

Moses talks Him down, but when Moses sees the idol for himself, he smashes the tablets, burns the calf, grinds it into powder, mixes it into water, and makes the Israelites drink it. He then tells the Levites to take their swords and "slay every man his brother...and neighbor." Three thousand people die.

Once again, the Israelites' short attention spans are on display. They can't go 40 days without a miracle before turning to idol worship. God, despite repeatedly warning them not to backslide, seems shocked by this, and the punishment is brutal: not only do they have to drink powdered idol, but thousands are killed by their own people. Ironically, one of the Ten Commandments they just received was "Thou shalt not kill."

The expanded laws in Exodus 21–23 reflect the Bronze Age setting: they're heavy on livestock, servants, and what to do if you have sex with a virgin. Witches suddenly become an important concern.

Interestingly absent in the latest barrage of rules are prohibitions against homosexuality or rape. The law against usury and the instruction to treat foreigners with compassion are surprisingly progressive. After all, Moses himself had been "a stranger in a strange land." If one insists on taking the Bible literally, then surely these laws about protecting widows, orphans, and immigrants must be taken seriously too.

Exodus 33-40

After the Golden Calf debacle, God is still not placated. In Exodus 33, He tells Moses that He will not personally accompany the Israelites to the land of milk and honey because, as He puts it, "you are a stiff-necked people; I might destroy you on the way." The Israelites, sobered by this divine threat, remove their ornaments in mourning.

Moses pitches a tent outside the camp where he meets with God. When the cloud descends over it, the people know the Lord is present and keep their distance, praying. Then we hit a puzzling contradiction: Exodus 33:11 claims God spoke to Moses "face to face, as one speaks to a friend," yet just nine verses later, in 33:20, God insists, "no one may see me and live." To reconcile this, God hides Moses in a crevice, covers him with His hand, and allows him to glimpse only His back as He passes by. A literal description of God's backside would've added some color here, but the text remains coyly ambiguous.

Next, God tells Moses to carve out a new pair of stone tablets and climb Mount Sinai again. Unlike the first set, which were inscribed by the "finger of God," this time, Exodus 34:27 makes it clear that Moses himself is to write down the commandments as God dictates.

But here's the twist: Exodus 34:10–26's commandments are not the familiar moral directives from Chapter 20. It's a different list altogether, one that focuses far more on ritual observance, agriculture, and cultic practice. It's less Charlton Heston, more *Children of the Corn*. Scholars often call this the Ritual Decalogue, and it includes the following:

1. Worship no other god, for Yahweh is a jealous god.
2. Do not make molten idols.
3. Observe the Feast of Unleavened Bread.
4. Dedicate the firstborn of every womb, human or animal, to God.
5. Do not work on the Sabbath, although the earlier exhortation to "keep it holy" (Ex. 20) is notably missing.
6. Celebrate the Feast of Weeks and other harvest festivals.
7. All men must appear before the Lord three times a year (whatever that means).
8. Bring the first fruits of your land to the house of God.
9. Do not offer the blood of a sacrifice with anything leavened.
10. Do not boil a young goat in its mother's milk.

Not only are the two sets of commandments radically different, but it's hard to even keep track of how many commandments the second list has. We must infer where one commandment ends and the next begins. Embedded within the ban on worshiping other gods are additional rules, like tearing down pagan altars and avoiding treaties with foreign nations. Is that one commandment or three?

Frankly, commandments 3 and 6 are both about harvest festivals and could've been combined. The overall effect is disorganized, archaic, and firmly rooted in the religious customs of a tribal society. Yet Exodus 34:28 explicitly calls these "the Ten Commandments." So, when modern Christians demand that the Ten Commandments be posted in public schools, they almost certainly mean Exodus 20, but biblically speaking, Exodus 34 is equally "the Ten."

Moses remains on the mountain for another 40 days and 40 nights, neither eating nor drinking, and returns to the Israelites, who are stunned by the radiance of his face, and shredded abs.

The final six chapters of Exodus provide an exhaustive account of how the Israelites constructed the ark, tabernacle, candlesticks, and altar. Skilled artisans were recruited, and the people contributed freely. Just a taste of the detail, from Exodus 37:17–19:

> And he made the candlestick of pure gold: of beaten work made he the candlestick; his shaft, and his branch, his bowls, his knops [ornaments], and his flowers, were of the same: And six branches going out of the sides thereof; three branches of the candlestick out of the one side thereof, and three branches of the candlestick out of the other side thereof.

It's telling that the Bible devotes chapter after chapter to the tabernacle's measurements and priestly garments, yet only a handful of verses to the creation of the cosmos. Maybe they didn't know, or didn't think their audience would care, how the universe began. But they would damn sure know how to build a lampstand.

Let's revisit the Commandments. Can't we all come up with a better, more just list that would better speak to modern concerns? Here's mine:

1. If you are lucky enough to live in a democracy, you must vote and be informed.
2. Respect women's bodily autonomy, and do not discriminate based on race, gender, sexuality, or religion.
3. Treat animals used for food humanely and minimize suffering.
4. Support fair wages, worker protections, and social benefits.
5. Love and honor your family.

41

6. Do not murder. Take life only in clear self-defense or defense of others.
7. Do not steal.
8. Public officials must serve the people, not their own interests.
9. Always tell the truth about important matters.
10. Protect the Earth for your grandchildren's grandchildren.

LEVITICUS

Leviticus 1-15

We start *Leviticus* with arcane priestly rules and regulations, veer sharply into some horrific violence, and are then presented with a laundry list of clean and unclean animals that lumps together birds and bats because they both have wings. After that, we are subjected to a lengthy discourse on quack treatments for leprosy. Oh, joy.

Aaron is now a priest, an unlikely assignment given his role in the Golden Calf debacle; he and his two sons, Nadab and Abihu, play a central role in the sacrifices in the new tabernacle. There are a series of sacrifices, starting with a sin offering, then a burnt offering, then a ram of ordination, and then a fellowship offering, from what I can decipher. Here's how the sin offering is described in Lev. 8:14–15:

> And he brought the bullock (bull) for the sin
> offering, and Aaron and his sons laid their
> hands upon the head of the bullock for the
> sin offering. And he slew it; and Moses took
> the blood, and put it upon the horns of the
> altar round about with his finger, and purified
> the altar, and poured the blood at the bottom
> of the altar, and sanctified it, to make
> reconciliation upon it.

During the Ram of Ordination, a wafer (bread made without yeast) is added to the altar to be burned. I assume this is the origin of the wafer used at Communion.

After the Sin Offering, God sends a fire to consume the altar, causing the assemblage to shout and fall to their faces. In an ill-advised move, Aaron's sons created their own fire, and God "devoured them, and they died before the Lord." God orders the children of Aaron's uncle to carry the charred bodies out of sight. Moses then tells Aaron to not to show any emotion, to avoid "letting your hair become unkempt," lest he, too, is murdered. The reason for Aaron's sons' lapse is hinted at in Lev. 10:9, where God says no more wine is to be served.

Then God speaks to Moses and Aaron, defining what is meant by clean and unclean animals (Lev. 11:13–19). This is a long list, but the gist is that to be considered "clean," an animal must have both a divided hoof and chew the cud (cattle, sheep, goats, and deer). Unclean animals, on the other hand, include pigs, camels, rabbits, rodents, and most shellfish. A rabbit is considered impure because, although it chews the cud, it does not have cloven hooves (fun fact: rabbits don't actually chew the cud). To be considered clean, a fish would need fins and scales. Birds are generally clean except for scavengers. Bats are lumped in with the unclean birds. This type of guidance would have been helpful when God instructed Noah to take seven pairs of clean and one pair of unclean animals onto the ark.

Most Americans are not that exercised about eating bats, but let's consider pork. God's instruction is clear: "You will regard the pig as unclean," yet Christians happily slaughter and consume pigs by the million.

Lev. 12–15 deals with how to handle clean and unclean people. Unclean people are mostly, but not exclusively, women and lepers. Lev. 12 specifies that if a woman bears a boy, she must get him circumcised on the eighth day and cannot touch any hallowed thing for 33 days. If she has a girl, this changes to 36 days. In each case, she must sacrifice a lamb. Don't have a lamb? Not to worry: two turtledoves or two young pigeons can be substituted.

Lev. 15 says that if a woman has her period, she is unclean for seven days, and a man she has sex with is also unclean for seven days. Anything she touches or lies upon is also unclean. She can become clean by taking turtledoves and pigeons to the priest, who will sacrifice them on the eighth day. Men with genital discharge, or perhaps semen, are also unclean and are instructed to wash themselves with water, being clean again in the evening of the same day.

The entirety of Lev. 13 and 14 describe the symptoms and treatment for leprosy. Lev. 13:4 starts a series of steps to ascertain if the patient is unclean: "If the bright spot be white in the skin of his flesh, and in sight be not deeper than the skin, and the hair thereof be not turned white; then the priest shall shut up him that hath the plague seven days." It is possible to be clean: Lev. 13:17: "And the priest shall see him: and, behold if the plague be turned into white; then the priest shall pronounce him clean..." The treatment for leprosy is an entirely holistic medicine that would probably be approved by RFK, Jr. Lev. 14 describes how a leper can become clean, which starts with dipping one bird in the blood of another, then releasing the bird, then having the leper shave, bathe, then sacrifice a lamb, then take some oil and pour it onto their left hand, and then finally putting the oil on the leper's head. There are some steps after this, but I...just...can't....

This is some strange and unpleasant material, but I think it's important not to gloss over it. If the Bible is to be taken seriously, we must persevere through the material, realizing it won't be one long Joseph and the Amazing Technicolor Dreamcoat. As with the very detailed instructions in Exodus on how the Tabernacle is to be constructed, the Bible in Leviticus describes the priestly wardrobe and process in considerable detail. This must have been very important to the Israelites. God is very prescriptive and easy to anger, as when he incinerates Aaron's sons for having the audacity to produce their own flame. It's a chilling touch that Aaron is instructed not to show emotion, or he must suffer the same fate. What possible moral virtue can we take from this story?

Leprosy must have been a significant concern, given its communicability, crowded living conditions, and the lack of modern medicine. The disease-causing bacteria, *Mycobacterium leprae*, are passed via contact or airborne droplets. It's not as easy to transmit as the common cold, and most people do not become infected even if exposed, so the isolation recommended as a treatment in Leviticus 14 would have been a useful step, but more than seven days would have been required. Without antibiotics, there was no cure, so the pronouncement that lepers could so easily become "clean" would not have been effective. In fact, it would have allowed infectious people to needlessly spread disease.

Leviticus 16-27

We continue with the elaborate priestly ceremony of atonement. Leviticus 16 describes the sacrifices in detail, starting with the instruction for the priest (Aaron) to wear simple woolen coats and linen breeches. But God warns them not to approach the Ark at any time they choose, only when allowed by God, lest they die (and God already incinerated Aaron's two sons, so this is not an empty threat). Sin and burnt offerings are made, and goats, rams, and bulls are sacrificed.

There's a lot of bloodletting, but also one lucky goat (the scapegoat) that takes the sins of the congregants. This goat is to be released into the wild (where it would probably soon die of dehydration or be killed by predators).

More commandments. In Lev. 17, it is forbidden to drink blood. Incest is a no-no. From Leviticus 18:6-23, we get a long list of prohibitions relating to sexual conduct. One must not carnally know ("see the nakedness" of) your father, your mother, sister, son's daughter, father's sister, mother's sister, father's brother, daughter-in-law, son in-law, or neighbor's wife. Also, no mother/daughter action or worshiping Molech (the Canaanite god of child sacrifice). The well-known admonition against gay sex is in Lev. 18:22: "Thou shalt not lie with mankind, as with womankind: it is an abomination." A similar statement appears in Lev. 20:13, which prescribes the death penalty for such actions. The text is mute on lesbianism. Sex with animals is also an abomination.

If these sins are committed, it's not just the sinner that gets the blame; it is the entire land. Lev. 18:25: "And the land is defiled: therefore, I do visit the iniquity thereof upon it, and the land itself vomiteth out her inhabitants." Remember when Noah was so angry at Ham after his son had "seen his nakedness" when he was drunk? It sure seems like seeing your father's nakedness means having sex with him. I now understand why Noah's encounter with Ham didn't sit well with him.

In Lev. 19, we are told to keep the Sabbath, have no molten gods (He just can't let the Golden Calf thing go!), not to steal, fudge weights and measurements, swear, defraud, curse, mar the corners of your beard (that's a new one...), prostitute your daughter, or wear clothes that have both wool and linen. Interestingly, God also instructs us not to disrespect the poor or unnecessarily respect the wealthy. Lev. 20 focuses on the need to stone anyone who supports Molech or makes curses.

Apparently, incest had not been sufficiently addressed in earlier chapters, so we are told again that the following warrant the death sentence *for both* of the parties: adultery, sex with your father's wife, sex with a daughter-in-law, men/men sex, mother/daughter sex, sex with beasts (yes, the beast is to be killed even though it probably didn't consent), and sex with your sisters. If you have sex with a woman on her period, it's unclean; if you have sex with your uncle's wife or brother's wife, you will be sterile. Wizards are to be stoned to death.

Priests get special laws in Lev. 21, including not shaving the corners of beards, using profanity, or taking whores for wives. If a daughter of a priest is a whore, she is to be burned. Priests are only to marry a virgin, never harlots or divorcees. Priests must not have blemishes, be lame, have flat noses, broken bones, be dwarfs, or have their stones broken (testicles?). Blemishes are also not allowed on sacrificial animals.

There is much more to say on religious ceremonies, including the Sabbath, Feast of Pentecost, and Day of Atonement in Lev. 23 and 24, although Lev. 24 finishes with rephrased commandments, including not to murder, compensation for taking of beasts, and the need to have common laws for anyone on Israeli land. There is also an extended passage about a jubilee occurring every 50 years, a time of rest, reconciliation, and the return of land to its original owners. After that, we dive back into more laws (commandments), including not making graven images, engaging in usury, or violating the Sabbath. The rewards for observing these laws include rain in the season due, the expulsion of evil beasts, and the submission of all enemies. But if the commandments are not honored, it won't be fun: God promises to send pestilence, eat the flesh of sons and daughters, destroy high places, and lay waste to cities.

Leviticus concludes with a complex passage on the value of commitments made to the Lord, which might be the value of gifts offered to the priest. There are different valuations based on age and sex. For example, a 50-year-old male's commitment is valued at 50 shekels, and a woman of the same age is only 30 (presumably, she can't work as hard in the fields). However, a boy aged less than four years is worth 5 shekels, and a girl of the same age is only worth 3 (presumably because she's a girl).

NUMBERS

Numbers 1-9

True to its name, we start the *Book of Numbers* with a lot of numbers. God instructs Moses and Aaron to conduct a census, really a military draft registration with the tribes: Reuben, Simeon, Judah, Issachar, Zebulun, Ephraim, Manasseh, Benjamin, Dan, Asher, Gad, and Naphtali. All males over age 20 were liable to serve in the army, and the total count was 603,550 (Num. 1:44–46). The locations of each camp are specified, and the number of soldiers per tribe is enumerated.

The Levites, the smallest of the tribes at 22,000 males, were set aside only to run temple procedures and were not liable for the draft; anyone other than a Levite trying to operate the temple would be killed. Moses and Aaron (both are Levites) oversee the Tabernacle, along with Aaron's surviving sons, Eleazar and Ithamar (his other sons, Nadab and Abihu, were

49

incinerated by God). There is also a temple tax of five shekels to be paid to Aaron and Moses. It's an interesting turn of phrase in Num. 3:51: "And Moses gave the money of them that were redeemed unto Aaron and to his sons, according to the word of the Lord, as the Lord commanded Moses." In other words, Moses says God told Moses to give money to Moses' brother.

We then review additional temple procedures, starting in Num. 4. The Kohathites and Gershonites, aged 30–50, who are part of the Levites, are tasked with caring for the holy things. God speaks to Moses, saying that He is entitled to the firstborn of each family, but instead, He will take the Levites for temple duty. Their responsibilities are very specific: Num. 4:25: "And they shall bear the curtains of the tabernacle, and the tabernacle of the congregation, his covering, and the covering of the badgers' skins that is above upon it, and the hanging for the door of the tabernacle of the congregation."

Num. 5 starts by saying that unclean people must be excluded from the temple, basically lepers, people with discharges, and anyone who has been around dead people. In Exodus, there was a long discussion on lepers, women on their periods, and men with discharges, so counting these as unclean is expected. But why is having a dead person nearby an unclean act?

The next topic is dark. In Num. 5:11–31, we are presented with the scenario where a man suspects his wife of cheating. She must appear before a priest, who prepares a potion consisting of water and the dust of the temple floor. The woman takes an oath and must drink the concoction. If she is innocent, the mixture will have no effect. But if she is guilty, it will cause her "thigh to rot." Num. 5:28 says, "And if the woman be not defiled, but be clean; then she shall be free, and shall conceive seed." So, it seems if the woman is innocent, she can bear more children, but if guilty, God will abort her pregnancy. This barbaric practice is precisely the type of action Leviticus and Exodus would have labeled witchcraft.

Despite all the commandments regarding sexual activity, this is the first time abortion has come up. And Numbers is not taking a firm "anti-abortion" stance. Surely, if the writers of the Old Testament were concerned about the early termination of pregnancy, they would not have limited their critique to this gobbledygook. Maybe they accepted the practice, recognized that life was hard, pregnancies often failed, and that all bets were off until a baby was born and took its first breaths.

Num. 6 deals with a separate vow of a Nazarite that the Israelites could take. This extra commitment involved not drinking alcohol, shaving, or touching the dead (there we go again with the dead being unclean). Various sacrificial procedures and vows are described. The next three chapters provide detailed descriptions of the offerings the tribes presented, primarily consisting of shekels, goats, lambs, and incense. We gain more specifics on how Levites conduct services, including the fact that they can only serve between the ages of 25 and 50.

As with Leviticus, the first chapters of the Book of Numbers, with their focus on temple procedures, are a challenging read. The total male population over the age of twenty was 603,550, matching the numbers in Exodus, so we can assume the total Israelite population was approaching three million, including women and children, a massive number of people for that time and place.

Onward, we go into Numbers, starting with Chapter 9, which reiterates the need to celebrate the Passover with a familiar outline: the unclean need to stay away, it's to occur on the 14th day of the correct month, and that a single ordinance should apply to residents and visitors of the land. This chapter concludes with the description of a supernatural cloud that would sit upon the tabernacle. So long as the cloud persists ("two days or a month or a year"), the Israelites would not venture outside their tents.

Numbers 10-17

In Num. 10, God commands the creation of two silver trumpets to be used for sounding the alarm and specifies the order of march for the various tribes, a sort of military deployment order. There was a three-day march, preceded by the Ark of the Covenant, but when they settled down, tensions arose as the Israelites fondly remembered the fish and melons they ate in Egypt. As a punishment for this kvetching, God consumes them in fire, only interrupted when Moses intervenes. Honestly, I can understand the desire to walk away from an empty desert under the leadership of an unpredictable God who sometimes burns his followers to death.

Moses also complains about the burdens of leadership, so God tells him to gather his seventy top elders at the Tabernacle. Then, in a divine fit of sarcasm, God declares that the people won't be eating meat for just a day or two—"but even a whole month, until it comes out at your nostrils and becomes loathsome to you"—because they've despised him and longed for Egypt (Num. 11:19).

God then causes a wind that directs piles of quails to the camp. The Israelites begin to chow down on the birds, but God is again sent into a rage and sends a plague because of their gluttony. Even with its non-OSHA-compliant construction industry, Egypt would seem appealing right about now.

Miriam and Aaron now speak to Moses, seemingly questioning why God had only spoken with Moses. Miriam, we learn, is Moses' older sister, who observed him in the basket on the Nile. Why she was not named earlier is unexplained. Anyway, God is not pleased, gives her leprosy, and kicks her out of the camp.

Moses then sends spies into Canaan as a prelude to the planned invasion, but their report is not encouraging: Although it is indeed a land of milk and honey, the Amalekites, Jebusites, Amorites, Canaanites, and Hittites that live there are strong in their walled cities; indeed, some are giants (are we being set up for the tale of David and Goliath?). How did a race of giants survive the flood?

This report is most unwelcome to the Israelites, who openly wonder if they need to appoint a new captain and return to Egypt. Only Caleb and Joshua remain loyal, and it takes an appearance from God to prevent them from being stoned to death by the Israelites. Moses intervenes and talks God out of killing everyone, lest the Lord's name is no longer to be respected for having launched the ten plagues. God says the Israelites will "wander in the wilderness forty years" before they can reach the Promised Land.

At least it's clear now that this inter-generational journey was not due to poor maps but was instead mandated by God. Despondent over the situation, some of the Israelites decide to attack the Canaanites, but when Moses and the Ark stay at camp, they are swiftly defeated.

Num. 14:18 states that "The lord is long-suffering, and of great mercy, forgiving iniquity and transgression, and by no means clearing the guilty, visiting the iniquity of the fathers upon the children unto the third and fourth generation." The first part of this statement seems at odds with the rest of Numbers: God is not long-suffering at all and seems to have no mercy. The second part of the statement seems excessive; why is it just to punish children for the actions of their parents or grandparents? This seems like a cruel overreaction.

If you were pining for more tabernacle and priestly procedures involving olive oil, rams, and goats, you're in luck! In a bit of a twist, wine is now added to the mix, rounding out a sacrificial recipe that applies not just to native-born Israelites but also to foreigners—sojourners living among the tribes— who wish to make an offering. After detailing the ritual, God clarifies an important legal principle: there's a difference between knowingly and unknowingly breaking the law. Num. 15:27 puts it this way: "And if any soul sin through ignorance, then he shall bring a she goat of the first year for a sin offering." The distinction between being unaware of the law and deliberately violating it is a noteworthy development.

After all, it is not fair to penalize someone who has familiarized themselves with a law but to excuse someone who has not bothered to study it. Yet, at the same time, there are differences. A jury could find that a novice in the real estate market might not appreciate legal subtleties that a veteran could be aware of. But if you know the laws and break them, the results are far more serious.

A horrific example of the application of the Law is found in Num. 15:31, where an unfortunate man was collecting kindling on the Sabbath and was brought before Moses and Aaron for violating the 4th Commandment (Exodus 20). The Lord instructs Moses to execute the man for his sin, which is carried out by the congregants, who stone him to death, "Because he hath despised the word of the Lord, and hath broken his commandment..." With God, there is no middle ground. The poor person was only trying to support his family, yet his punishment was the same as a murderer.

The tensions from earlier chapters remain unresolved, and Korah, Dathan, and Abiram openly challenge the authority of Moses and Aaron. The usurpers accuse Moses of being a failed and prideful leader (honestly, they had a point), and agree to hold competing ceremonies to see which authority is backed by God. God is not pleased and opens the earth to swallow the leaders of the insurrection. He then sends a fire to wipe out the top 250 insurrectionists, but He's still not done. A plague sweeps through the camp, killing 14,700 more before Aaron rushes into the congregation, lights incense, and atones for the people's sins. To reinforce Aaron's authority, God has each of the twelve tribes present a staff. Aaron's rod blossoms as a sign of divine endorsement.

The Israelites, despite the constant stream of miracles that allowed them to flee oppression, rout the Egyptian army at the Red Sea, and get food and water in the desert, realize their situation remains perilous. Earlier, God killed two of Aaron's sons, and now He has incinerated more people when they remembered the good life in Egypt. As frustration simmers, God starves the Israelites and then causes gluttony as a punishment, then a plague. With their advanced party reporting the strength of the opposition and the ill-advised attack that resulted in defeat from the Canaanites, it is clear that there will be no immediate arrival in the land of milk and honey. The character of leaders is revealed in times of great stress, so we will see how God and Moses can guide the Israelites through these troubled times.

Numbers 18-22

Chapter 18 is a bit of a slog, dealing with the responsibilities of priesthood, the special duties of the Levites, and the system of tithes. God specifies that the Levites must give a tithe of the tithe they receive—ten percent of the offerings brought by the people. This portion, God says, must be the "best" of what is collected, whether grain or produce.

Numbers 19 opens with the unusual command to sacrifice a red heifer, whose ashes are to be used in a purification ritual. The rest of the chapter revisits the theme of ritual impurity: contact with a corpse (or even a human bone) renders a person unclean for seven days.

Numbers 20 begins with more grumbling about the lack of water. At Meribah, God instructs Moses to take his staff, gather the people, and speak to the rock to bring forth water. But Moses, clearly frustrated, scolds the people and strikes the rock twice instead. Though water still gushes out, God is super displeased with Moses for not following instructions to the letter. As punishment, God forbade Moses from entering the Promised Land.

Moses then sends a diplomatic request to the king of Edom for safe passage through their territory but is summarily refused. Next, God calls Moses, Aaron, and Aaron's son Eleazar up Mount Hor, where Aaron dies and his priestly garments are passed to Eleazar. God accuses Aaron of having "rebelled against my word at the water of Meribah," so it seems he's being blamed alongside Moses for the rock-smacking incident. A small offense, perhaps, but the consequences are severe. Though Aaron is mourned for thirty days, it feels as though he dies in disgrace—an ungracious dismissal of a loyal servant by a petty and tyrannical deity.

Moses is soon back in action, defeating Arad the Canaanite. But the Israelites are still complaining about hunger and thirst, and God once again lashes out. Numbers 21:6 reads: "And the Lord sent fiery serpents among the people, and they bit the people, and much people of Israel died."

To stop the plague, God offers an odd cure: Moses is to make a bronze serpent (how is this not a forbidden idol?) and mount it on a pole. Anyone who looks at it will be healed. This snake-entwined staff becomes an enduring symbol of healing, still seen today in medical emblems, and it echoes earlier snake symbolism in Greek myth and future Biblical scenes.

The Israelites' request to pass through Amorite territory is also denied, with the same result as at Arad: Israel wages war and captures "all the cities of the Amorites, in Heshbon, and in all the villages thereof." They then battle the king of Bashan, Og, and defeat him as well, killing him and his sons and leaving "none left him alive."

The simmering tensions of earlier chapters persist. The people continue to complain about Moses and Aaron, as well as the ongoing scarcity of food and water. The earth swallowed previous dissenters; now, complainers are bitten by snakes. Maybe these military victories in Numbers 21 will finally take some pressure off Moses—and, perhaps, cool the Israelites' dissatisfaction with God himself.

Numbers 23-36

Israel's growing military success is not lost on King Balak from Midian, and he sends for the sorcerer Balaam to improve the odds. But God speaks to Balaam and allows him to go to Balak, if Balaam supports God's people. En route, Balaam's donkey can see angels that Balaam is blind to and is whipped repeatedly for taking evasive action. Finally, the donkey begins to speak, asking, "What have I done unto thee that thou hast smitten me these three times?" which is one of the more intelligent questions posed in the Book of Numbers. The angel is finally visible to Balaam and instructs him to continue his journey to King Balak but only speak what God tells him.

The tale of the talking donkey provides a much-needed comedic break from the constant gloom and doom of Leviticus and Numbers. Although the snake in Gen. 2 conversed with Eve, the donkey in Num. 22 has a larger speaking role and is a remarkably sympathetic character. It's the first time there has been any sense of the inner life of animals. Not only does the aggrieved donkey express his concerns as a human would, he seems to see things that people can't, such as the angel that was invisible to Balaam. Throughout the Bible, animals are treated as food or sacrifices; they have no feelings, agency, or purpose other than to serve and die for humans. Perhaps the donkey indicates that even in a harsh environment, the Israelites had not lost their sense of humor.

In Num. 23–24, we are presented with a series of parables relating to King Balak and Balaam. The gist is that Balak continues to try to induce Balaam to curse the Israelites despite Balak's constructing the required sacrificial altars. There is some interesting symbolism. Num. 23:24: "Behold, the people shall rise up as a great lion, and lift up himself as a young lion: he shall not lie down until he eat of the prey, and drink the blood of the slain," and Num. 24:9: "He couched, he lay down as a lion, and as a great lion: who shall stir him up? Blessed is he that blesseth thee, and cursed is he that curseth thee." At the end of Num. 24, Balak and Balaam part ways.

Things have still not been resolved in the Israelite camp. At Shittim (I'm not making that up), Moab women hook up with the Israelite men, and God springs into action. He instructs Moses to slay every whoring man, and then for good measure, He sends a plague that kills 24,000 in the camp. When priest Phinehas observed one woman, Cozbi, disappearing into the tent of Zimri, a member of the Simeonites, he took a javelin and killed them both, earning God's praise.

The plague seems to have been an important event, kicking off the need for another census, which (as did the first census years ago) counted all men 20 years or older (except for Levites, who were exempt from military service). In the first census, there were 603,550 men; in this one, 601,730, a loss of 1,820. I guess it's impressive that the population was flat, given the mass casualty events that God had inflicted. The census also appears to have occurred towards the end of the 40 years of wandering, as they anticipate finally arriving in (conquering) Canaan.

In the next few chapters, we get a mix of topics. In Num. 27, the daughters of Zelophehad ask that they not be disinherited just because their father died without a male heir. God clarifies that they should indeed get their father's property in this case. God also summons Moses to go to Mount Nebo so that he can see the Promised Land.

This seems like a passing of the guard, where Joshua takes command from Moses. There are still hard feelings about what happened in Meribah, where Moses "rebelled against my commandment," a failure which God also held against Aaron, even in death. Numbers 28 and 29 describe the sacrifices to be made at Passover, New Year, and the feast of the Tabernacles. In Numbers 30, we are told that vows to God must be kept, although vows made by wives can be overridden by their husbands.

The passing of time has been hard to track. Many events seem disassociated from any timeline, for example, the lengthy description of how priests can induce abortions (Num. 5), the inheritance rights of daughters (Num. 27), or the sections that detail tabernacle and sacrificial procedures. These are sprinkled across the first 30 chapters, but they are independent events that could appear anywhere. It's strange that the writers of Numbers didn't create a clearer chronology.

God and Moses continue to control the Israelites with fear and violence. A partial list of the crimes they commit against their followers include giving Miriam leprosy; burning to death people who pined for life in Egypt; sending a plague that kills 24,000 for fornicating with the daughters of Moab; the stoning of a wood collector who worked on the Sabbath; and deadly serpents.

Surely, the census Moses conducted in Num. 26 would have had more favorable results if God could have resisted His murderous impulses. It's a wonder that these mass killings didn't cause desertion and the disintegration of the entire project, but it seems that God's reign of terror has worked. After forty years in the desert, the Israelites are on the threshold of entering the Promised Land. As their wandering ends, the torch is passed from Moses to Joshua, and a new census is conducted, which will be used to allocate the soon-to-be conquered lands among the tribes.

In Numbers 31, Moses unleashes the dogs of war on the Midianites near Jericho. Led by Phinehas, each tribe has contributed 1,000 soldiers to the cause, resulting in a total force of 12,000. While receiving *no losses* (Num. 31:49), they burned the enemy cities and exterminated all the Midian soldiers and kings, including Balaam, the unlucky sorcerer with the aggrieved talking donkey (who we hope was able to talk his way out of any trouble with the Israelite army). Phinehas led the triumphant procession of slaves, booty, and animals before Moses but must have been startled by his reception at camp. Instead of gratitude, Moses was furious.

Citing the whoring of the Moab women, his instruction is explicit: Num. 31:17–18: "Now, therefore, kill every male among the little ones and kill every woman that hath known man by lying with him. But all the women children that have not known a man by lying with him keep alive for yourselves." In other words, you messed up. Finish killing all the boys and wives and keep the virgins for your own pleasure (there were 32,000 of them per Num. 31:35). The instruction is to rape *all* the girls regardless of age. I guess we know why ethnic cleansing didn't make it into the 10 Commandments....

After a dispute over the cattle lands of Gilead, we are presented with a travelogue of Moses' journey from Egypt to their current location outside of Canaan. Num. 33:55 finishes with a warning that if all the locals aren't cleared from the land, they will surely be a "prick in your eyes, and thorns in your sides" that will cause ongoing headaches. Num. 34 describes the boundaries that the various tribes will be assigned in Canaan. The high priest Eleazar and Joshua are appointed to lead the apportioning of the land.

In Numbers 35, there is a long-overdue clarification on the issue of killing. If someone strikes impulsively or hurls an unaimed rock that kills someone, it's not automatically a death sentence. Instead, the assailant can go to a sanctuary city and plead their case. The need to differentiate between murder and manslaughter seems obvious, so it's strange it wasn't addressed earlier. It's almost like Moses is making it up on the fly.

So concludes the Book of Numbers: a messy, violent, bureaucratic slog through the desert, littered with corpses, contradictions, and commandments. Some are just, others plainly horrifying. Canaan was on the horizon, a reward that must have shimmered as a tantalizing yet forbidden vison to Moses. He had led the Israelites out of bondage but would never set foot in the Promised Land.

DEUTERONOMY

Deuteronomy 1-10

The title *Deuteronomy* is derived from a Greek term meaning "copy" or "repeat," which it wastes no time in doing. Deut. 1:1 opens with: "These be the words which Moses spake unto all Israel on this side Jordan in the wilderness, in the plain over against the Red Sea, between Paran, and Tophel, and Laban, and Hazeroth, and Dizahab." In other words, we're listening to Moses deliver a lengthy sermon to his people (all three million of them?), a recap of what happened in earlier books of the Bible.

In Deut. 1:10, Moses reminds the Israelites that God has multiplied them "as the stars of heaven" and then urges them to follow the appointed tribal leaders, who serve as judges and wise men. The next few chapters recount conflicts with the Amorites, the King of Bashan, the Moabites, Gilead, and other tribes.

61

In Deut. 2:34, Moses reminds the people that Sihon was defeated and that "we took all his cities at that time, and utterly destroyed the men, and the women, and the little ones, of every city, we left none to remain"—just in case anyone forgot how defeated adversaries were to be handled. In Deut. 3:28, Moses backs Joshua's leadership: "for he shall go over before this people, and he shall cause them to inherit the land which thou shalt see." In Chapter 4, Moses restates that he will die in the current land and not cross over the Jordan.

Much of Deut. 4 and 5 is a restatement of the Ten Commandments, with particular emphasis on the prohibition against making graven images. Deut. 4:16–18 prohibits making any "similitude of any figure," including beasts, birds, or fish. The list of commandments here aligns with those in Exodus 20, rather than the alternate list in Exodus 34.

Deut. 6:22 provides an interesting summary of the plagues: "And the Lord shewed signs and wonders, great and sore, upon Egypt, upon Pharaoh, and upon all his household, before our eyes."

Deuteronomy 7 is a lengthy reiteration that victories are conditional upon obedience. If the Israelites follow God's laws, none will be barren, their livestock will thrive, and the plagues of Egypt won't be repeated. Enemies will be "consumed," and no pity should be shown to them. No graven images are allowed in Israelite homes—they are "abominations" and "cursed things."

The sermon continues, revisiting key moments from earlier chapters, including the giving and preservation of the Ten Commandments in the Ark. Deuteronomy 10 closes with a call for obedience: "Keep the commandments and fear the Lord, and praise the Lord." There's also a bizarre exhortation in Deut. 10:16: "Circumcise therefore the foreskin of your heart, and be no more stiff-necked." Now *that* would make a good bumper sticker or placard at a sporting event.

If Moses was the author of the Pentateuch (the first five books of the Bible), how could he have written, "These are the words which Moses spake…"? The scholarly consensus is that Deuteronomy was written around the 6th century BCE, so someone supposedly living centuries earlier wouldn't have been its author. Someone else is narrating. Did Moses even exist? It seems unlikely, as there's no record of him outside the Bible. He may be an amalgam of figures or legends familiar to early Israelites. For example, King Sargon of Akkad was a historical figure from Samaria around 2300 BCE, and, according to legend, he was found as an infant floating in a basket on the Euphrates. Sound familiar?

Reading Deuteronomy is a strange experience. It's like going to a Billy Joel concert where nobody wants new material—they just want *Piano Man* on a loop. What is the point of Deuteronomy? If the names, places, and events are mostly a retelling of Exodus, Leviticus, and Numbers, what new insight does it offer?

Take Deut. 10:19: "Love ye therefore the stranger: for ye were strangers in the land of Egypt." This adds little to Leviticus 19:34: "But the stranger that dwelleth with you shall be unto you as one born among you, and thou shalt love him as yourself: for ye were strangers in the land of Egypt." Leviticus is already clear that migrants are to be treated with kindness and equality.

However, when repeated material in Deuteronomy differs from earlier instructions, it raises questions. For example, what exactly is a graven image? Exodus 20's second Commandment says: "Thou shalt not make unto thee any graven image or any likeness of anything that is in heaven above, or that is in the earth beneath, or that is in the water under the earth." But Deut. 4:17–18 lists specific examples: "the likeness of any beast that is on the earth, the likeness of any winged fowl that flieth in the air…that creepeth on the ground…or fish that is in the waters." So, is it okay to paint pictures of birds and fish? Exodus leaves some room for artistic interpretation; Deuteronomy seems to shut that down.

These conflicting passages have helped shape different religious views on representational art. Islamic art, for example, tends to avoid images of living creatures, relying instead on calligraphy and geometric design. Most Christian traditions, by contrast, embrace representational art, some quite enthusiastically. In fact, many Christians seemed unbothered by the giant golden statue of Donald Trump wrapped in an American flag and openly adored at the 2021 CPAC conference.

Deuteronomy 11-25

We continue our review of well-worn themes and judgments: Keep the Commandments; destroy rivals and hew down their graven images; don't drink blood; only eat meat; stone competing prophets to death; avoid unclean animals; don't boil a kid in its mother's milk; forgive debts and free slaves every seven years; eat no leavened bread during Passover; observe the Feast of Tabernacles; don't sacrifice animals with blemishes; two eyewitnesses are required to establish guilt; don't wear clothes made of mixed fabrics; and, of course, the penalty for adultery is death.

But Deuteronomy introduces new material starting in Chapter 15. Slaves are to be released every seven years, but only if they're Hebrew. Foreign slaves don't get the same courtesy. And even Hebrew slaves don't just walk away: if their master gave them a wife during their servitude and they had children, the slave can only go free alone. The wife and kids remain the property of the master. If the slave decides to stay for love of his family, his ear is pierced with an awl, and he becomes a slave for life. "And it shall not seem hard unto thee," the text says, "when thou sendest him away free from thee; for he hath been worth a double hired servant" (Deut. 15:18). Translation: Slavery's a bargain, don't feel bad about it.

In Deuteronomy 22, we get a wide array of new laws, some disturbingly specific. A man who takes a woman captive in war must let her shave her head and mourn for a month before marrying her. If a man has multiple wives and the unloved one bears a child, he must still grant that child a proper inheritance. A "stubborn and rebellious" son who is also a drunkard may be stoned to death. Oxen and donkeys are not to be yoked together. And in Deuteronomy 22:5, we're told it's an abomination for a man or woman to wear clothes associated with the opposite sex. Off-putting maybe, but an abomination?

Verses 13–21 of the same chapter offer a stomach-turning glimpse into biblical sexual ethics. If a man claims his new bride wasn't a virgin, her parents must produce a "token of virginity," commonly understood to mean a bloody bed sheet. If they can't, the woman is to be stoned to death "because she hath wrought folly in Israel, to play the whore in her father's house." But wouldn't the husband, not her parents, be in a better position to confirm what happened? And how reliable is a single night's laundry as legal evidence? Also, let's note that not all women bleed during their first sexual encounter. It's almost as if this law was written by primitive men who didn't understand female anatomy.

Verses 22–30 add to the discomfort. If a woman is raped in the city but doesn't scream, both she and her rapist are to be executed. The assumption is that she must have been complicit. But if the rape occurs in the countryside, only the rapist dies because screaming wouldn't have helped. No consideration is given to whether the woman could scream, or whether she was physically restrained. If a man is caught having sex with an unmarried woman, he must pay her father a fine, marry her, and is forbidden from ever divorcing her.

Deuteronomy 23 lists those barred from public worship: eunuchs (defined as anyone who's had their "privy member cut off"), bastards, Moabites, and Ammonites—though Egyptians are allowed, "because thou wast a stranger in their land." In military camps, anyone who has a nocturnal emission must wash and stay outside until evening. Also, everyone is required to carry a trowel to bury their own waste.

One surprising standout in this chapter is Deut. 23:15–16, which says that if a runaway slave comes to you, you must not return them to their master. Instead, you're to let them stay where they want, and "thou shalt not oppress him." In a book filled with punitive laws, this feels… almost progressive. It also contradicts Exodus 21 and Leviticus 25, where slavery is affirmed, and runaway slaves are not protected. So how did Southern slaveholders, who loved quoting the Old Testament, skip right over this part?

Chapter 23 also includes financial and social regulations: you can't charge interest on loans to fellow Israelites, but you can charge foreigners (23:19). Deuteronomy 24 expands on various civil laws. Newlywed men are exempt from military service for a whole year so they can stay home and "cheer up" their wives (24:5). Daily wages must be paid promptly to poor laborers (24:15), and a portion of the harvest must be left for widows and orphans (24:21). But not all of it is compassionate: a woman who's been divorced and remarried may not return to her first husband; doing so is "detestable" (24:4).

Deuteronomy 25 continues with penalties and curious commandments. Punishments of up to 40 lashes are permitted (25:3), and while you can eat grapes from your neighbor's vineyard, you better not carry them off in a basket. And in a particularly vivid and vindictive statute: if a woman intervenes in a fight by grabbing a man's genitals, her hand is to be cut off, and "thine eye shall not pity her" (25:11).

Elsewhere, the language of ownership is chillingly casual. Slaves are treated as family assets, gifted or inherited, and Deuteronomy offers no real challenge to the idea that humans can be owned. Foreigners can be permanently enslaved (Lev. 25), and women captured in war—grieving, widowed, shaved, and likely traumatized—can become wives, and sexual partners, after 30 days. The line between war bride and sex slave is, at best, hazy.

I had expected Deuteronomy to simply rehash what came before, but starting in Chapter 15, it veers into new and often unsettling territory. Some laws, like protections for widows, exemptions for newlyweds, and compassion toward runaway slaves, seem genuinely humane. Others, especially those concerning women, sex, and slavery, not so much.

There's an obsession with male anatomy: eunuchs are banned from worship, women who grab testicles get mutilated, and soldiers who experience nocturnal emissions are disqualified for the day. One wonders who was expected to staff the army if that rule were strictly enforced.

And for all the talk of justice, there's precious little room for nuance. Virginity is presumed provable. Rape is judged based on how loud the victim was. Death is meted out for drunken sons and ambiguous sexual missteps. It all reflects a worldview that is rigid, punitive, patriarchal—and, in many ways, shockingly out of touch with both morality and reality.

Deuteronomy 26-34

We start with an admonition: "Thou shalt not muzzle the ox when he treadeth out the corn." This verse is often interpreted as a nod to animal and human dignity, though that may be a generous reading. If the Bible's point is that animal and human deserve fair treatment, it could've just said so plainly. Instead, we get this curious agricultural metaphor, leaving modern readers to squint for meaning.

Next, we're back to sex and marriage. If two brothers live together and one dies childless, the surviving brother is required to marry the widow. If he refuses, she must follow a very specific ritual: Deut. 25:9–10 says she is to approach him before the town elders, remove his shoe, spit in his face, and declare, "So shall it be done unto that man that will not build up his brother's house." No guidance on whether it's the left or right shoe. The symbolism is colorful, the shame public, and the patriarchy fully intact.

We then shift to the topic of tithing. The first fruits of the harvest must be given to God, who, being incorporeal, delegates the collection to His priests. Every third year is a designated "tithing year," with specific instructions to care for strangers, orphans, and widows. It's unclear whether this is a one-time annual event or a year-long obligation. Deut. 26:15

includes part of the prayer said during tithing: "Look down from thy holy habitation, from heaven, and bless thy people of Israel..." This is arguably the first time heaven is described as God's physical residence. Up to this point, divine action has been mostly terrestrial: plagues, fire, food from the sky, parted seas but little mention of an actual celestial address.

In Deuteronomy 27, after crossing the Jordan, the Israelites are instructed to build stone monuments and participate in a call-and response ceremony where the priests read the laws and the people affirm with an "Amen." Many of these declarations take the form of curses. Deut. 27:22, for example, says: "Cursed be he that lieth with his sister, the daughter of his father, or the daughter of his mother." This type of doubling— saying "your sister" and then explaining "daughter of your father"—is common in the Bible.

Chapters 28 and 29 outline a familiar biblical formula: follow the rules and prosper, break them and suffer. The list of blessings (like being exalted above all nations or enjoying ample rain) is relatively short. The list of curses, however, is extensive and graphic: disease, drought, military defeat, insanity, betrayal, and famine. Highlights include being struck with "consumption, fever, inflammation, and extreme burning" (28:22), having one's wife sleep with another man (28:30), worms eating your grapes (28:39), and resorting to cannibalism of your own children (28:55). In Deut. 30:19, we finally get the boiled-down message: "I have set before you life and death, blessing and cursing: therefore choose life." In short: obey and live, disobey and die.

Deuteronomy 31 is Moses's farewell address. Now 120 years old, he assures the Israelites that Joshua will lead them to victory, just as they defeated the Amorite kings. Moses reminds them—again—that he will die before entering the Promised Land. God confirms this and adds that, once the people rebel, "My anger shall be kindled against them... and I will forsake them" (Deut. 31:17). As a safeguard, Moses is instructed to write a poem, the *Song of Moses*, and store it in the Ark of the

Covenant to remind future generations of God's promises and threats.

After delivering the song, Moses climbs Mount Nebo to die. God is still angry over the waters of Meribah and refuses to let him enter the Promised Land. Moses blesses the twelve tribes and dies, and we're told in Deut. 34:10: "There arose not a prophet since in Israel like unto Moses, whom the Lord knew face to face."

The final chapters of Deuteronomy cover a wide range of material, laws on sex, marriage, offerings, and rituals, but they also include some important theological developments. For the first time, heaven is clearly referenced as God's "holy habitation," which hints at the future development of an afterlife or celestial reward system.

We end Deuteronomy with the Israelites on the threshold of conquest. But where Numbers ends with a bloodied sword raised, Deuteronomy leaves us with a funeral and a passing of the torch. Moses, who began as the voice of God and lawgiver on Sinai, is now dead. The people mourn for 30 days. Joshua, untested, prepares to lead them into Canaan.

Curiously, we are informed that "These are the words which Moses spake" and that "There arose not a prophet since... like unto Moses," both indications that someone other than Moses wrote Deuteronomy. Whoever the actual author was, they wrote after the events described, which makes Deuteronomy not just a religious document, but an early example of retrospective mythmaking: revering the past while reasserting the covenant.

JOSHUA

Joshua 1-8

Finally, the Israelites are ready to begin their conquest of the Promised Land. Joshua sends two spies to reconnoiter Jericho, and they decide the best location for surveillance is a whore house run by a woman named Rahab. She hides them from the authorities and makes a deal: in exchange for her help, they agree not to harm her or her family. After three days, the spies return, light up cigarettes, and brief Joshua on all they'd seen and done. Most of it, anyway.

The Israelite army, 40,000 strong, arrives at the banks of the Jordan River, led by the Ark of the Covenant. As the Ark approaches, the river miraculously parts, and the force crosses without getting their feet wet. After reaching a hill near Gilgal, Joshua decides that now, on the eve of a major military campaign, is the perfect time to disable his entire army. According to Joshua 5:5, none of the men born during the forty years in the wilderness had been circumcised. So out come the flint knives, and the mass procedure is performed at the Hill of Foreskins. Presumably, it got the name after, not before, the operations were conducted.

Jericho, heavily fortified, looms ahead. Joshua unveils a foolproof battle plan: the Ark leads a procession of seven priests with seven rams' horns, who circle the city once a day for six days. On the seventh day, they do seven laps, blast the horns, and the people shout. Just like that, "the wall fell down flat" (Josh. 6:20). The Israelites storm the city, killing everyone—men and women, young and old, even the animals. Only Rahab and her household are spared. All gold and silver is taken for God's treasury.

But amid the holy slaughter, a real crime occurs. Achan, son of Carmi, secretly keeps a cloak and some valuables. Joshua, unaware, sends a small force to attack the next city, Ai, but they're repelled. Distraught, Joshua falls into despair and asks God how such a failure could happen. Given that Ai was a minor set-back, his reaction seems too full of self-pity. God informs him that the covenant has been violated. Achan is found out, stoned to death, and then burned—because, apparently, God can overlook mass murder but not petty theft from His divine loot chest.

With God's wrath appeased, Joshua plans a more serious assault on Ai. This time, he sends 30,000 troops and sets a trap. One force lures the defenders out by pretending to retreat, while another slips into the unguarded city and slaughters everyone. A total of 12,000 die, and the king of Ai is hanged from a tree. According to Joshua 8:28, the town was burned and left "a desolation unto this day."

It's cathartic to finally see the Israelites take action, though you wouldn't want to be on the receiving end. At Jericho, they kill every man, woman, child, and animal. At Ai, they spare the livestock but still kill all the people. As in earlier conquests, the text presents genocide with a matter-of-fact tone, as if it's just divine housekeeping. The only acknowledged "crime" is a soldier pocketing silver and punished with death by stoning and fire.

For the first time, the narrative suggests actual military tactics. An army of 40,000 is plausible—Alexander the Great invaded Persia with approximately 50,000 troops. Joshua's initial mistake at Ai (sending too small a force) is believable, and his later feigned retreat and ambush strategy is textbook battlefield deception. The king of Ai fell for it and paid with his life.

But the fall of Jericho feels far less grounded. Ancient sieges were long, miserable affairs. Inside the walls, defenders suffered from food shortages and constant fear. Outside, attackers dealt with exposure, disease, and exhaustion. Walls didn't just tumble at the sound of trumpets, they were undermined, battered, or outlasted. The Ai campaign reads like real warfare while Jericho hinges on a miracle.

Speaking of miracles, I hadn't realized the Israelites parted not one, but two bodies of water—the Red Sea and the Jordan—on cue. That's a useful skill to have when launching an invasion. Also notable is the text's subtle admission that it was written long after the events: monuments "still stand today," and ruins remain "a desolation unto this day." It's an acknowledgment that we're not hearing eyewitness testimony.

Joshua 9-24

After hearing about Joshua's successes at Jericho and Ai, the Gibeonites resort to trickery. Claiming to be travelers from a distant land, they approach the Israelite camp in worn-out clothes with moldy provisions and ask for a treaty. The Israelites, apparently not big on background checks, agree to a non-aggression pact, only to discover days later that the Gibeonites live just down the road. It's a lazy negotiation strategy on Joshua's part, and the Israelites get played. Still, Joshua honors the agreement, though he demotes the Gibeonites to perpetual servitude as woodcutters and water carriers.

Ironically, Joshua then defends these new vassals when five local kings unite to punish Gibeon for their defection. Joshua launches a surprise attack, routing the enemy coalition. In a dramatic climax, the defeated kings are captured and made to lie prostrate before Joshua, who places his foot on each of their necks, gives them a humiliating dressing-down, and then executes them.

One curious detail in this battle is celestial: "The sun stood still, and the moon stayed, until the people had avenged themselves upon their enemies...so the sun stood still in the midst of heaven and hasted not to go down about a whole day" (Josh. 10:13). That's one way to buy more daylight.

What follows is a string of victories over other Canaanite tribes, with outcomes just as bloody as Jericho's. Entire populations, including civilians and animals, are slaughtered. Joshua 12 offers a roundup of the carnage: 31 kingdoms destroyed.

Despite the rapid-fire narrative, the conquest of Canaan seems to have taken some time. In Joshua 13, God reminds Joshua that he's getting old and there's still land to be claimed. The rest of chapters 13–18 details how the land is divided among the twelve tribes, with maps of territorial allotments. Chapter 20 addresses cities of refuge—places where those who killed accidentally could flee for trial—and the allocation of Levitical cities, which were assigned separately from tribal inheritances.

In Chapter 23, Joshua, now near death, reminds the Israelites to stick with God, avoid pagan worship, and refrain from intermarrying with the neighbors they hadn't yet killed. He gathers the tribal leaders at Shechem and recounts the highlights of his and Moses' accomplishments in a kind of farewell address, a condensed version of Moses' lengthy goodbye in Deuteronomy. After this, Joshua dies at age 110, and the long-carried bones of Joseph are finally buried at Shechem.

There's a notable downward trend in biblical lifespans. Noah lived to 950, Abraham to 175, Isaac 180, Jacob 147,

Joseph 110, Moses 120, and Joshua 110. At some point, people must have realized that humans living nearly a millennium was a stretch. Ages hovering around 100 may have seemed improbable, but not impossible, and would have made the story more believable.

The same could be said of Joshua's military feats. There's no archaeological evidence for any of the battles described in the book, but some of the tactics sound plausible. Feigned retreats to lure enemies, sieges of fortified cities, and overwhelming troop numbers are all attested in ancient warfare. A 40,000-man army is large but within the realm of possibility. The brutal treatment of captured cities, including the killing of noncombatants, was, sadly, not unique to the Israelites. What stands out is the theological framing: genocide not as crime but as divine command.

Even if the claim that 31 tribes had been annihilated is exaggerated, it probably preserves the echoes of real battles. The Israelites believed they were entitled to the land, and God was on their side. Their war crimes were sanctified into holy deeds. Notably, there's a tonal shift between Deuteronomy and Joshua: the former deals in sweeping declarations, while the latter details boots-on-the-ground methods—ambushes, siege tactics, psychological warfare. Israel's leaders are no longer just prophets and priests; they're battlefield strategists, combining divine guidance with practical military acumen and unapologetic brutality.

The end of Joshua feels like the end of an era. Moses brought the people to the edge of the Promised Land, but Joshua took them across the finish line. The land has been divided, the enemies vanquished, the bones buried—but the legacy of bloodshed in God's name has only just begun.

JUDGES

Judges 1-10

After Joshua's conquest, you'd think the Israelites would be done. But evidently, the job wasn't finished. Judah and his brother Simeon lead the charge against the remaining Canaanites and Perizzites. In Judg. 1:7, there's a grotesque little anecdote where King Adoni-bezek, now their prisoner, admits: "Seventy kings with their thumbs and big toes cut off used to pick up scraps under my table. Now God has paid me back." In other words, he's been maimed in the same way he once mutilated others.

The Israelites continue their conquest, capturing cities like Jerusalem, Hebron, Debir, and Bethel. But they fail to drive out all the local inhabitants. An angel shows up, scolds them for their half-hearted extermination campaign, and warns that foreign gods will soon lead them astray.

And, surprise surprise, the Israelites immediately start worshipping Baal and intermarrying with the locals. As foreign powers press in, the Israelites once again cry out for help. This time, God's spirit falls on Othniel, the first of Israel's "judges," a title that blends military, political, and religious authority. Othniel drives out the king of Mesopotamia and ushers in 40 years of peace.

Then comes another relapse. The Israelites sin again (details vague), and this time God allows them to be oppressed by Eglon, king of Moab. When the Israelites repent, God sends a left-handed assassin named Ehud from the tribe of Benjamin. Ehud hides a sword on his right thigh (a place guards wouldn't check if expecting a right-handed threat), gains a private audience with the obese king, and stabs him so deeply that the handle disappears into Eglon's belly. Ehud escapes while the palace guards assume their king is just…on the toilet. A short battle follows in which Israelite forces kill 10,000 Moabites.

Next up: Deborah, a prophetess and the only female judge, a rare leadership role for a woman in ancient Israel. She calls on Barak, a hesitant military leader, to muster an army against the Canaanite general Sisera. Barak agrees only if Deborah goes with him. They rout Sisera's army, and he flees on foot to the tent of Heber the Kenite, a neutral party. There, Heber's wife Jael offers him refuge, lulls him into sleep, and then hammers a tent peg through his skull, fulfilling Deborah's prophecy that a woman would claim the glory. Judges 5 recounts the victory in a rousing and poetic *Song of Deborah*.

Do the Israelites now remain loyal to God? Of course not. After another 40 years, they're back to worshipping Baal. This time, God allows the Midianites to dominate them. An angel appears to Gideon, a reluctant farmer from the tribe of Manasseh, and calls him to lead the resistance. Gideon is skeptical. But after the angel miraculously ignites a meat-and-bread offering with fire, he's convinced—sort of. He still wants more proof, so he sets up a test: he places a fleece outside overnight and asks that in the morning the fleece be wet with dew while the ground remains dry. God obliges. Still not satisfied, Gideon reverses the request the next night, this time asking for the fleece to stay dry while the ground is wet. With this foolproof test completed, preparations for war can begin.

Gideon selects his attack force by having the men drink from a river. Those who cup water in their hands and lap it "like dogs" are selected for an elite force of 300. Those who kneel to drink are sent home. It's a confusing selection method, but it gets results. Gideon's 300 launch a surprise nighttime attack, causing panic in the Midianite camp and scattering their forces. Eventually, Gideon captures and kills the Midianite leaders, Zebah and Zalmunna, and defeats what is described as a 120,000-man army, although clearly, Israel's larger forces must've played a role offstage.

Gideon goes on to father 70 sons through many wives and another son, Abimelech, with a concubine. He dies "old and full of years," probably also full of exhaustion. And yes, the Israelites immediately return to Baal worship.

Abimelech, hungry for power, conspires to make himself king. He slaughters his 70 brothers—potential rivals—except for the youngest, Jotham, who escapes. From a mountaintop, Jotham delivers a pointed parable: the trees of the forest seek a king. The olive tree, fig tree, and grapevine all decline, preferring to continue producing oil, fruit, and wine rather than rule over others. But the thornbush accepts, offering shade to those who obey and threatening fire to those who don't. The message is clear: no good or fruitful leader would stoop to rule in this way, so the people are left with a worthless, dangerous ruler like Abimelech.

And sure enough, Abimelech's reign ends in disaster. After three years, his own allies turn against him. During a siege, a woman drops a millstone on his head from a tower. Mortally wounded, Abimelech begs his armor-bearer to kill him, so it won't be said that a woman struck the fatal blow. (Spoiler: it's still said.)

We wrap up Chapter 10 with Israel worshipping Baal again and wondering why God is mad.

Despite occasional successes, the Israelites under the judges never seem to learn. God no longer rains fire and brimstone but uses foreign oppression as discipline. The judges themselves are an eclectic bunch: some are valiant, others violent or vain, and a few barely register. With its vivid tales of betrayal, violence, talking trees, and odd divine tests, the Book of Judges echoes the surrealism of Genesis but lacks its sense of cosmic scale. It feels like we're filling in narrative gaps, documenting the tribal chaos between Joshua and the eventual rise of monarchy.

One can't help but wonder about Gideon's 300: was this a retroactive echo of Leonidas and his Spartans at Thermopylae in 480 BCE? If so, it would suggest that this part of Judges was written, or rewritten, after the classical Greek period.

Judges 11-21

There's a lot of colorful and troubling storytelling in the last half of Judges. Jephthah, born to Gilead and a prostitute, was a successful raider but a social outcast. When the Ammonites threatened Gilead (both the region and the name of the chieftain), the elders made him an offer he couldn't refuse: lead the fight and become their ruler.

Before battle, Jephthah cuts a reckless deal with God: "Whatsoever cometh forth of the doors of my house to meet me, when I return in peace...shall surely be the Lord's, and I will offer it up for a burnt offering" (Judg. 11:31). So, basically, the first thing to greet him at home is getting sacrificed. What could go wrong?

Naturally, he wins. And naturally, the first to greet him is his only daughter, dancing with a tambourine. Devastated but unwilling to break his vow, he tells her the news. She calmly accepts her fate but asks for a two-month reprieve to mourn her virginity with her friends in the mountains. The text says she "knew no man" when she returned, which is biblical code for "still a virgin." I call BS on that, but either way, her reward for being a good daughter was to be murdered and burned on an altar.

Jephthah then goes to war with the Ephraimites—fellow Israelites—and slaughters those who can't correctly pronounce *Shibboleth*. It's gruesome linguistics-as-loyalty-test stuff. While his mother's background made him a pariah, Jephthah was still from Gilead, part of the tribe of Manasseh. Why he ended up as a judge over all Israel isn't entirely clear, but he served for six years.

He's followed by Ibzan, who fathered sixty children, then Elon, and then Abdon, who had forty sons and thirty grandsons who rode seventy donkeys. That's one donkey per kid, not seventy each, though either way, it seems intended as a flex.

The cycle repeats: the Israelites fall into idolatry, and the Philistines take over. An angel appears to a barren woman from the tribe of Dan, telling her she'll give birth to a child who will save Israel and that she must never cut his hair. Enter Samson.

Samson grows into a hot-tempered strongman who falls for a Philistine hottie named Timnah and demands she be his wife. On the way to visit her, he kills a lion and later finds bees making honey in its carcass. At the wedding, he makes a riddle about it—"Out of the eater came something to eat…"—which confounds the guests. Timnah gets the answer out of him and tells her family, and Samson flies into a rage. He murders thirty men and storms off.

Then things escalate. He ties torches to the tails of 300 foxes and releases them through Philistine fields. He slays a thousand soldiers with a donkey's jawbone. How? No detail provided. Eventually, he falls for Delilah, who's bribed to find the source of his strength. After several tries, he tells her it's his Fabio-length hair. She shaves it while he sleeps, and the Philistines seize him, gouge out his eyes, and imprison him. Oddly, they allow his hair to grow back. With one last burst of strength, he pulls down a temple, killing himself and countless enemies.

Then comes a confusing side tale. In Ephraim, a man named Micah creates a silver idol and hires a wandering Levite as his personal priest. The Danites show up, steal both the idol and the priest, and then wipe out a peaceful town called Laish. The narrative offers no moral, but the tribal infighting is escalating.

And then we arrive at Judges' most grotesque moment. A Levite, his concubine, and a servant are traveling from Bethlehem when they stop in Gibeah, a Benjamite town. An old man offers them lodging, but during the night a mob surrounds the house and demands, "Bring forth the man that came into thine house, that we may know him" (Judg. 19:22).

Angry gay mobs seem to be a recurring problem in the Bible. This scene echoes Genesis, where men surround Lot's house in Sodom. (It's interesting that these parallel tales are both in Chapter 19 of their respective books. Is an ancient scribe winking at us?) In Sodom, angels intervene. Here, there is no divine rescue. The old man offers his virgin daughter instead, but the mob isn't interested. The Levite then tosses his concubine to them. She is gang-raped all night. In the morning, he finds her collapsed at the doorstep and says, "Up, and let us be going." When she doesn't respond, he cuts her body into twelve pieces and sends one to each tribe, demanding retribution.

Here's what's insane: his outrage comes only after her death, not during the rape he permitted. A concubine in biblical times had recognized status. Children from such unions had legal rights. The Levite handed over his long-term partner to be brutalized and then had the gall to demand vengeance from the other tribes. But his grotesque PR campaign works. The Israelites muster an army of 400,000 to punish the Benjamites, who field just 26,000. After some initial defeats, the Israelites wipe out the tribe, killing 25,000 and destroying their cities. Then they panic: oops, we might have gone too far.

To fix this, they identify a town—Jabesh-gilead—that didn't join the war, and slaughter all its inhabitants except the virgins, whom they give to the Benjamites. Still short, they steal more virgins during a festival in Shiloh. It's forced marriage by massacre and kidnapping.

The murder of Jephthah's daughter, the rape and dismemberment of the concubine, the attack on Jabesh, and the abduction of the Shiloh women are continuations of the over-the-top brutality of earlier books. But the war stories here are even more implausible than in Joshua. A 400,000-man army in the Iron Age would have been logistically impossible.

Judges closes with a chilling summary: "In those days there was no king in Israel: every man did that which was right in his own eyes." Which, in this context, includes mass rape, child sacrifice, and civil war. But I'm sure things will be better when kings rule Israel.

Honestly, I'm relieved to be done with Judges. It's not quite the slog that Leviticus was, but it comes close. Who are these miserable people who burn their daughters, decimate tribes, hack concubines to death, and then act like they hold the moral high ground? It's a wonder God didn't just let them worship Baal and reboot with a less bloodthirsty species.

RUTH

The *Book of Ruth* is an endearing vignette of grace wedged between the carnage of Judges and the dynastic drama of Samuel. Ruth and her sister-in-law Orpah are both widowed in Moab. Their mother-in-law, Naomi, decides to return to Judah and urges the two younger women to stay behind with their families. Orpah tearfully complies, but Ruth clings to Naomi and insists on going with her, pledging, in one of Scripture's most beautiful declarations: "Whither thou goest, I will go; and where thou lodgest, I will lodge: thy people shall be my people, and thy God my God: where thou diest, will I die, and there will I be buried: the Lord do so to me, and more also, if ought but death part thee and me" (Ruth 1:16–17).

Ruth and Naomi settle in Bethlehem. To support them, Ruth goes out to glean in the fields—a practice allowed by law for the poor—and catches the eye of Boaz, an overseer and relative of her deceased husband. He offers her protection and extra grain. Naomi sees potential. She tells Ruth to perfume herself and approach Boaz at night, lying at his feet. Boaz gets the message. He negotiates for the land—and the right to marry her—and soon they marry. Ruth gives birth to a son, Obed, who is later identified as King David's grandfather.

After the pointless cruelty, violence, and implausibility of Judges, we needed this palette cleanser. Ruth is a quiet, redemptive story of love and loyalty—not just between a woman and a man, but between two women who endured grief, migration, and economic upheaval together. Also, the affection between Ruth and Boaz is understated but mutual. Ruth doesn't just need to marry, she wants *this* marriage.

The final genealogy serves a strategic function: it roots David in Bethlehem and lays the groundwork for later Christian authors to trace Jesus's lineage to this moment. That detail alone suggests later editorial involvement, but for once, the redactors left the heart of the story untouched. So, let's take a moment to appreciate it on its own terms as a moving, hopeful tale of survival, fidelity, and second chances.

1 SAMUEL

1 Samuel 1-15

Samuel's father, Elkanah, has two wives, Peninnah, who was fertile, and Hannah, who was barren. Hannah, despondent over her inability to conceive, prays in earshot of Priest Eli. God allows her to give birth to Samuel, while Eli's sons are delinquents who exploit pilgrims (it's always the preacher's kids, isn't it?). A mysterious man (God?) shows up and tells Eli that Israel will be blessed, but his sons will die by the sword. Later, when Samuel is serving under Eli, God speaks to him, telling him to inform Eli (in 1 Sam. 3:14), "The iniquity of Eli's house shall not be purged with sacrifice nor offering forever," meaning that no atonement is possible for their sins. It's not clear why Eli needs to be given this message twice or why God outsourced the second message to the child Samuel.

A battle between the Israelites and the Philistines follows, and Israel loses 4,000. Then they use the Ark to lead them into battle, but that doesn't work, and they lose another 30,000, including Eli's sons (prophecy fulfilled!) and the Ark itself, which is captured. Upon hearing the news, Eli falls off his seat and breaks his neck, dead. But like Frodo's ring, the Ark *wants to return to its master*. It causes tumors and panic until the Philistines can't get rid of it fast enough.

Twenty years pass, and Samuel urges the Israelites to stop worshiping Baal, and God smashes a Philistine incursion. Samuel goes on to have a long career as a judge and prophet, and his stature probably rivals that of royalty. When Samuel is old, his two sons take over, but they are corrupt bribe-takers, and the Israelites yearn for a king instead of more judges.

Saul, from the tribe of Benjamin, has lost his family's donkeys and finds his way to Samuel, who realizes Saul is the future king. Samuel assembles the tribes, and they appoint Saul king—even though he's hiding in the baggage. "God save the King," they cry. Honestly, Saul doesn't seem like great king material.

His leadership is immediately tested when the Ammonites give the tribe of Jabesh an ultimatum: surrender or have their right eyes cut out. Saul gets the news while in the fields with his oxen, which he slaughters and sends out in pieces to the tribes with a message: come help Jabesh, or you'll end up like this ox. In Judges, the Levite sent pieces of his concubine to the tribes, and now Saul sends slices of an ox. Seriously, why can't they just send letters?

Anyway, Israel assembles an army of 300,000 and slaughters the Ammonites. Samuel gives his farewell speech in 1 Samuel 12:14: "If ye will fear the Lord, and serve him, and obey his voice, and not rebel against the commandment of the Lord, then shall both ye and also the king that reigneth over you continue following the Lord your God." In other words, God's support is conditional on obedience.

After the Philistine governor is killed, the Israelites again go to war with their oppressors. Saul forms an army, but it begins to melt into the desert. He also errs by making a burnt offering without waiting for Samuel. Saul's son Jonathan charges forward, kills some of the enemy, and panic spreads among the Philistines. Saul's men rally. Saul forbids anyone from eating until the battle ends, but Jonathan eats some honey, and later the rest of the soldiers feast on oxen and sheep. Jonathan offers to die for breaking orders, but the Israelites acclaim his leadership, and his life is spared.

More battles and victories follow, but Saul's luck runs out when God orders him in 1 Sam. 15:3: "Now go and smite Amalek, and utterly destroy all that they have, and spare them not; but slay both man and woman, infant and suckling, ox and sheep, and camel and ass." Saul's army slaughters the Amalekites but spares the best sheep and cattle—and captures their king, Agag. Samuel reminds Saul that God had demanded *total* destruction. Saul begs forgiveness and grabs Samuel's cloak as he turns away, tearing it. Samuel, apparently fed up with everyone's disobedience, hacks Agag to pieces and storms out of camp. 1 Sam. 15:35 concludes with God expressing regret that he had "made Saul king over Israel."

Ugh, I was hoping for more *Ruth* and less *Judges*, but we're back to fanciful battles, wandering livestock, and divine commands to slaughter everything that breathes. The era of judges is clearly ending, and a monarchy is beginning to take shape, but it's not clear whether God initiates this shift or merely allows it. Samuel, for his part, thinks the whole idea is a mistake. When he asks God, he's told that the people aren't rejecting him (Samuel), they're rejecting God himself. Samuel warns them about the dangers of kings—taxation, conscription, corruption—but the people insist. Eventually, Samuel relents and anoints Saul with God's apparent blessing.

Saul's decision not to kill all the animals after the Amalekite battle was pragmatic, but God had mandated *absolute* slaughter: so Saul was no longer fit to be king. I think Saul was treated unfairly. If blind obedience is the ultimate test of leadership, Saul may have failed. But if good judgment and battlefield success matter, his record was excellent. Instead of being defenestrated, Saul deserved a promotion.

1 Samuel 16-31

Samuel is in a funk because Saul has lost God's favor, but God has a plan B. He tells Samuel to anoint someone else—David, the son of Jesse in Bethlehem. The Bible describes David as a comely, beautiful creature with a ruddy complexion. Meanwhile, Saul is having trouble dealing with his fall from grace and calls for someone who can lift his spirits. Enter David, a skilled harpist. Saul quickly grows fond of him, "loved him greatly," and makes him his armor-bearer.

Soon, the Israelites are squaring off against the Philistines across a valley, and a giant named Goliath steps forward to challenge any Israelite to single combat. In 1 Samuel 17:4–7, Goliath is described as wearing a brass helmet and thick greaves, and his spear is "like a weaver's beam," which excited and impressed David and Saul. How tall was Goliath? The Masoretic Text says "six cubits and a span," nearly 10 feet tall, but the Septuagint (an earlier Greek translation) records his height as "four cubits and a span," around 6 feet 9 inches. Still a towering figure, but not a Marvel character.

David volunteers for the job. Armed with nothing but a sling, he lands a stone squarely in Goliath's forehead, then races forward, decapitates him, and brings the severed head back to Saul—who strangely seems not to know who David is. 1 Sam. 17:58: "And Saul said to him, Whose son art thou, thou young man? And David answered, I am the son of thy servant Jesse the Bethlehemite." Jonathan is immediately smitten too, giving David his cloak, bow, and belt. Nothing untoward happening here, folks; we should just move on.

Saul quickly becomes jealous of David's popularity and military prowess. He sends him on dangerous missions against the Philistines, hoping David won't survive. However, David is a skilled warrior and returns with piles of enemy foreskins like a deranged cat dropping gifts at his master's feet. Saul rewards him by giving his daughter Michal in marriage, but the danger hasn't passed.

As Saul's paranoia grows, David flees to Samuel for protection. Michal tries to fool Saul's men by putting a goat-hair dummy in the bed, a classic decoy they learned from *Home Alone*. Later, at a ceremonial dinner, Jonathan warns David that Saul still wants him dead. David escapes again, this time into Philistine territory. There, he becomes an outlaw-turned-mercenary, raiding surrounding towns and offering his services to the enemy. The Philistines, skeptical of his loyalty, later send him to chase down Amalekite raiders rather than fight alongside them.

Saul, increasingly desperate, orders the massacre of the priests of Nob who had helped David. Eventually, Saul and David find themselves in the same desert cave, where David sneaks up and cuts the corner off Saul's cloak—proof that he could have killed him but didn't. Saul, in a rare moment of clarity, says: "Thou art more righteous than I: for thou hast rewarded me good, whereas I have rewarded thee evil" (1 Sam. 24:17). David promises not to erase Saul's name or destroy his kin.

Samuel dies in Ramah while David continues to build his forces. After being insulted by the surly camel-merchant Nabal, David is placated by Nabal's wife Abigail, who supplies provisions. Nabal later dies after a night of heavy drinking, so Abigail becomes David's newest trophy wife.

The tension with Saul isn't over. Another near-miss: David sneaks into Saul's camp and makes off with his spear and water jug, again demonstrating mercy. But Saul remains king, and David continues operating on the fringes.

As the Philistine threat looms, Saul turns to the occult, seeking help from a witch at Endor. She's understandably nervous, since Saul has outlawed sorcery, but she summons the ghost of Samuel anyway. The prophet tells Saul the Philistines will win, and that Saul and his sons will soon be joining him in the afterlife.

Meanwhile, David is sent to fight Amalekite raiders, and so he misses the main Philistine-Israelite showdown at Mount Gilboa. It's a disaster for Israel. Saul's sons, including

Jonathan, are killed. Saul, gravely wounded, falls on his own sword to avoid capture.

While David's victory over Goliath was dramatic, it wasn't a decisive end to the Philistine threat. They had defeated Israel before and would again as long as the unfortunate Saul remained in charge. Saul never fully recovers from a prior misstep: sparing some Amalekite livestock that God had ordered destroyed. He also violates his own ban on witches and violates other commandments too. His relationship with David, romantic or not, has raised eyebrows for centuries.

It's also strange that the text retains two separate stories of David sparing Saul's life: one in the cave, another in the desert. These near-identical scenes feel like narrative padding. One would have been enough to prove David's restraint.

2 SAMUEL

2 Samuel 1-11

David gets the news of Saul's death from a refugee of the battle who claims to have personally helped to dispatch Saul, prompting David to tear his own clothes in grief. David then has the refugee killed. The people of Jabesh accept David as the king, where he remains for 7 years and 6 months before the battle of Gibeon. The civil war battle between the House of David and the House of Benjamin (loyal to Saul) is sometimes believable and, other times risible. Each side sends out twelve soldiers, who face each other and then move forward, grabbing their opposite number by the head and simultaneously knifing him in the side. I assume there were no left-handers.

Probably stunned by the stupidity of the first wave, additional forces join the battle, and Abner (Saul's military leader) flees the scene. Losses are 19 men for David and 360 for Benjamin (Abner), numbers that speak to the nature of the limited war between the two houses. Despite this setback, Abner assumes control of Saul's forces but is accused of having sex with one of Saul's concubines and flies into a rage. He becomes a turncoat, pledging his support for David, but is killed by one of David's officers, Joab.

Some enterprising officers from the House of David kill one of Jonathan's sons (Jonathan was the son of Saul) and bring his head as a gift to David. They expect a reward, but David has them killed, their hands and feet cut off, and their bodies hanged.

The civil war ends, and David, at the age of 30, becomes king of Israel. He would go on to rule for 40 years. The new king then moves against Jerusalem, where the Jebusite defenders taunt the Israelites by saying "the blind and lame" could defend the city against David. David conquers the city, but the account of the battle is skeletal: He takes the city's citadel, and the king of Tyre builds him a palace. David also defeats the Philistines and uses his downtime to take on several more (unnamed) wives and concubines.

David then brings up the Ark, but the ox that tows it missteps, and one of the handlers named Uzzah touches the Ark to steady it, which sets God into a tizzy. 2 Sam. 6:7: "And the anger of the Lord was kindled against Uzzah, and God smote him there for his error, and there he died by the ark of God." This seems to have given David second thoughts about how to deploy the ark. He initially shunts it off to the Obed-Edom family, but upon seeing the blessings it provides them, he brings it into the city. David wears a loincloth and whirls and dances at the head of the ark's procession, prompting his wife Michal to tell him he is acting like a fool. Michal was barren, which seems like a punishment for criticizing her husband, but I get the feeling she was just fine with that.

After prophet Nathan predicts God's support and David offers a prayer, David goes on a streak of military victories. He defeats the Philistines (again) as well as the Moabites, whom he forces to lie prostrate in two lines, killing everyone in the first line and allowing the second line to live. He also defeats the king of Zobah and the Edomites, capturing 1,000 chariots, 700 horsemen, and 20,000 foot-soldiers. David continues to have a soft spot for Saul's defeated clan and allows Jonathan's son, Mephibosheth, to eat at the royal table.

After the death of the Ammonite king, David sent ambassadors to convey his condolences, but the Ammonites misinterpreted his intentions—and honestly, I think they can be forgiven for this. They humiliated the envoys by shaving off half their beards and sent them packing. The Ammonites then enlisted the Aramaeans, but Joab, David's general, routed them. In a second clash, Joab reportedly killed 40,000—biblical body counts being what they are.

But while Joab was busy winning battles, David was getting into mischief back home. One evening, while walking on the palace roof, he spots the beautiful Bathsheba, wife of the soldier Uriah the Hittite, bathing. He summons her to his room for sex. Later, she sends word that she's pregnant, and David panics. If he can get Uriah to come home and sleep with her, no one (other than Bathsheba) will know the child isn't his. David orders Uriah to leave his post and return home, but Uriah is too loyal and refuses to enjoy the comforts of home while his comrades remain in battle. So David sends him to the front lines, where he's predictably killed. After a brief mourning period, David marries Bathsheba, and she gives birth to their son.

Why was Abner upset by being accused of taking one of Saul's concubines? Women were property, so wouldn't his control of the deceased Saul's women be taken for granted? Also, what are we to make of the engagement where 24 soldiers die when they all grab their opponents by the head and stab with their right hand? Maybe we overestimated the sophistication of ancient combat, or we should acknowledge that the writers were unfamiliar with or unconcerned by the literalness of their accounts.

The scale of David's victories is unlike those of earlier military achievements, and we receive some degree of detail on the battles; yet, the taking of Jerusalem is surprisingly brief. The defenders show David contempt by saying "the sick and lame" could repel an attack, yet when he defeats them, we learn nothing about what transpires. David is happy to murder the prostrate Moabites, so what does he do with the insolent Jerusalemites? We aren't told, but I assume it wasn't pretty.

The story of the Ark is head-scratching. Why doesn't David lead his army with the Ark rather than having it follow? And what is up with God's wrath at Uzzah, who was killed after trying to prevent the Ark from toppling over? If God was so concerned about someone touching the Ark (other than priests), why did He allow people to walk at its sides in the first place? This is another cruel and arbitrary action by a god with anger management issues.

Also troubling is David's appalling use of Bathsheba. How many wives and mistresses does he need to not chase the next shiny object he sees? Not only does he cheat with her (rape her, in truth), but he conspires to get her loving husband killed. Perhaps David has secured God's blessing to the degree that Saul never did, and he is certainly more militarily successful; however, David is becoming less honorable by the day. He is no longer the man Saul admired after their desert-cave encounter.

2 Samuel 12-24

I was not the only one to be angered by David's treatment of Bathsheba. The prophet Nathan uses a parable about a rich person taking a poor man's lamb for slaughter as a way of telling David he's broken God's law by raping Bathsheba and killing her husband. God won't kill David but will instead hold his yet unborn son to pay the price. The child only survives seven days. David is inconsolable, at least until he sleeps with Bathsheba again, and she gets pregnant with Solomon. Note that God didn't punish David for David's crime, instead causing his innocent son to be a sort of blood sacrifice for the sins of his father.

Moving along, David's son Amnon is an apple that has not fallen too far from his father's tree. He notices the beauty of his sister Tamar, entices her into his room, and rapes her. David is angry about the assault, just not enough to do anything about it. Two years later, another of David's sons named Absalom takes matters into his own hands, luring Amnon to a party and then murdering him.

Absalom then sets sights on his father's kingship, ultimately causing David to flee Jerusalem for the remote desert. David is on the run but has left his ten concubines in Jerusalem at the mercy of Absalom, who publicly rapes them on the palace roof, in full view of all Israel. It was a horrific crime whose victims were not David, but those close to him. This is the second time God has punished David's family for crimes he committed, yet David himself walks free.

There is an interesting interlude where someone named Shemi yells at David, cursing him and tossing rocks. David tells his soldiers to ignore the threats and carry on—an unexpected forgiveness of free speech. A major battle at the Forest of Ephraim follows, and Absalom is defeated. David has given instructions to "deal gently" with Absalom if he is encountered, an order his general, Joab, ignores. Absalom is left dangling when his hair got caught in a tree branch, making him an easy target. Joab put three darts through his heart, and for good measure, ten more guards attacked and killed him. This is the second time Joab has killed people David wanted to spare. Joab earlier stabbed turncoat Abner, a valuable new ally for David, and now has killed the king's son, yet there are no consequences. Is David's hold on his army slipping?

David is beside himself over his son's death, moaning in 2 Sam. 18:33: "O my son Absalom, my son, my son Absalom! Would God I had died for thee, O Absalom, my son, my son!" You can feel the pain of the loss of a beloved son, the betrayal by his generals who disregarded his orders, and, perhaps, regret about how he had governed Israel. Let's face it, though, there was no universe where Absalom would have been pardoned for attempted regicide. But the threat to David's rule is not over. Sheba (a Benjamite) and Amasa form another threatening army. Joab tricks Amasa into embracing him but then runs a sword through his belly. The citizens of the walled city of Abel-Beth-Maacah surrender Sheba, and his head is delivered to the victorious Joab.

A three–year famine strikes, and David asks God its cause. The reply is that the late Saul had dishonored the Gibeonites. It seems like Saul can't win, even in death. You'll recall that Joshua had made a treaty with the Gibeonites (in Joshua 9), but I guess Saul had reneged, and now David and his people were being held accountable by God. David asks the aggrieved tribe of Gibeon what can be done to make amends and is told a blood sacrifice of Saul's descendants would do the trick. God lifts the famine after seven of Saul's descendants have been ritually slaughtered.

The Philistines remain a menace, and a series of battles ensues, one featuring a second Goliath whom Elhanan kills and another involving a warrior with six fingers on each hand and six toes on each foot. There's an interesting story from a battle at Bethlehem, where David has grown weary yet declines the water offered by his bodyguards who have fought their way from a well: 2 Sam. 23:17: "Be it far from me, O Lord, that I should do this: is not this the blood of the men that went in jeopardy of their lives? Therefore, he would not drink it."

God's anger is rekindled against the Israelites (I'm not sure why), and David orders a census, which he regrets undertaking (also not sure why). The results are that there are 800,000 fighting men for Israel and 500,000 more in Judah. The prophet Gad tells David that he can choose one of three penalties to be forgiven: seven years of famine, being chased by an invading army for three months, or three days of pestilence. David chooses pestilence, and 70,000 of his subjects perish. Perhaps he chose…*poorly*. But just as God's angel is about to lay waste to Jerusalem, he has a change of heart and stops the plague. As with God killing David's newborn son, He is again causing the death of David's people for sins they didn't commit.

King David is a horrible role model. His son Amnon has gotten the message that rape is ok, and he violates his own sister. David, no longer the violent but fundamentally moral actor that Saul encountered, does nothing to hold Amnon to account, but his other son, Absalom, does. David's crime with Bathsheba cost him the life of his infant son and nearly his kingdom to boot. David's trials are not over, though, and he must deal with more insurrections, famine, and pestilence. Why did God again lay waste to His people, and why was a census an offense that David had to atone for?

There appears to be an increased use of prophets, first Nathan and then Gad, who serve as intermediaries between the king and God. Why are these people necessary when there has been plenty of direct king–God dialogue in the past? Witches are to be killed, so how are these prophets, with their riddles about future doom, so different?

I am struck by the similarity between David's refusal to take water at Bethlehem and a (presumably) later story about Alexander the Great. According to the Roman historian Arrian, Alexander was offered water while his army was suffering in the Gedrosian Desert (modern-day Pakistan) on the return march from India. An infantry squad collected the water from a gully and presented it to the king, but Alexander refused to drink, emptying it onto the sand. Alexander's message was clear: if my soldiers can't drink, I won't either. Was the refusal of water a common trope associated with great leaders? Was the David story a copy of Alexander, or was Alexander's story inspired by the Bible?

Finally, how can the Philistines find so many freakish six-toed giants to unleash against David?

1 KINGS

1 Kings 1-11

The focus of the first half of the *Book of 1 Kings* is Solomon, but when we start, David is still on the throne. Now "old and stricken in years," David grew cold in the evenings and needed someone to keep him warm, so he selected a beautiful "young virgin," Abishag, to snuggle with. He "knew her not," although I'll bet he gave it a go.

Sensing weakness, David's son Adonijah began acting like he'd already inherited the crown. But David, ever politically savvy, had promised Bathsheba that her son Solomon would succeed him. He reaffirms that promise publicly, has Solomon anointed king, and then quietly exits stage left after a 40-year reign.

While other Old Testament luminaries get long, reflective sendoffs, David does not. Yet his life was nothing if not eventful: he killed Goliath, navigated a toxic (possibly romantic) relationship with King Saul, ascended to power, won countless military victories, and crushed a civil war. He was also a rapist and a war criminal. Still, in popular culture, David looms large. In medieval France, he was immortalized in playing cards alongside Alexander the Great, Charlemagne, and Augustus as one of the four kings.

With David dead and buried, Solomon wastes no time cleaning house. Adonijah, hoping for a consolation prize, asks if he can marry Abishag—the same human hot water bottle who'd kept Dad comfortable. Solomon sees this for what it is: a not-so-subtle power play. He has Adonijah executed. General Joab, who had backed the wrong horse, is also killed, as is Shimei, the desert stone-thrower whom David had once pardoned. 1 Kings 2:46 sums up this purge nicely: "And the kingdom was established in the hand of Solomon."

With his position secure, he married the (unnamed) Egyptian pharaoh's (unnamed) daughter. Then God appeared to Solomon in a dream and asked him what he most longed for. Solomon replied that as an inexperienced leader, he wanted discernment over riches or longevity. That's a really good answer! Sure enough, God grants his wish, a gift the king displays in the Judgment of Solomon. The case involves two prostitutes who lived in the same house and had both just given birth. One of the babies died, yet both claimed the surviving child was theirs. What to do? Solomon said the baby should simply be cut in two, and the real mother immediately said she'd surrender the child to save it, while the other woman said it would be just fine to cut it in half. Solomon gave the child to the first woman, proving his wisdom.

Solomon's holdings became vast, including 4,000 stalls for his chariots. He established good relations with Hiram, king of Tyre, and access to the cedars from Lebanon that would be needed for the grand temple he wanted to construct. Several chapters are dedicated to the construction of the Temple, the Holy of Holies (the most sacred area of the Temple, set aside for the Ark), the doors, and Solomon's palace.

The Ark is brought to the Temple, and a lengthy prayer is offered by Solomon, after which he sacrifices 22,000 oxen and 120,000 sheep. God reminds him to keep the Commandments and not worship other gods. Forced labor of the defeated Amorites, Hittites, and Perizzites was used for the giant construction project (the Israelites are unconcerned about slave labor when they're in charge...), and some of the land was freed up by the Pharaoh (Solomon's new father-in-law), who massacred indigenous settlements for a land dowery.

The Queen of Sheba paid Solomon a visit and was impressed by his wisdom and wealth, which he demonstrated by drinking from gold goblets and sitting on a throne made of gold and ivory. Another display of his vast appetite was his 700 wives and 300 concubines, some of whom were from strange lands and worshipped other gods. The now elderly Solomon began to worship "Ashtoreth the goddess of the Zidonians and after Milcom the abomination of the Ammonites" (1 Kings 11:5), which does not go over well with God. Hostile forces begin to form, including Jeroboam, who had been visited by a mystic who foretold his rise to power. Solomon's rule (like his father David's) lasted 40 years, and when he died, his son Rehoboam succeeded him.

Solomon, upon becoming king, had quickly and effectively cleared the field for his new administration and established a reputation for good judgment. But like Wall Street barons in the 1980s, he lived by the motto "greed is good." He constructed extravagant buildings, arranged the sacrifice of 142,000 animals in one sitting, and maintained 1,000 wives and concubines. Early in his reign, he was focused and disciplined, but later, he lacked inhibition and worshipped other deities despite all the blessings he'd received from God.

1 Kings 12-22

The conflict between Rehoboam and Jeroboam, which had been bubbling at the end of Chapter 11, explodes in Chapter 12. Rehoboam decides to double down on his father Solomon's repression of the tribes, telling them (1 Kings 12:10–11), "My little finger shall be thicker than my father's loins…my father hath chastised you with whips, but I will chastise you with scorpions" and that the punishments will continue until morale improves. The tribes of Judah and Benjamin are loyal to Rehoboam, but the other tribes back Jeroboam, who is still unsure of his position and constructs golden calves for worship. He also allows common people (not just Levites) to be priests.

A "man of God" shows up in Bethel and causes the altar to burn. When Jeroboam reaches out his hand in protest, his arm withers. He pleads with the man of God, and his arm is restored. Jeroboam offers him food, but he declines, saying God has forbidden him to eat. Another prophet hears this story and meets the man of God, assuring him God has said it's ok to eat, and they share a pleasant meal. On the way out of town, the man of God is killed by a lion, which leaves the man's donkey unscathed. Jeroboam "returned not from his evil way" after this incident, probably because he was confused about what it meant, other than lions want you dead. They really do.

Jeroboam's son Abijah becomes ill, and he sends his wife to mystic Ahijah. God instructs Ahijah to inform her that her son will perish as soon as she arrives home and that trouble awaits. 1 Kings 14:15: "For the Lord shall smite Israel, as a reed is shaken in the water, and he shall root up Israel out of this good land, which he gave to their fathers, and shall scatter them beyond the river because they make their groves (idols), provoking the Lord to anger."

Sure enough, her son Abijah dies as soon as she's home. Jeroboam's reign of the Northern Kingdom was 22 years, and his son Nadab succeeded him. Rehoboam ruled the Southern Kingdom of Judah in Jerusalem for 17 turbulent years. 1 Kings 14:24: "And there were also sodomites in the land: and they did according to all the abominations of the nations which the Lord cast out before the children of Israel." The Egyptian king Shishak took advantage of a weakened Jerusalem, raided the Temple, and carted off valuables, including bronze shields (what about the Ark?).

The next several chapters review the rulers of Judah and Israel over several hundred years. Abijam was sinful; Asa expelled male prostitutes and suffered from a foot disease; Nadab was sinful; Baasha was sinful; Elah worshipped idols; Zimri was overthrown; Omri was sinful; Ahab worshipped Baal and provoked God. The prophet Elijah tells Ahab there will be three years of drought, and Elijah hightails it for the desert, where he is at first given food by ravens but then goes to a poor woman at Zarephath. She's reluctant to give Elijah any food lest she and her son starve, but Elijah insists she make bread.

Magically, the flour and oil the woman used are replenished. Then her son dies, but Elijah raises him from the dead in 1 Kings 17:21: "And he stretched himself upon the child three times, and cried unto the Lord and said, O Lord my God, I pray thee, let this child's soul come into him again," after which the child was revived. I'm not sure what stretching yourself upon a child means, but it can't be good.

Elijah then convenes a meeting at Carmel with King Ahab's Baal-worshiping priests. They agree to a competition where each side prepares a bull for a burnt offering, and may the better God win. The Baal priests go first, yet nothing happens. Elijah mocks them in 1 Kings 18:27 by saying of their god: "Either he is talking…or he is in a journey or sleeping and must be awaked." It's Elijah's turn, and sure enough, a flame from heaven engulfs his offering. Elijah kills all the false priests, and then the drought abates. Elijah meets God in a cave and is given his marching orders to anoint Jehu as King of Israel and Elisha as the new prophet.

Soon, a Samarian king, Ben-Hadad, threatens Israel. He tells Ahab to be ready to surrender all his gold and silver, which Ahab agrees to. However, when Ben-Hadad asks for the wives and children, Ahab balks. A prophet materializes and tells Ahab that despite being outnumbered, he will win. There's a battle where Ahab is victorious, but he stops before it turns into a slaughter and offers his chariot to the defeated Ben-Hadad. The prophet predicts destruction for having allowed his enemies to survive, a concern that God had also raised in the Book of Judges when His armies didn't entirely destroy opposing tribes.

Meanwhile, Ahab wants the vineyard belonging to Naboth, but Naboth won't sell. Ahab's wife Jezebel has Naboth stoned on trumped-up charges, and Elijah informs Ahab that was a big mistake. 1 Kings 21:25: "But there was none like unto Ahab, which did sell himself to work wickedness in the sight of the Lord, whom Jezebel his wife stirred up." Ahab apologizes and stays in power until he agrees with Jehoshaphat, the king of Judah, to attack Gilead. Ahab asks his prophets for their advice, and they all agree a victory is in the offing, except for Micaiah, who predicts defeat. Micaiah is rewarded by being thrown into prison and given only bread and water.

Ahab goes into battle dressed as a common soldier, but Jehoshaphat dresses as a king. The enemy has been given orders to only shoot at the king of Israel, so they target the conspicuous Jehoshaphat, but an errant missile hits Ahab, killing him. Ahab's son Ahaziah becomes king and starts to worship Baal.

After the unification under David and Solomon, the second half of the Book of Kings depicts a fractured Israel, with Jerusalem leading the Southern Kingdom, comprising the tribes of Judah and Benjamin, and the other ten tribes forming the Northern Kingdom (Israel). Although the two kingdoms sometimes found common ground, they also sometimes went to war with each other.

Prophetic messages are becoming more prevalent, starting with the man of God, whom a lion kills. Prophets also appear before battles at Gilead and Samaria, as well as during drought forecasts. The most prominent of these prophetic voices is Elijah, whose powers seem to grow throughout 1 Kings. His first miracle is to replenish flour and water, but then he raises someone from the dead and then causes God's fire to devour a burnt offering. The prophet Micaiah learns what happens to those who don't follow the company line, and he's sent to jail.

The continued appeal of Baal is remarkable. If we are to believe it, Ahab's priests are murdered for their misplaced belief in Baal, yet Ahab's son loses no time before forsaking God. You'd think such a strong demonstration, as provided by Elijah, of God's superiority would make an impression.

Let's celebrate that the Egyptian king Shishak, who sacked Jerusalem, is called by his name rather than just "Pharaoh." In *Raiders of the Lost Ark*, Harrison Ford's character states that Shishak is responsible for bringing the Ark to the Well of Souls in Egypt after it was plundered in Jerusalem. The Bible only says valuables were looted, but it's hard to imagine the Ark would have been left alone by the Egyptians. There was indeed a Pharaoh named Shishak, and various reliefs of his conquests have been unearthed in Karnak, Amum, and Megiddo. However, the inscriptions make no mention of Jerusalem. Previously, when the Ark fell into enemy hands, it had caused diseases and was returned to the Israelites, so why would it have found comfort in Egypt?

2 KINGS

2 Kings 1-8

After Ahab died in battle, Moab rebelled against Israel. New King Ahaziah fell through some latticework and was near death. He sent messengers to find a Baal healer to ask if he'd survive, but the prophet Elijah intercepted them and told them to tell the king he was doomed. The messengers report all of this to the king, adding that Elijah was a hairy man wearing a girdle. Did that make the story more believable? Anyway, Ahaziah wants to see Elijah and sends in the army. Two companies of soldiers are burned alive by Elijah, but the third company commander gets the message, pleads for mercy, and brings Elijah to the king—who promptly dies.

Elijah and Elisha are then en route to the Jordan River. In 2 Kings 2:1–12, Elijah parts the waters with his rolled-up cloak, allowing them to cross easily, but he knows his end is near. Soon, a chariot of fire descends and takes him away in a whirlwind directly to heaven. **Elijah** was gone, but he hadn't died; it was a change-of-address card, not a notification to the Social Security Administration.

Elisha takes up the mantle—literally—and parts the waters using Elijah's cloak. Nearing Bethel, he's mocked by 42 children for his baldness. Elisha can either tell the kids he makes bald look sexy or react violently. He chooses the latter, causing two she-bears to rip the children to shreds. We all know that kids can be cruel, but this seems like an overreaction.

The kings now are Jehoshaphat for Judah and Joram for Israel. The two strike a deal to attack the king of Moab, but they run into trouble after failing to find water. They turn in desperation to Elisha, who asks why on earth he should help them. (I can think of a reason: he'd die without water too.) Elisha relents and tells them to dig in a dry stream bed, and water will appear. The Moabites see the water and believe it's blood from a slaughter, so they attack. The Israelites win, and the Moabite king sacrifices his son.

More Elisha miracles follow. He makes olive oil for a widow, resurrects a dead child, makes a pot of stew edible, and multiplies loaves of bread to feed a crowd of prophets. The account of raising the dead child is in 2 Kings 4:34: "And he went up, and lay upon the child, and put his mouth upon his mouth, and his eyes upon his eyes, and his hands upon his hands: and he stretched upon the child: and the flesh of the child waxed warm." Then Elisha gave the child a candy bar and told him not to tell Mommy what had just happened.

A Syrian general, Naaman, suffers from leprosy, and Elisha cures him. Later, Elisha strikes his own servant Gehazi with the disease after Gehazi tries to collect payment from the general. Another miracle is less impressive: a helper loses an ax head in a stream, and Elisha makes it float.

Elisha can magically discern the disposition of the Syrian forces and relay this information to the Israelites. The Syrians think they've surrounded Elisha, but he conjures chariots of fire and strikes the enemy blind. He then captures them, restores their vision, feeds them, and releases them, thereby securing temporary peace. Samaria later is besieged by the

Syrians, and people resort to cannibalism (one of Moses' earlier curses for disobedience). Elisha predicts deliverance, and sure enough, the Syrians flee in terror at what they think is a massive army. It's actually just four diseased soldiers trying to escape. Elisha's prophecies continue. The King of Syria sends a messenger, Hazael, to ask if the king will survive. Elisha says the king will die and that Hazael will become a ruthless enemy of Israel.

There seems to be a Rap Battle between prophets Elijah and Elisha. Both raise the dead, multiply oil, part the Jordan, and summon fire-chariots. Maybe Elisha's murder-by-bear episode put him ahead on shock value, but Elijah wins on style—ascending to heaven without dying, palms sweaty, knees weak, arms heavy.

The names don't help modern readers: Jeroboam is opposed by Rehoboam, Elijah precedes Elisha, and Jeroboam's son Abijah interacts with the mystic Ahijah. Whatever was being signaled by these near-matches is now lost to time. The miracles and themes such as resurrections, feeding multitudes, and curing leprosy feel more like the New Testament than the gritty Old. But let's not get ahead of ourselves. Also, can we go back to the 42 children murdered by bears? How did that work? If they'd divvied up the work evenly, each bear would have had to maul 21 children, and surely each mauling would take several minutes. Wouldn't the kids have scattered in all directions rather than sheltering in place and waiting for SWAT to arrive?

2 Kings 9-25

Elisha, still smarting from his loss in the Rap Battle to Elijah, instructs another prophet to anoint Jehu as king and tell him to eliminate King Joram. Jehu sets off and meets Joram and King Ahaziah on the battlefield. Joram asks whether Jehu comes in peace, and Jehu replies in 2 Kings 9:22, "What peace, so long as the whoredoms of thy mother Jezebel and her witchcrafts are so many?" Probably thinking a simple "no" would have sufficed, Joram turns his chariot around and flees, but Jehu shoots him in the back and kills him. King Ahaziah fares no better and dies fleeing the scene. That leaves Jezebel.

Jehu finds her defiant and glamorized. She's done up her eyes and styled her hair, perhaps knowing the end is near. Her palace officials, clearly reading the room, chuck her out the window. Her body splatters on the ground, and Jehu runs her over with his chariot for good measure.

But Jehu's thirst for blood isn't satisfied. He demands the execution of 70 of Ahab's descendants living in Samaria. Their heads are delivered in baskets. Later, when Jehu encounters some relatives of Ahaziah, he gives an unambiguous command to his soldiers in 2 Kings 10:14: "Take them alive." The soldiers do this but then immediately kill all 42 of them at the pit near the shearing house. This again raises questions about the standards of biblical communication. If you want prisoners alive, maybe don't immediately kill them? And there's that number again—42—the same number of children mauled by bears after Elisha got roasted for being bald.

In the seventh year of Jehu's reign over Israel, Joash rules in Jerusalem (Judah). He tries to stave off the Syrians with a bribe but is ultimately assassinated. Then comes King Jehoahaz of Israel, who worships idols and gets hammered by the Syrians. More kings come and go, but at this point, even the biblical authors seem bored. Several entries conclude with a casual, "For more details, consult the Book of the Chronicles of the Kings of Israel," which is the ancient version of "Google it."

One notable event is Elisha's death. On his deathbed, he gives King Jehoash an odd prophetic demonstration. He tells him to shoot an arrow out the window—it represents victory over Syria. Then he instructs him to beat the ground with arrows. Jehoash strikes three times. Elisha is furious: 2 Kings 13:19: "Thou shouldest have smitten five or six times...now thou shalt smite Syria but thrice." OMG, just tell him how many fucking times to hit the ground!

Then Elisha dies. However, his body still retains some strength. When Moabite raiders toss a corpse into Elisha's tomb, the body touches Elisha's bones and springs back to life. It's a short, weird, zombie miracle that reminds us this prophet still had juice, even postmortem.

Meanwhile, Israel keeps slipping into idolatry. The Assyrians begin dismantling the Northern Kingdom, deporting Israelites en masse. Down south, King Hezekiah of Judah takes the throne. He institutes reforms, restores worship, and even destroys Moses's old bronze serpent, which had become an object of veneration.

Still, Jerusalem isn't safe. The Assyrians show up and demand surrender, boasting they've crushed far stronger nations. Hezekiah seeks help from the prophet Isaiah, who tells him to stand firm. Then, in 2 Kings 19:35 we are told God comes to the rescue: "And it came to pass that night, that the angel of the Lord went out, and smote in the camp of the Assyrians an hundred thousand fourscore and five thousand (185,000): and when they arose early in the morning, behold, they were dead corpses." Assyrian King Sennacherib retreats in ignominy and is assassinated by his sons.

Isaiah isn't done, though. He also predicts that Babylon will eventually conquer Jerusalem. Hezekiah is succeeded by Manasseh, who reverts to idol worship. God responds by promising to wipe Jerusalem off the map.

Later, King Josiah rises to power and finds an ancient scroll during Temple renovations. It contains laws and funding instructions for temple repair. A prophet clarifies that priests should be bypassed, and money should go straight to the workers. Josiah takes this as a sign to purge the land. He tears down pagan altars, kills the priests of these high places, and burns human bones on the desecrated altars. 2 Kings 23:20: "And he slew all the priests of the high places...and returned to Jerusalem." So, a budgeting memo leads to mass murder? Either Josiah was looking for a reason to justify things he already planned, or it's an incredibly disproportionate reaction.

Eventually, Josiah dies in battle at Megiddo—fighting the Egyptians, not the Babylonians. But it's Babylon that seals Jerusalem's fate. Nebuchadnezzar invades, destroys the Temple, and ships off the skilled classes to Babylon in exile. The final chapter of 2 Kings leaves Judah under a Babylonian-appointed governor, the real power now firmly in Mesopotamian hands. The Babylonian conquest of Judea, the experience of the Jewish exiles, and the ultimate repatriation after Cyrus the Great defeated Babylon will loom large over the rest of the Old Testament, particularly the prophets who foresee (or retroactively comment on) these dramatic events.

Elisha's end feels anticlimactic. He and Elijah were parallel figures—miracle-working prophets, chariot protectors, God's chosen—but their exits diverge. Elijah gets the cinematic "chariots of fire" departure straight to heaven. Elisha? He dies offscreen in Judea after a confusing arrow-counting session. Chariots of fire showed up to protect Elisha once, but not at the end. That image of supernatural protection—borrowed by the 1981 film *Chariots of Fire* about British Olympians and their God-glorifying runs—was apparently a one-time-only perk.

If God created heaven in Genesis, where was He living before that? The biblical writers don't say. But by 2 Kings, heaven isn't just a cosmic ceiling, it's a real destination. Elijah's fiery exit moves us one giant leap closer to the later Christian notion that heaven is where the righteous go. That idea isn't fully baked yet, but the ingredients are starting to come together.

1 CHRONICLES

Like Deuteronomy, *1 Chronicles* repackages and sometimes revises key biblical events. It falls into the same trap we saw in Deuteronomy, where laws from Exodus are reviewed and subtly edited from their original form. This raises an obvious question: if the information is the same, or nearly the same, why repeat it? And if it's different, why wasn't it included in the original account, where it might have made for a more coherent narrative? Although 1 Chronicles revisits material from Genesis, Exodus, and Leviticus, its focus is on King David, as previously described in 1 and 2 Samuel and 1 Kings.

We begin all the way back in Genesis: Adam was the father of Seth, Seth was the father of Enosh, and so on. We're given similar genealogical rundowns for the descendants of Ishmael, Esau, Edom, Judah, King David, Jerahmeel, Caleb, the high priests, and the Temple musicians. This consumes a considerable amount of space, and it's hard to see how it's necessary or helpful.

We then get descriptions of the Temple guards and the priestly duties of the Levites. 1 Chronicles 9:28–29 states:

> Certain of them had the charge of the
> ministering vessels, that they should bring
> them in and out by tale. Some of them also
> were appointed to oversee the vessels, and all
> the instruments of the sanctuary, and the fine
> flour, and the wine, and the oil, and the
> frankincense, and the spices.

Thank God they covered these topics and didn't leave us hanging.

In Chapter 18, David's military campaigns are revisited. We're told he defeated Moab and captured 1,000 chariots, 7,000 horsemen, and 20,000 foot-soldiers. In the original account (2 Samuel 8:4), the numbers are the same except for the horsemen—only 700 were reported there. Which is correct? Maybe it is a scribal error, but I think it's more likely an attempt to enhance David's military reputation by inflating the size of the army he defeated.

The story of Saul's death is also revised. In 1 Samuel 31, Saul dies bravely in battle alongside his sons. The Philistines mutilate his body, but the people of Jabesh retrieve it by night and mourn him for seven days. In 1 Chronicles 10:13, the battle death remains, but the ending shifts: "So Saul died for his transgression which he committed against the Lord…and also for asking counsel of one that had a familiar spirit, to enquire of it." In other words, Saul didn't die a tragic hero; he died because he sinned—most notably, by consulting a witch the night before the battle.

David's famous Ark procession is also altered. In 2 Samuel 6, David wears only a linen cloth around his waist while dancing; Michal looks on in disgust; and we're told she is barren afterward. In 1 Chronicles 15:27–29, David is described as wearing a full robe of fine linen (an ephod), Michal still looks on in disgust, but there's no mention of her barrenness. It feels like an effort to make David's dancing seem less bizarre (less…gay?) and to reframe Michal's reaction as excessive or petty. By dropping her barrenness, God also seems less vindictive, though frankly, He's got plenty of that elsewhere.

Another twist comes in the census David orders. In 2 Samuel 24:9, Israel has 800,000 fighting men and Judah 500,000. The census angers God, though the reason is vague. 1 Chronicles 21:1 supplies the missing motive: "And Satan stood up against Israel, and provoked David to number Israel." So the devil literally made David do it!

But if Satan really wanted to harm God's people, surely he could have come up with something more destructive than a headcount. Also, the numbers don't match. 1 Chronicles reports 1,100,000 for Israel and 470,000 for Judah, an increase of 300,000 in Israel and a 30,000 drop in Judah. This could be another copying error, or it could be a narrative tweak meant to enhance David's (i.e., Judah's) accomplishments by making Israel look more populous and threatening by comparison.

Then there's the matter of David's punishment. After the census, David is given three options in both 2 Samuel 24 and 1 Chronicles 21: famine, military defeat, or plague. However, in 2 Samuel, the famine would last seven years, while in 1 Chronicles, it's only three. Which is it, seven or three? My vote goes to 2 Samuel. Why? Because seven years is the same duration as the famine in Joseph's story from Genesis, and biblical authors love numerological consistency.

2 CHRONICLES

2 Chronicles focuses primarily on the reigns of the kings of Judah, beginning with Solomon and ending with the Babylonian exile. It parallels and expands upon events found in 1 Kings and 2 Kings, but with a pronounced emphasis on temple worship, priesthood, and God's covenant with Judah. The book highlights the construction of Solomon's Temple, the religious reforms of kings like Hezekiah and Josiah, and the consequences of Judah's faithfulness (or lack thereof) to God. Like 1 Chronicles, it zeroes in on the Southern Kingdom, mentioning the Northern Kingdom of Israel only when it intersects with Judah's story. It also has a habit of whitewashing earlier accounts to flatter some of its protagonists.

There is no mention that Solomon killed his own brother, or that Solomon maintained a harem of 1,000 wives and concubines, leaving him remembered solely for his wealth, wisdom, and role in constructing the Temple. Also absent is the famous "Judgment of Solomon" story, in which he threatens to cut a baby in half to reveal its true mother. This is strange, given it's one of the most iconic stories of "wisdom" in the Old Testament. Was this omission an editorial decision by later compilers who found the original tale less than compelling, or perhaps too unsettling for their purposes?

A subtler alteration can be found in the account of the Temple dedication. In 1 Kings 8:10–11 we read:

> And it came to pass, when the priests were
> come out of the holy place, that the cloud
> filled the house of the Lord, so that the priests
> could not stand to minister because of the
> cloud: for the glory of the Lord had filled the
> house of the Lord.

But in 2 Chronicles 5:13–14, the scene is reworded:

> For he is good; for his mercy endureth
> forever: and then the house was filled with a
> cloud, even the house of the Lord; so that the
> priests could not stand to minister by reason
> of the cloud: for the glory of the Lord had
> filled the house of God.

The addition of "good" and "mercy" subtly reframes the narrative, offering a more overt theological spin to what had been a straightforward (if mystical) description of divine presence.

After the dedication, God offers Solomon a warning in 2 Chron. 7:13–14:

> When I shut up the heavens so that there is
> no rain, or command locusts to devour the
> land, or send a plague among my people, if
> my people, who are called by my name, will
> humble themselves and pray and seek my face
> and turn from their wicked ways, then I will

hear from heaven, and I will forgive their sin
and will heal their land.

Not to get ahead of ourselves, but this verse suggests that what God requires is repentance and prayer—not blood sacrifice—for forgiveness. That has some theological implications down the line.

Another example of sanitized storytelling appears in 2 Chron. 32, describing the Assyrian siege of Jerusalem. In 2 Kings 19:35, the angel of the Lord kills 185,000 Assyrian soldiers overnight, a number that strains credibility. In 2 Chronicles, the angels still repel the attack, but it omits this implausibly high body count.

The book ends with the decree of the Persian king Cyrus, who permits the exiled Israelites to return to Jerusalem and rebuild the Temple, a transition that leads directly into the Book of Ezra.

Ultimately, it's unclear how much new ground 2 Chronicles covers after slogging through 1 and 2 Kings. Sure, omitting some of Solomon's darker traits may make him seem more pious, but it also flattens his character. Doesn't the extravagant detail—his thousand wives and concubines, his ruthless consolidation of power—help us grasp the sheer scale and decadence of his reign?

EZRA AND NEHEMIAH

Ezra

The next two books, *Ezra* and *Nehemiah*, were originally presented as a single text but were later split. The Book of Ezra opens with a royal decree from Cyrus, emperor of Persia (which had conquered Babylon and now controlled Jerusalem), authorizing the repatriation of the Israelites and the reconstruction of the Temple. Ezra 1:2: "Thus saith Cyrus king of Persia, The Lord God of heaven hath given me all the kingdoms of the earth; and he hath charged me to build him a house in Jerusalem, which is in Juday."

This decree is presented as the fulfillment of a prophecy from *The Book of Jeremiah*. However, Jeremiah 25:11–12 mentions a 70-year exile, and while the biblical editors treat this as a forward-looking prophecy, the Book of Jeremiah was likely compiled and finalized after the exile began—if not after Cyrus's rise. So it reads less like a miraculous prediction and more like an after-the-fact alignment, a "prophecy" being retrofitted to match historical events.

Anyway, numbering 42,360 Israelites plus 7,337 servants (maybe life in exile wasn't so bad after all), the returnees begin rebuilding the Temple. But local officials, perhaps less than thrilled by this repopulation project, send a letter to King Artaxerxes complaining about the Israelites' rebellious history. Artaxerxes is persuaded and tells the Israelites to halt construction. The Israelites ignore the order and resume building. Another complaint is filed, prompting a review of Persian archives. Emperor Darius locates Cyrus's original decree and orders that the reconstruction proceed.

Artaxerxes later commissions the priest Ezra to travel to Jerusalem and ensure that God's law is being upheld. Not only is Ezra's trip fully funded, but he is granted sweeping authority, including the power to imprison or execute anyone who obstructs him. This may seem odd—why would a Zoroastrian emperor back a Jewish priest with the power of life and death? Ezra 7:23 gives a hint: "Whatsoever is commanded by the God of heaven, let it be diligently done for the house of the God of heaven: for why should there be wrath against the realm of the king and his sons?"

Artaxerxes wasn't necessarily a believer; he just didn't want to anger any potentially vindictive deity. It's basically a bribe. Then again, why would a Persian emperor feel the need to placate a minor desert god and a nerdy civil servant? There's a narrative shift as well. Until Ezra enters the scene, the story is told by an omniscient narrator. Once Ezra arrives, it switches to first-person—"*I, Ezra*"—a rare POV move in the Old Testament.

Upon reaching Jerusalem, Ezra is appalled to find widespread intermarriage between Jewish men and foreign women, a clear violation of the law as he interprets it. He responds by ordering mass divorces. Wives and children must be abandoned to preserve Israel's purity, a stark reminder that sometimes in scripture you can either follow God's law or act ethically, but rarely both. Ezra calls a public assembly to enforce the decree, but the weather is bad and attendance is poor. He gives them a few extra days. Eventually, he slut-shames the offenders by name, demands animal sacrifices, and sends the foreign wives and their children packing.

Here's a list of the main emperors of the Achaemenid Empire, founded by Cyrus. (A few with very short reigns are omitted.)

- **Cyrus II (The Great):** 550–530 BCE. Founder of the empire. Issued the decree in Ezra 1.
- **Cambyses II:** 530–522 BCE. Not mentioned in Ezra.
- **Darius I (The Great):** 522–486 BCE. Oversees the archival search and authorizes the Temple rebuild (Ezra 6). Also known for getting spanked by the Greeks at Marathon.
- **Xerxes I (The Great):** 486–465 BCE. Mentioned in Ezra 4. Locals complain to him, but nothing happens. He may have been busy fighting Spartans—see *300*.
- **Artaxerxes I:** 465–424 BCE. Stops construction (Ezra 4) but later commissions Ezra and Nehemiah.
- **Darius II:** 423–404 BCE. Possibly referenced indirectly.
- **Artaxerxes II–IV** and **Darius III:** 404–330 BCE. Later rulers; not directly referenced in Ezra.

The Book of Ezra reads like a clunky time-travel novel: the timeline jumps around, cause and effect get scrambled, and a parade of Persian emperors issue conflicting orders. Ezra 4, in particular, includes a confusing flash-forward: it references opposition during the reigns of Xerxes and Artaxerxes even though those events haven't happened yet in the story. Then Ezra 4:24 abruptly snaps back to the reign of Darius I, who finds Cyrus's original decree and gives the go-ahead to finish the Temple. Only *after* that, during Artaxerxes' reign, are Ezra and Nehemiah dispatched to enforce religious law and rebuild the city walls. The scribes may have intended to stitch multiple reforms into one cohesive redemption arc, but what we're left with feels like *Ezra-Nehemiah: The Director's Cut*, complete with deleted scenes shuffled out of order.

It's also a bit absurd to imagine these Achaemenid emperors—rulers of the largest empire on earth, worshiped like gods—fretting over a scattered minority in a dusty province. And yet we're asked to believe they not only honored a decades-old decree from a long-dead predecessor but did so with urgency and divine fear.

Nehemiah

Nehemiah, a wine steward for Artaxerxes, becomes aware of the dire state of the rebuilding effort in Jerusalem. He prays to God, expresses remorse for his people's turning away from God, and hopes the dispersed people will return home. It's a prayer mixed with foreshadowing, which (of course) is fulfilled when the Israelites can return to Jerusalem.

When he's serving wine to the emperor and his wife, the emperor asks why the long face, and Nehemiah tells him of the rebuilding needed in Jerusalem and how he would like to take a sabbatical to fix things. The emperor (of course) grants his wish, gives him authority to travel and requisition timber, and makes him the governor of Judah.

Once in Jerusalem, Nehemiah gets the tribal leaders together and explains his vision for rebuilding the city walls. They (of course) enthusiastically drop everything to help with the project. There is a l-o-n-g list naming everyone involved. The local non-Israelites are distrustful, and the workers split shifts on the walls and on security details. Nehemiah is dedicated to his work and says he refused the food and wine he was authorized to have so that nothing would distract him (the first part of the Book is written in Nehemiah's first person).

There is another long list of each clan that returned from Persia with the number of people. The priest/scholar Ezra makes an appearance. He gathers all the Israelites and reads them Moses' laws from dawn until midday, and the people (of course) listen rapturously. There is a Festival of Shelters where they live in temporary huts and confess their sins, and there's a long prayer of confession followed by a list of the clan leaders that signed an agreement. Here, there is a shift from first person back to the omniscient author. The agreement addresses tithes, offering dough and wine to the priests, canceling debts every seventh year, observing the Sabbath, and prohibiting intermarriage with foreigners.

It's been twelve years since Nehemiah left Persia, so it's time to update the (very patient) emperor. He departs, leaves Eliashib in charge, and makes his report to Artaxerxes. Upon returning to Jerusalem, Nehemiah is stunned to find the Israelites have backslidden. The account shifts again to his first person as he rants about temple procedures being disregarded, that some of the townspeople who had moved into the city have left, and that intermarriage has returned (it must not have been a short visit to Persia). Nehemiah is furious. Nehemiah 13:25: "And I contended with them, and cursed them, and smote certain of them, and plucked off their hair, and made them swear by God…"

Although Nehemiah had earlier made sure we understood he was unpretentious, he didn't really want to labor in obscurity. Neh. 13:31: "And for the wood offering, at times appointed, and for the first fruits. Remember me, O my God, for good." Pay attention to me, he's saying to God.

The timeline and narration continue to confuse. Why was Artaxerxes surprised by Nehemiah's sadness if he'd already sent Ezra to Jerusalem to enforce God's laws? Or did Artaxerxes send Nehemiah first, then Ezra? The emperor must have had great confidence in his sommelier if he made him governor, or Judah was so inconsequential that it didn't matter.

Nehemiah's relationship with the emperor and with God is strangely intimate. His prayers to God are lengthy and heartfelt. I don't recall prayers elsewhere in the Bible being as personal and self-centered. He fully expects and assumes his prayers will be granted. It's also odd that Artaxerxes would have so easily granted the request that a servant be given carte blanche to travel, secure materials, and govern a province. Although Nehemiah saw an opening when the emperor asked him why he was sad, it was an impossibly risky move for him to make such an indulgent request. There is no Persian or other ancient evidence apart from the Bible to attest to any of this, and Nehemiah's own account stretches credulity. What wine is best paired with such exaggeration?

ESTHER

In the third year of King Xerxes' reign, he threw a massive party. Drinks flowed from golden cups, and the bar was open. To impress his guests, he ordered the beautiful Queen Vashti to parade before them, but she refused. Instead of simply asking her why, Xerxes convened his advisers and ended up sending a decree to all 127 provinces declaring that wives must honor their husbands. His counselors then proposed a beauty contest to find a new queen. This sounded like a swell idea to Xerxes.

A year-long grooming regimen was set up for the virgins brought into the palace. Each woman got one night with the king; afterward, she was shunted off to the harem and forgotten. But one young woman wasn't going to be discarded so easily. Esther, a nice Jewish girl raised by her cousin Mordecai, took tips from the palace eunuchs on how to appeal to Xerxes (I think we can guess what this advice might have featured). After a memorable roll in the hay, Xerxes crowned Esther queen and banished Vashti for good.

Cousin Mordecai, a minor palace official, refused to bow to Haman, the king's right-hand man. Enraged, Haman decided that killing Mordecai wasn't enough—he would orchestrate the extermination of every Jew in the Persian Empire. Esther 3:13 lays it out: "And the letters were sent…to destroy, to kill, and to cause to perish, all Jews, both young and old, little children and women, in one day…and to take the spoil of them for a prey." Seems like an overreaction.

Haman got Xerxes to approve the plan, unaware that Esther was herself Jewish. But Esther had a counterplot. She needed the king's favor, and when she approached him uninvited—a risky move—Xerxes gently extended his golden scepter, sparing her life and probably leading to another roll in the hay.

Esther invited Xerxes and Haman to a private banquet. Meanwhile, Haman was busy constructing gallows to hang Mordecai. At the feast, Esther revealed that her people were marked for annihilation and named Haman as the mastermind. Xerxes stormed out in a rage, realizing the treachery of his right-hand man—and perhaps fearing a disruption in the supply of Doc Yahweh's Little Performance Poppers. When he returned, he found Haman begging Esther for mercy and assumed he was raping her, which was an outrage reserved for the king alone.

Haman was hanged on the very gallows he had built for Mordecai. Xerxes gave Mordecai his job and authorized a violent reversal: the Jews were granted permission to take vengeance on their enemies. Esther 9:5 says: "Thus the Jews smote all their enemies with the stroke of the sword, and slaughter, and destruction, and did what they would unto those that hated them." Altogether, 75,000 Persians were killed. Xerxes might've reflected that the sex had been memorable but wasn't worth the murder and carnage that had been unleashed across his kingdom.

The book ends with praise for Xerxes (of course) and the promotion of Mordecai. It reads more like a tale from *One Thousand and One Nights* than biblical history. Without Esther's and Mordecai's ethnicity, it's unclear why it belongs in the

Bible at all. God is never mentioned. If taken as history, the story strains credibility. But as a fable, it's a hoot. The Festival of Purim (named for the *Pur*, or lots, Haman cast to determine the date of the massacre) is still celebrated on the 13th of Adar. It may have predated the story itself, suggesting this tale was crafted to justify a holiday, not the other way around.

JOB

We open the *Book of Job* as the Devil goes down to Georgia—well, to the land of Uz, home to a successful farmer named Job. Satan and God are having a Zoom call where God brags in Job 1:8: "Hast thou considered my servant Job, that there is none like him in the earth, a perfect and upright man..." Satan, like Elon Musk, is a disrupter who delights in inflicting unnecessary pain on people living in red states. He proposes testing Job's faith by stripping away his wealth and comforts to see if he'll curse God. God thinks this sounds like a fun diversion and agrees, with one caveat: Satan must not kill Job.

Disasters follow in quick succession. Lightning strikes, raiders attack, storms rage, fields are destroyed, and his children die. Only Job and his wife survive. Still, Job doesn't curse God.

God and Satan reconvene, and Satan ups the ante. They agree to afflict Job with a painful, disfiguring skin disease to see if that breaks his spirit—again, without killing him. Job's wife has had enough and urges him to "curse God and die," which might've been a mercy. But Job holds firm.

What follows is a poetic dialogue, beginning with three exchanges between Job and his friends Eliphaz, Bildad, and Zophar. In the first cycle, Job laments his birth and wishes he had died in the womb. Eliphaz tells him to repent and turn to God. Bildad says Job's children must have sinned. Zophar insists that God sees all wrongdoing. In the second cycle, Job maintains his innocence while the friends accuse him of arrogance and denial. The same pattern repeats in the third.

Job then delivers his closing argument. In Job 31:2, he asks, "For what portion of God is there from above? And what inheritance of the Almighty from on high?" And in 31:6: "Let me be weighed in an even balance, that God may know mine integrity." His point: God may judge, but why punish someone who hasn't done anything wrong?

At this point, a younger bystander named Elihu jumps in. He criticizes Job for claiming innocence and his friends for their shallow arguments. Elihu insists that suffering is part of God's mysterious plan, claiming that the same God who sends rain to water crops can also send pain to discipline or instruct.

Then God enters the scene, speaking from a whirlwind— also in poetry. He bombards Job with questions: Has he seen the storehouses of hail? Does he know when mountain goats give birth? I'm guessing the answers to those were "no," followed by "yes." God also takes credit for creating two mythical beasts: the Behemoth, a massive, grass-eating land creature with powerful limbs, and the Leviathan, a terrifying, armor-plated fire-breathing sea monster.

God reprimands Job's three friends for misrepresenting Him and tells them to offer seven bulls and seven rams as a sacrifice. Job is rewarded: his fortunes are restored twofold, and he lives another 140 years.

Some of the poetry in the book is haunting and beautiful:
- **Job 8:9:** "For we are but of yesterday, and know nothing, because our days upon earth are a shadow."

- **Job 9:25–26:** "Now my days are swifter than a post: they flee away, they see no good. They are passed away as the swift ships: as the eagle that hasteth to the prey."
- **Job 18:18:** "He shall be driven from light into darkness, and chased out of the world."

The phrase "the patience of Job" has come to mean enduring suffering with grace, but Job didn't do that. He was horrified. His wealth was destroyed, his children killed, and his health wrecked for no obvious reason. He spends most of the book protesting that he did nothing wrong and that righteousness should be rewarded. But in the Bible, that's rarely how it works. Scoundrels thrive while God incinerates or petrifies people for minor offenses.

So what are we supposed to learn? Job's grudging patience is eventually rewarded, but the lesson is murky. God and Satan set the terms for a cosmic bet, then Satan vanishes without explanation. The whole setup feels more like Mount Olympus than monotheism. Do God and Satan have regular meetings? And if Satan had killed Job, would God have punished him? If He has that power, why hasn't He used it?

In the end, God seems bored, Job is shattered, and the friends are useless. The only truly compelling figures are Job's steely wife and Satan. Mrs. Job dares to say what no one else will: that this divine experiment is cruel and death might be the only mercy. And Satan? He's the only one with a consistent goal and a coherent arc. He challenges authority, exposes flaws, and walks away untouched. God gets manipulated, Job gets crushed, and the friends ramble, but it's the Devil and a grieving woman who emerge as the most complex, morally grounded, and narratively compelling characters in the book.

PSALMS

This long book of poems and songs is a refreshing change from much of the Bible's stilted prose, violence, and tedium. With its 150 chapters spread across five collections, the *Book of Psalms* has room to maneuver.

Some readers find prophetic messages embedded in certain passages, and while it's not impossible to interpret some verses using that lens, prophecy is a distinct literary genre in the Bible. As a rule, Psalms is not prophecy, just as *Ezekiel's* prophetic statements involving horse ejaculate (I am not making that up) are not meant to be sung about in Sunday School.

1) Hymns of praise and worship (Psalms 1–41)

These prayers exalt God's righteousness and emphasize the need to praise Him. For example, Psalm 7:10–11: "My defence is of God, which saveth the upright in heart. God judgeth the righteous, and God is angry with the wicked every day."

Jesus famously quoted Psalm 22:1 while on the cross, saying, "My God, my God, why hast thou forsaken me?" (Matthew 27:46; Mark 15:34). This psalm, traditionally attributed to King David, expresses deep anguish but ultimately ends with hope and renewed trust in God. By invoking it, Jesus may have been channeling the despair David felt in his own suffering. Many Christians also see Psalm 22 as prophetic.

In Psalm 22:16, David writes: "For dogs have compassed me: the assembly of the wicked have enclosed me: they pierced my hands and my feet." At first glance, this sounds like a crucifixion. But David is not making a prediction, he's describing a present moment of agony. If this were intended as prophecy, we might expect the future tense: They *will* pierce. More intriguingly, the word "pierced" doesn't appear in all translations. The New Jerusalem Bible renders verse 16 as: "A pack of dogs surrounds me, a gang of villains closing in on me as if to hack off my hands and feet..."

That sounds less like crucifixion and more like an ambush. While Psalm 22 is a powerful lament, its prophetic status is questionable, and it certainly doesn't offer a literal description of Jesus' death on the cross.

Then we arrive at Psalm 23, perhaps the most evocative and beloved passage in the Old Testament—and arguably one of the most beautiful in all English literature:

> The Lord is my Shepherd; I shall not want.
> He maketh me to lie down in green pastures:
>   he leadeth me beside the still waters.
> He restoreth my soul: he leadeth me in the
>   paths of righteousness for his name's sake.
> Yea, though I walk through the valley of the
>   shadow of death, I will fear no evil; for
>   thou art with me; thy rod and thy staff they
>   comfort me.

Thou preparest a table before me in the presence of mine enemies: thou anointest my head with oil; my cup runneth over.

Surely goodness and mercy shall follow me all the days of my life: and I will dwell in the house of the Lord forever.

2) Prayers for help and protection (Psalms 42–72)

These include the memorable Psalm 49:16–17: "Be not thou afraid when one is made rich, when the glory of his house is increased: For when he dieth he shall carry nothing away: his glory shall not descend after him." This is essentially the biblical version of "You can't take it with you." It's both a self-evident truth and a theological statement: in death, no one holds an advantage over another.

3) Pleas for forgiveness (Psalms 73–89)

One example: Psalm 78:38: "But he, being full of compassion, forgave their iniquity, and destroyed them not: yea, many a time turned he his anger away, and did not stir up all his wrath." Fair enough. But didn't God once kill a man just for trying to keep the Ark of the Covenant from toppling?

4) Songs of thanksgiving (Psalms 90–106)

Psalm 100:3 is typical of this category: "Know ye that the Lord he is God: it is he that hath made us, and not we ourselves; we are his people, and the sheep of his pasture."

5) Petitions for punishment (Psalms 107–150)

Psalm 137 is especially striking: "By the rivers of Babylon, there we sat down, yea, we wept, when we remembered Zion…Happy shall he be, that taketh and dasheth thy little ones against the stones." The New Jerusalem Bible adds some rhetorical punch: "Daughter of Babel, doomed to destruction, a blessing on anyone who treats you as you treated us, a blessing on anyone who seizes your babies and shatters them against a rock!" It's a shocking and barbaric image, but should we be surprised? Moses ordered the killing and rape of captives. So did Joshua. This is par for the biblical course.

Much of Psalms was designed for ceremonies—group recitations, songs, or temple services—and likely works well in those settings. But if you're reading it for literary originality or philosophical insight, it often disappoints. Many of the lines blend into a kind of devotional boilerplate: Don't abandon me to my enemies. Punish the wicked. Hear me, merciful Lord. Clap your hands for joy. Worship no other gods. O Lord, how great you are.

The writers of Psalms could have given us Psalm 23 and called it a day. That single poem achieves what much of the Bible fails to do, or never even attempts. It presents God not as a vengeful warrior or capricious tyrant but as a nurturing shepherd. It offers comfort during fear, assurance in hardship, and a promise of peace beyond life's slings and arrows. It's easy to see why it remains a source of solace in moments of deep stress—one of the constants of the human experience.

This is also one of the few places where the King James Version truly outshines modern translations. Consider the difference: Modern: "Even if I go through the deepest darkness…" King James: "Yea, though I walk through the valley of the shadow of death…" The former is accurate. The latter is unforgettable.

And yet, how consistent is Psalm 23 with what we've learned about God so far? Is this the same God who slaughters firstborns, drowns armies, torches cities, and punishes generations for their ancestors' sins? In the Bible, sheep aren't comforted, they're slaughtered, burned, and offered on altars. If this were my shepherd, I'd sleep with one eye open.

PROVERBS

The *Book of Proverbs* contains over 900 verses, divided into 31 chapters. Traditionally, King Solomon is credited as its author, but this attribution is highly suspect. More likely, the book is a compilation of aphorisms from multiple authors, assembled over many years. Some chapters have a particular focus: Chapter 1 offers advice to young men; Chapter 5 warns against adultery; and Chapters 4 and 8 explore the nature and value of wisdom. Most of the other chapters are more freewheeling.

What advice is offered to young men? Sons are urged to fear the Lord, listen to their parents, help their neighbors, and avoid the company of murderers. The wise are encouraged to pursue good doctrine, recognize that unreliable men can't be trusted, avoid foolishness, educate themselves, and—as in Prov. 4:17—steer clear of criminals who "eat the bread of wickedness, and drink the wine of violence." Prov. 4:23 is a standout: "Keep thy heart with all diligence; for out of it are the issues of life." In other words, be careful how you think; your thoughts shape your life.

Chapters 5–7 focus heavily on warnings against "loose women." Prov. 6:26 warns, "For by means of a whorish woman a man is brought to a piece of bread: and the adulteress will hunt for the precious life," suggesting a man can buy a prostitute, but adultery will cost him everything. Prov. 6:28 continues the theme with the rhetorical question, "Can one go upon hot coals, and his feet not be burned?" Men are advised to remain loyal to their wives; children with other women are portrayed as suspect; and immoral women are said to seduce men with myrrh, aloes, and cinnamon. It's worth noting that in the story of the two prostitutes who come before Solomon, he renders his decision without passing moral judgment on their profession. Perhaps the Bible doesn't have an issue with prostitution per se, only with men who cheat with another's wife.

Chapters 10–22 are attributed to Solomon and contain a grab bag of maxims, many self-evident: laziness leads to poverty; excessive drinking leads to foolishness; wise people take advice; wealth can be protective; the Lord hates dishonest scales; gossips are untrustworthy; happy people smile; and again, fair weights and measures are essential in commerce (someone must have been shorted at the deli counter at Whole Foods…).

Some of the proverbs remain memorable:
- **Proverbs 16:18** – "Pride goeth before destruction, and a haughty spirit before a fall."
- **Proverbs 22:6** – "Train up a child in the way he should go: and when he is old, he will not depart from it."
- **Proverbs 22:15** – "Foolishness is bound in the heart of a child; but the rod of correction shall drive it far from him."

The first two continue to resonate. The third has not aged well. Today, corporal punishment is widely regarded as a harmful method of discipline. Studies show that those subjected to childhood violence often perpetuate the cycle, repeating the "lessons" their parents beat into them. They do not, in fact, depart from it.

The closing chapters reflect on how wisdom, or the lack of it, affects governance. Prov. 28:2 states, "For the transgression of a land many are the princes thereof: but by a man of understanding and knowledge the state thereof shall be prolonged." In other words, wise leadership promotes national stability. Ain't that the truth?

Prov. 29:18 reads: "Where there is no vision, the people perish; but he that keepeth the law, happy is he." I once saw the first half of this proverb hanging in the boardroom of a nonprofit I used to frequent, but the second half was conveniently left out. Taken in full, the "vision" is clearly tied to God's law. Perhaps they didn't want to spark a conversation about laws requiring the stoning of rebellious children or the killing of witches.

The book ends with a poem about the "virtuous woman," a capable wife who rises early, manages the household, and makes belts to sell on Etsy.

Proverbs covers a lot of ground, but many topics important to us today are not discussed. It devotes significant attention to instructing young men but offers little for young women beyond "don't be promiscuous." There is no guidance on how to treat the earth or its non-human inhabitants. The value of wisdom is emphasized, but rarely is the process of becoming wise laid out. The importance of God's laws is a recurring theme, but it lacks the fervor of earlier biblical books. One suspects that the deists of the Enlightenment would have found the God of Proverbs palatable. Like the Book of Esther, most of Proverbs could function just fine without religion.

As with other parts of the Bible, it's telling that the writers added rather than refined. The 900+ proverbs could easily be condensed into a few dozen. How can anyone keep track of so many? Earlier books included hundreds of laws, but most people remember only the Ten Commandments—a list that may be morally problematic but, as a piece of branding, is a masterpiece.

Still, there are timeless and evocative sayings here. That shouldn't surprise us. Ancient writers were fully capable of insight and depth. They had the same cognitive capacities we do and weren't constantly distracted by parrots whistling like R2D2 on TikTok.

ECCLESIASTES

Ecclesiastes claims to be written by Solomon, the king, preacher, and philosopher of Jerusalem, and wastes no time establishing itself as the Debbie Downer of the Old Testament. Eccles. 1:2 opens with a refrain that becomes its thesis: "Vanity of vanities, saith the preacher, vanity of vanities; all is vanity." In other words: it's all pointless. Life is meaningless, repetitive, and absurd. Generations come and go, the sun rises and sets, the wind blows south, then turns around and goes north (which, meteorologically speaking, isn't how air currents work...). Eccles. 1:9 adds, "The thing that hath been, it is that which shall be...and there is no new thing under the sun."

A standout line comes in Eccles. 1:15: "That which is crooked cannot be made straight: and that which is wanting cannot be numbered." The world is broken, and there's no fixing it. The Philosopher then explains how he sought pleasure, amassed slaves, livestock, wealth, and women—yet concluded it was all for nothing. We all meet the same fate. Life, he says, is like chasing the wind.

It's odd that Solomon is credited with this bleak perspective, given how his biblical story is anything but modest. He built the Temple, commanded armies, dazzled foreign dignitaries, and ploughed his way through a thousand wives and concubines. And yet here, the world is declared crooked, justice is a mirage, and everything is ultimately meaningless.

Chapter 3 delivers the most famous passage in the book, later adapted into the song *Turn! Turn! Turn!* by Pete Seeger and popularized by The Byrds in 1965. Eccles. 3:1–8:

> To everything there is a season, and a time to
> every purpose under heaven: A time to be
> born, and a time to die;
> A time to plant, and a time to pluck up that which
> is planted…A time to love, and a time to hate.

It sounds profound, but is it really? It's a list of obvious life events. Yes, there's a time to be born and die, but does that mean life is just a set of alternating-opposites? Isn't experience messier than that? And must love be balanced with hate? Hopefully not. Eccles. 3:20 reminds us again where all this is going: "All go unto one place; all are of the dust, and all turn to dust again."

Then comes a fascinating question in 3:21: "Who knoweth the spirit of man that goeth upward, and the spirit of the beast that goeth downward to the earth?" Is there a difference between human and animal souls? Maybe. Maybe not. The author doesn't claim to know whether the dead are conscious at all. Better, he says, to be a live dog than a dead lion.

In Eccles. 4:4, he observes that much achievement stems from envy: "I considered all travail, and every right work, that for this a man is envied of his neighbor. This is also vanity and vexation of spirit." So, ambition is driven by jealousy. That's honest, but it seems to undermine the 10th Commandment, which forbids coveting your neighbor's goods. Here, envy isn't just acknowledged; it's practically treated as the engine of human effort.

Chapter 7 takes a misogynistic turn. The writer says he found "one man among a thousand" to respect, but "a woman among all those have I not found" (Eccles. 7:28). That's bleak. And if Solomon really wrote this, it's particularly ironic—he had no trouble finding hundreds of women to sleep with, just none worth admiring, apparently.

Later chapters advise on kingship, wisdom, and the joys of youth. You shouldn't badmouth a king, even privately, because "a bird of the air shall carry the voice" (Eccles. 10:20). That's good advice. Punishments should be swift. Sometimes the wicked prosper while the good suffer. And the young? They're told to enjoy themselves, to eat, drink, be merry, before old age arrives, with trembling limbs and dimming eyes. But just in case they're having too much fun, they're reminded again: life is meaningless. Utterly meaningless.

Then comes the twist ending. Eccles. 12:13 declares: "Let us hear the conclusion of the whole matter: Fear God, and keep his commandments: for this is the whole duty of man."

What? After all that despair, cynicism, and existential uncertainty, we're supposed to fear God and follow the rules? That feels tacked on. The book reads like the Bible's great secular meditation on the futility of life yet suddenly veers into Sunday School moralizing. It's likely this conclusion was added later, possibly to bring Ecclesiastes in line with orthodoxy and ensure it wasn't left on the cutting room floor.

SONG OF SOLOMON

There are four love poems spread over the book's eight chapters, each alternating between the voices of the woman and her lover. Most stanzas begin with the female speaker, though the male voice takes the lead in Chapter 4.

The first poem sets the tone in *Song of Songs* 1:2, when the woman says: "Let him kiss me with the kisses of his mouth: for thy love is better than wine." The man replies in 1:9, "I have compared thee, O my love, to a company of horses in Pharaoh's chariots." Quite the smooth operator!

The second poem (Chapter 2) continues the lyrical exchange between the lovers, filled with natural imagery, longing, and romantic flattery. The woman modestly calls herself a "rose of Sharon" and a "lily of the valleys," but her lover elevates her: "As the lily among thorns, so is my love among the daughters." She in turn admires him, likening him to an apple tree.

The third song (chapters 3–5) introduces more sensual imagery: the woman's breasts are compared to twin fawns, and the men whom she favors are Solomon's elite swordsmen, emerging from a cloud of myrrh-scented smoke, and riding chariots crafted from the cedars of Lebanon. I'm pretty sure I've seen this show advertised on the Las Vegas Strip.

The final section (chapters 6–8) brings a mix of longing and erotic frustration. In one scene, the woman hesitates to open the door to her lover, leading to separation and yearning. In 8:1, she wishes for a world where love could be shown openly: "If only you were to me like a brother, who was nursed at my mother's breasts! Then, if I found you outside, I would kiss you, and no one would despise me." This suggests that public displays of affection between unmarried lovers were frowned upon.

What a palate cleanser after the doom and gloom of Ecclesiastes! Like the Book of Esther, The Song of Solomon makes no mention of God. Its erotic poetry is an odd addition to the Bible, one that serves no nakedly theological purpose. The King James editors gymnastically dodge the obvious, comically labeling each chapter as an allegory of divine love. For example, the heading on Chapter 4 reads: "The love of the church to Christ; the church prayeth for Christ's coming." With enough rest, perhaps even a second coming.

ISAIAH

Isaiah 1-39

The prophet Isaiah most likely refers to Isaiah ben Amoz, who lived in Judah during the 8th century BCE and appears in 2 Kings and 2 Chronicles as a court prophet during King Hezekiah's reign.

This section of the *Book of Isaiah*, now called First Isaiah (chapters 1–39), reflects that period's political turmoil—namely, the looming threat of Assyria. Isaiah opens with a fiery sermon about Jerusalem's coming judgment, likening its leaders and people to those of Sodom and Gomorrah. Isaiah 1:10: "Hear the word of the Lord, ye rulers of Sodom; give ear unto the law of our God, ye people of Gomorrah." God is fed up with the people's ritual sacrifices, despite having commanded them in earlier books, and calls them worthless. Jerusalem, he says, has become a whore, and the divine wrath is coming. Still, hope is offered: if the people repent, God might forgive them. One of the most quoted verses follows in Isaiah 2:4, envisioning a peaceful future:

> And he shall judge among the nations, and
> shall rebuke many people: and they shall beat
> their swords into plowshares, and their spears
> into pruninghooks: nation shall not lift up
> sword against nation, neither shall they learn
> war any more.

I'll believe that one when I see it.

Isaiah doesn't have much good to say about the leadership in Jerusalem. Isaiah 3:4 declares, "And I will give children to be their princes, and babes shall rule over them." (A prophecy of DOGE's management by teenage influencers?) Women are also singled out for God's judgment, punished not for actual sins, but for their pride, jewelry, and ankle bracelets. God will strip them bare and shave their heads. But after the judgment, Isaiah promises a glorious future where God's presence will shield the city from storms and suffering.

Chapter 6 gives us Isaiah's dramatic origin story: he sees God enthroned and is overwhelmed by his own unworthiness. A seraph touches his lips with a burning coal, purifying him. God then tells Isaiah to speak in a way that ensures the people won't understand: "Make the heart of this people fat, and make their ears heavy, and shut their eyes..." (Isa. 6:10). Yet the inference is clear: the people must endure suffering before they recognize the error of their ways.

Chapter 7 contains one of the most misunderstood verses in the Bible, one central to Christian theology. Isaiah 7:14 (KJV) reads: "Behold, a virgin shall conceive, and bear a son, and shall call his name Immanuel." This verse is trotted out every December in Christmas pageants as a messianic prophecy about Jesus. But that interpretation depends heavily on translation. The Hebrew word *almah* simply means "young

142

woman," not "virgin." The Greek Septuagint—a translation of Hebrew scripture into Greek made in the 3rd–2nd centuries BCE—renders it as *parthenos*, meaning "virgin," which is the version quoted in the Gospel of Matthew. The New Jerusalem Bible, for example, renders it: "The Lord will give you a sign in any case: It is this: the young woman is with child and will give birth to a son whom she will call Immanuel."

In context, Isaiah is speaking to King Ahaz of Judah, who is terrified of an impending attack. The prophecy is meant as reassurance: before this child is old enough to know good from evil (maybe around age 10 or 12), the military threat will have passed. This has nothing to do with Mary, a miraculous birth, or a messiah centuries later.

Chapter 11 imagines a rejuvenation of the Davidic line—a stump of a tree that will regrow. It paints a poetic image of peace: "The wolf also shall dwell with the lamb, and the leopard shall lie with the kid; and the calf and the young lion and the fatling together; and a little child shall lead them" (Isa. 11:6). Note: it does not say "the lion shall lie down with the lamb," though that misquote has become famous. Later verses imagine lions eating straw and infants playing near deadly snakes. (Presumably just once.)

Then comes a long string of oracles (prophetic declarations) that foretell doom for Israel and its neighbors:

- **Babylon:** Stars will go dark, foreigners will be slaughtered, infants dashed to pieces, women raped, and the city turned into a swamp haunted by owls.
- **Assyria:** The Lord will trample invaders.
- **Philistia:** Famine will kill everyone.
- **Moab:** Cities destroyed overnight, mass slaughter.
- **Damascus (Syria):** Reduced to rubble.
- **Israel:** Judged harshly for idol worship.
- **Cush/Sudan:** Corpses devoured by wild animals.

143

- **Egypt:** A devastating drought will hit; its leaders and gods will fail, though Hebrew will be spoken in five cities.
- **Arabia:** Advised to shelter refugees.
- **Jerusalem:** Rather than defend the city, its warriors party, saying, "Let us eat and drink, for tomorrow we shall die."
- **Phoenicia (Tyre):** The port will be forgotten for 70 years.

As for Isaiah's "let us eat and drink..." line, it's often interpreted as a call to seize the day. But that misses the point. The soldiers weren't embracing life, they were ignoring God's warnings. They should've been repenting, not partying.

Isaiah doesn't stop there—he has apocalyptic visions of the Earth itself being devastated: "Behold, the Lord maketh the earth empty, and maketh it waste, and turneth it upside down..." (Isa. 24:1). Grapes will wither, lawlessness will spread, and the weight of sin will crush the world before it eventually rises again. But when Jerusalem is restored, there will be a huge party, and the dead will rise and join the living to celebrate the rebirth.

It's also notable that Isaiah, like the other prophets, had no insight into events beyond the Near East. No mention of China, India, or the Americas. It's almost like he had no idea the rest of the world existed.

Isaiah 40-55

The style shifts dramatically in Chapter 40. *Second Isaiah* (Deutero-Isaiah) is believed to have been written during the Babylonian exile, around 540 BCE. The tone becomes more hopeful, focused on comfort and redemption.

The next dozen chapters become a long poem revisiting earlier themes. Isaiah 40:11 offers a gentle image of divine care: "He shall feed his flock like a shepherd: he shall gather the lambs with his arm..."

False gods are mocked, and idolatry is ridiculed. The Jews' escape from Babylon is portrayed like a second exodus, with miraculous partings and safe passage. Jerusalem will become a beacon to the world, tested but ultimately restored.

Chapter 45 contains a striking political endorsement for Cyrus the Great, a pagan king who advanced God's interests even though he "hast not known" Him. This is the only time in the Bible a non-Israelite is referred to as Messiah (anointed one). Some modern Christian apologists have used this passage to claim that Donald Trump, the 45th president—irreverent like Cyrus—can still be God's instrument. It's an odd comparison. Cyrus is revered because he freed the Jews, founded an empire, respected religious freedom, and pioneered administrative reforms. Trump is worshipped because he's cruel to trans people.

The different styles and repeated themes in Isaiah make it hard to follow. Jerusalem is spared, then destroyed, then spared again depending on the chapter. Israel's enemies will be destroyed, but not before they get a few good hits in. Idol worship is always a threat. But ultimately, God will protect Jerusalem, bless it, and make it a shining symbol of divine favor.

Isaiah 56-66

Third Isaiah (Trito-Isaiah) likely dates from after the return from exile. The focus shifts to rebuilding society, observing proper worship, and warning against complacency.

We begin with the importance of observing the Sabbath, specifically refraining from traveling, working, or even engaging in idle conversation. This seems like a new level of detail about what constitutes acceptable Sabbath behavior. We already know from the Book of Numbers that God required the execution of a man for merely gathering wood on the Sabbath. So... is gossip now on par with that?

God also takes aim at adulterers, specifically those who undress, apply perfume and ointment, and climb into large beds with their lovers. That feels oddly specific. He further condemns child sacrifice, which was practiced in some ancient Near Eastern religions. But wasn't it God who told Abraham to sacrifice Isaac? Does He get a free pass because He canceled the execution at the last second?

Isaiah also rebukes the hypocrisy of fasting while ignoring the needs of the poor. Isaiah 58:7 asks: "Is it not to deal thy bread to the hungry, and that thou bring the poor that are cast out to thy house? When thou seest the naked, that thou cover him; and that thou hide not thyself from thine own flesh?" In other words, fasting should not be performative. You should feed the hungry, house the homeless, and care for your own kin as an expression of true moral conviction. This is a surprisingly enlightened and widely ignored instruction from the prophet.

In Isaiah 61:1, we get a well-known passage: "The spirit of the Lord God is upon me; because the Lord hath anointed me to preach good tidings unto the meek..." Surely Isaiah is telling the Jews they'll soon be freed from exile—possibly already underway at this point following Babylon's fall to Persia.

God promises to punish Judah's enemies, particularly Edom: "I have trodden the winepress alone...I will tread them in mine anger...and their blood shall be sprinkled upon my garments..." (Isa. 63.3). In other words, He'll turn them into crushed grapes and it's going to get messy.

But restoration is on the horizon. God promises to restore Jerusalem to glory, rescuing His people like a river in flood or a mighty wind. He'll appear in garments red with the blood of the vanquished, less "Prince of Peace" than "Avenger in Chief." Once Jerusalem is restored, foreigners will serve the Israelites, tending their vineyards and flocks. It's not a benevolent vision of reconciliation.

God's new creation will bring wealth and prosperity flowing like a river, and those who oppose Him will be swept away in the storm. It will be a new heaven, a new earth, and "...the voice of weeping shall be no more heard in her, nor the voice of crying" (Isa. 65:19). People will live at least until they are 100 years old. The book closes with a return to the imagery of the

Peaceable Kingdom: wolves and lambs dining together. I suppose that's technically possible, but I'd rather be the wolf than the lamb in that scenario.

Isaiah is a literary patchwork of different voices, styles, and historical contexts, making it hard to navigate and not much fun to read straight through. A recurring theme is that Israel faces both external threats (Assyria, Moab, Babylon) and internal ones (idolatry, gossip on the Sabbath, perfumed sex on oversized beds). But despite these trials, God's people will ultimately prevail. Jerusalem may fall, but it will rise again.

There's some vivid and memorable imagery here—lions munching hay, the dead walking around the city—but some of Isaiah's prophecies are obvious duds, like the promise that everyone will live past 100 or that nations will beat their swords into plowshares. Other "prophecies" likely describe events that had already happened, such as the Jews' return from exile after Cyrus defeated Babylon. And sure, if you give it long enough, Egypt, Sudan, or Syria will suffer—how impressive is that to predict? If Isaiah had predicted war and renewal in Europe, he'd probably seem just as prescient.

JEREMIAH

Jeremiah 1-31

The prophet Jeremiah is often portrayed as a compassionate figure, burdened by the harsh visions he was commanded to deliver to Israel. But I'm not sure his own account supports that view. If anything, Jeremiah comes off as deeply self-important. In Jer. 1:5, God says to him: "Before I formed thee in the belly I knew thee, and before thou camest forth out of the womb I sanctified thee, and I ordained thee a prophet unto the nations." That's quite a divine résumé, and Jeremiah doesn't seem particularly shy about it.

This same verse is sometimes leveraged by pro-life activists, who believe if God knows you in the womb, He surely would not want you to be aborted. But the context matters: God is telling an important prophet (at least a self-identified important one) about his divine mandate, not making a broader pronouncement about family planning. If God was pro-life, He could have mentioned it in the Commandments, not prescribed abortions in Numbers, and not repeatedly required the murder of captive children.

Like Isaiah before him, Jeremiah predicts Israel's backsliding, foreign occupation, and eventual vindication. The message is familiar: repent or be punished. But if the people turn from their wickedness, the Lord will bless all nations. In Jeremiah's telling, Judah will be surrounded by enemies, and destruction will be vast. In Jer. 4:24, he says: "I beheld the mountains, and, lo, they trembled, and all the hills moved lightly." Some will survive, but they'll live under the thumb of northern invaders—Ammonites, Arameans, Assyrians, or Phoenicians.

Jeremiah says he's troubled by these visions, that his heart is crushed and his spirit dismayed. Judgment isn't limited to Judah. God announces punishments for Egypt, Edom, and Moab, and warns that circumcision won't save them. Any nation that disobeys will be destroyed. As ever, idol worship is condemned, but Jeremiah also emphasizes ethical treatment of society's most vulnerable—aliens, orphans, and widows. He tries to drive home the message with metaphors: just as linen shorts rot in the Nile, Israel must cling to God, and like wine jars, the descendants of David will be smashed with no pity. It's worth noting that the Northern and Southern Kingdoms had already been split for centuries, so the vision of internal destruction and division isn't exactly revelatory.

In Jer. 11:18–23, Jeremiah claims that men from his hometown of Anathoth plotted to kill him, but God tipped him off. In return, God promises to kill the conspirators' young men and starve their children. Despite believing he was chosen before birth, Jeremiah rails against pride, at least in others. Still, he seems to know Israel can't really change. Jer. 13:23 asks: "Can the Ethiopian change his skin, or the leopard his spots?"—one of the Bible's rare direct references to skin color.

The later chapters contain prophecies about the Babylonian conquest. Jeremiah insists that Nebuchadnezzar's victory is not just inevitable, it's divinely ordained. In Jeremiah's view, Babylon isn't the enemy but God's chosen instrument. Those who surrender will be spared but sent into exile, all part of God's mysterious plan.

Unsurprisingly, this message is unpopular, and Jeremiah is put on trial (he was acquitted). To dramatize submission, he wears a wooden yoke. But eventually, the Lord promises the yoke will be broken, and the Israelites will return home—fulfilled, in part, under Persian King Cyrus. Another assassination plot appears in Jer. 18:18, as Jeremiah's opponents seek to silence him for being too disruptive. He presses on regardless.

To its credit, the book's prophecy about the Babylonian exile and return under Cyrus roughly tracks with history. Jeremiah likely lived from around 650 to 570 BCE, meaning he was alive for the destruction of Jerusalem in 586 but not the return from exile in 539. Scholars generally agree that while most of the material was written during his lifetime, later editing—possibly by his scribe and companion Baruch—helped the text align with historical events. And let's be honest: if you predict that a major city in the ancient Near East will be destroyed and then rebuilt, odds are you'll be right eventually.

Jeremiah revisits familiar themes from Isaiah: faithlessness, punishment, and divine mercy. He also echoes earlier commands not to mistreat the vulnerable, a moral thread that runs through the Law, the Prophets, and back to Moses, the original "stranger in a strange land." Despite its many jagged edges, the Bible does seem to have a soft spot for the powerless.

Still, while Isaiah has moments of dazzling poetry, Jeremiah tends to drone. His prophecies are repetitive, his imagery less vivid. But perhaps that's not his fault. After so many visions of doom and redemption, it's hard to keep things fresh.

Jeremiah 32-52

We start off with a real estate transaction, dutifully documented by Jeremiah's secretary and scribe, Baruch. Riveting material. Jeremiah then launches into a lengthy prayer and vision: God had once made Israel great, but the people spurned Him and turned to idol worship; now, trouble is on the way.

An example of Jeremiah's tedious style can be found in chapters 32 and 33. In 32:43, God says the land will be like a desert where neither people nor animals live; in 33:10, He again says the land will be desolate with no people or animals; and in 33:12, He repeats that it will be a desert where no one lives. We get it—it's a fucking desert. Baruch presumably took detailed notes on all three versions, just in case God decided to change metaphors.

Jeremiah receives yet another message to deliver to King Zedekiah. (Why can't God just send a dream?) The message: Zedekiah won't die during the Babylonian invasion, even as the city falls. The reasons for God's judgment include the usual—idol worship—but also a failed promise. The Israelites had agreed to free their Hebrew slaves but then reneged. They apparently thought this act of self-regulation showed maturity, but God disagreed. In Jer. 34:17, He declares, "I proclaim a liberty for you…to the sword, to the pestilence, and to the famine; and I will make you to be removed into all the kingdoms of the earth." The issue wasn't slaveholding per se, but the breaking of a covenant—specifically, the failure to release Hebrew slaves in the seventh year.

An Egyptian military advance briefly disrupts the Babylonian assault. Jeremiah, however, predicts it won't amount to anything, and he's right. Would Jerusalem have fared better under Egypt? We'll never know. In any case, the offensive fizzles, and Jeremiah ends up in jail. King Zedekiah secretly consults him for advice. I'm not trying to turn this into a detailed historical analysis, but the mention of a failed Egyptian intervention has the ring of authenticity.

Jeremiah, fearing for his life, hesitates to speak candidly. But Zedekiah reassures him: he won't be killed and is free to speak the truth, so long as he tells no one about their conversation. Jeremiah then delivers the hard truth: surrender to the Babylonians, and Jerusalem will be spared. Refuse, and it'll all go up in flames.

Zedekiah refuses. The city is sacked. The king flees, is captured, and has his eyes gouged out. Nebuchadnezzar, meanwhile, frees Jeremiah. Thus, Jeremiah's prophecy is "fulfilled," at least based on a private conversation with a deposed, blind, and imprisoned king. You'll just have to take Jeremiah's word for it.

Jeremiah keeps pushing his pro-Babylonian stance, begging the survivors not to flee to Egypt—another plea that goes nowhere. Reminiscent of Isaiah's grim tone, Jeremiah forecasts divine judgment on a long list of surrounding nations: Egypt (God will pour out His wrath), Philistia (Gaza will mourn), Moab (no town will escape ruin), Ammon (terror from all sides), Edom (destroyed like Sodom and Gomorrah), and Damascus (left deserted). Why do prophets never foresee progress, cooperation, or innovation? Perhaps because their experience was that things were always falling apart.

Chapters 50–51 present Babylon's fall to Cyrus of Persia as prophecy, though the detail and timing suggest it was written in hindsight, as prophecy often is. In 50:24, God says: "I have laid a snare for thee, and thou art also taken, O Babylon...because thou hast striven against the Lord." Babylon will be destroyed for its idolatry, but better days are ahead for the Hebrews in exile. Babylon, too, will be reduced to silence and sand. You guessed it: another desert. The final chapter appears to come from a different author and closely parallels the last chapters of 2 Kings. It provides a recap of the fall of Jerusalem, the destruction of the Temple, and the exile to Babylon.

The Book of Jeremiah has not exactly been a page-turner. The early chapters are clogged with repetitive, doom-filled visions, many likely written or retrofitted after the Babylonian conquest to appear prophetic. Jeremiah often comes across as proud of his own humility. The second half retains some of the same irritations but gains momentum as it tracks historical events toward the fall of Jerusalem.

Oddly, God urges surrender to Nebuchadnezzar but seems shocked that the Babylonians would worship foreign gods— or that the Jews might want to flee a war zone. Hindsight is 20/20, but expecting an invading empire to preserve your religion is like expecting Amazon to protect mom-and-pop bookstores. It's a charming delusion.

<u>LAMENTATIONS</u>

Lamentations is a short book made up of five poems mourning the destruction of Jerusalem by the Babylonians in 586 or 587 BCE. Although tradition attributes the work to the prophet Jeremiah, modern scholarship casts doubt on this. The tone and structure are different from the Book of Jeremiah, and the poetic voice here may belong to another anonymous eyewitness or survivor of the catastrophe.

The first poem, *The Sorrows of Jerusalem*, begins starkly in Lamentations 1:1: "How doth the city sit solitary, that was full of people! how is she become as a widow! she that was great among the nations..." The former grandeur of the city is gone. The Temple has been desecrated, the people scattered or enslaved, and the speaker offers a mournful reflection on the cost of, in their view, having spurned God's protection.

The second poem, *The Lord's Punishment of Jerusalem*, is even bleaker. It offers a grim portrait of life after the city's fall: darkness covers the land, elders sit in silence, children collapse in the streets, and enemies laugh. Lamentations 2:9 laments: "Her gates are sunk into the ground; he hath destroyed and broken her bars: her king and her princes are among the Gentiles: the law is no more; her prophets also find no vision from the Lord." There is no hope at the end, only grief, as the narrator says the children he raised and loved were slaughtered on the day of God's wrath.

The third poem, *Punishment, Repentance, and Hope*, shifts tone. Though the suffering continues, the speaker finds a sliver of meaning in endurance and patience. God is merciful, even if distant. But the desire for vengeance against the conquerors creeps in: "Give them sorrow of heart, thy curse unto them. Persecute and destroy them in anger from under the heavens of the Lord" (Lam. 3:65–66). So much for universal forgiveness.

The fourth poem, *Jerusalem After Its Fall*, returns to raw despair: mothers boil their own children for food; the living envy the dead. Yet there is a lingering hope for cosmic justice. Zion has paid for her sins, and maybe now God will turn His attention to punishing the enemies.

The final chapter, *A Prayer for Mercy*, is a desperate plea. Foreigners occupy their homes, the people are reduced to slavery, and starvation looms. Lamentations 5:21–22 closes with a powerful ambiguity: "Turn thou us unto thee, O Lord, and we shall be turned; renew our days as of old. But thou hast utterly rejected us; thou art very wroth against us." Is redemption still possible? Or has God's fury run out the clock?

As the title suggests, the book is an extended expression of grief over the destruction of Jerusalem. Its imagery of cannibalism, mockery, starvation, and silence is graphic, but also strangely dignified. The people suffer, but they hold onto the hope that God might still care. The fall of Jerusalem to Nebuchadnezzar is historically grounded, and while the scale of the devastation may be exaggerated for dramatic effect, the emotional core of the text feels deeply authentic. Invading armies in the ancient world were rarely merciful, especially

155

toward people who had resisted or held rival religious beliefs. The Babylonians were no exception.

Unlike much of the Bible, which is told from the perspective of kings, generals, and prophets, Lamentations offers what historians call "history from below": the view from the street, from the ruins, from the people crushed by the decisions of those in power. The poems give voice to suffering not as collateral damage, but as the central experience.

The poetry in Lamentations is among the most affecting in the Bible. It's not uplifting, but it feels urgent, dragging the reader into a world of collapse that feels eerily timeless. We can sympathize with these poor souls, whose only real crime was being born into the "wrong" tribe. But it also raises an uncomfortable question: Where was this empathy when they were the conquerors? Moses ordered the murder and rape of prisoners; Joshua presided over the extermination of entire cities. If we're morally outraged by the Babylonians, shouldn't we be equally appalled at the genocidal commands issued in earlier books of the Bible? Lamentations recognizes the suffering of the Israelites, but there is no monopoly on pain.

EZEKIEL

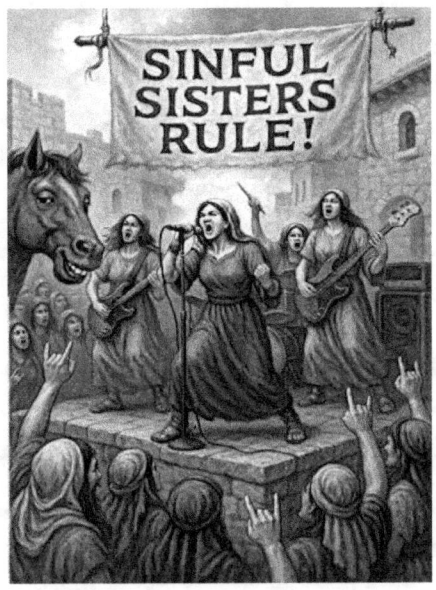

Ezekiel 1-24

Ezekiel was a Jew living in exile in Babylon before the fall of Jerusalem, an event also chronicled in the books of Jeremiah and Lamentations. Much of *Ezekiel* is allegorical, full of surreal imagery that later inspired the Book of Revelation. The book opens with one of the Bible's most bizarre visions, something out of a divine acid trip. Ezekiel sees a storm cloud approaching, flashing with lightning and fire, and then this:

> Also out of the midst thereof came the
> likeness of four living creatures...and every
> one had four faces, and every one had four
> wings. And their feet were straight feet; and
> the sole of their feet was like the sole of a
> calf's foot: and they sparkled like the color of
> burnished brass. (Ezekiel. 1:5–7)

157

Each creature had the face of a man, a lion, an ox, and an eagle. Nearby were four interlocking wheels, full of eyes, spinning and gliding through the air. Above them sat a throne made of sapphire, radiating a blinding light. God appears enthroned above it all, resembling polished metal from the waist up and fire from the waist down. Ezekiel hits the ground in terror. No surprise: God appoints Ezekiel as a prophet: "Son of man, I send thee to the children of Israel, to a rebellious nation that hath rebelled against me" (Eze. 2:3).

Ezekiel is to warn Jerusalem that they've sinned and God is about to drop the hammer. So far, standard prophet stuff, except then God temporarily paralyzes Ezekiel's tongue so he can't actually deliver the warning. It's a bold move, Cotton—let's see if it pays off.

Next, God orders Ezekiel to lie on his left side for 390 days, then on his right for 40 days. He's to eat a special bread made from wheat, barley, beans, lentils, millet, and fitches (spelt or emmer, probably). Ezekiel 4:9 is even marketed today as a brand of multigrain "biblical bread." In the original instructions, however, God tells Ezekiel to cook it over a fire fueled by human feces, a detail the modern marketing team wisely skipped. (God later relents and allows cow dung.) The number of days corresponds to the years of punishment for Israel and Judah.

Then comes the core message that the end is near: "An end, the end is come upon the four corners of the land" (Eze. 7:2). The land is full of violence, idolatry, and injustice. In a second vision, Ezekiel sees God—again appearing in semi-metallic, semi-flame form—leading him on a flying tour of Jerusalem's temple, now desecrated with pagan symbols. God forms a holy hit squad and orders them to kill the inhabitants of the city, showing no mercy to old or young. A man in linen (some sort of priestly figure) carries out the slaughter.

Ezekiel relays more warnings: obey God's law, ignore false (especially female) prophets, and destroy idols. God will unleash war, famine, wild beasts, and plague, punishments that are feeling rote by now. In Chapter 16, Jerusalem is depicted as an abandoned baby rescued and raised by God, only to grow up and become a nymphomaniac who worships foreign gods, commits adultery, and sacrifices her children.

Later comes a more reflective moment: Chapter 18 grapples with whether guilt is inherited. If a wicked man has a righteous son, should the son suffer for his father's crimes? Ezekiel says no: "The soul that sinneth, it shall die...the son shall not bear the iniquity of the father" (Eze. 18:20).

This ethic of individual responsibility contradicts earlier biblical texts like Exodus 20:5 and 34:7, where God says he'll visit the sins of the fathers upon their children to the third and fourth generation. Ezekiel's version is more palatable to modern readers, and frankly, more just.

Then there's a disturbing note in Ezekiel 20:25–26: "Wherefore I gave them also statutes that were not good...that I might make them desolate, to the end that they might know that I am the Lord." It sounds like God admits to giving Israel bad laws to make them suffer. Ezekiel may be referencing Numbers 3:13 ("All the firstborn are mine") and interpreting it to mean that God demanded child sacrifice as a test of loyalty. While some scholars suggest this is rhetorical or symbolic, Ezekiel seems to be saying the horror of such demands was the point.

Then comes *The Tale of the Sinful Sisters*—Oholah and Oholibah—stand-ins for the Northern and Southern Kingdoms, and a killer name for a heavy metal band. They are depicted as promiscuous women who lust after foreign men and pagan gods. Their punishment? Public humiliation, stoning, and burning. The metaphor hits its stride in 23:20: "For she doted upon their paramours, whose flesh is as the flesh of asses, and whose issue is like the issue of horses." The New Jerusalem Bible gives some more *umph* to the passage by describing the paramours as "big-membered as donkeys, ejaculating as violently as stallions."

Finally, God tells Ezekiel that his wife will die and he is not to mourn her. The wife represents Jerusalem: beloved, beautiful, and doomed to destruction by Babylon's invading armies. The lack of mourning signifies the stunned silence that will follow Jerusalem's fall.

Ezekiel is intense, graphic, hallucinatory, and oddly poetic in places. As prophecy, it blends trauma, theater, and theology into a brutal vision of judgment, laced with occasional flickers of moral progress (like personal accountability). At times, though, it's hard to know if you're reading a holy book or an ancient fever dream.

Ezekiel 25-36

After the parables and hallucinations of its early chapters, Ezekiel takes a tonal shift in Chapter 25. Adopting the fire-and-brimstone style of Isaiah and Jeremiah, he turns his focus to the destruction of Israel's neighbors and the dark days ahead, though eventually, there's a promise of future glory for Jerusalem.

First up: divine wrath for Ammon. God says he'll turn it into pastureland for cattle and sheep, which doesn't sound so bad. But then God really gets going: Moab will be erased as a nation, Edom will be punished with total slaughter, Philistia wiped out, and Sidon attacked from every direction.

Then comes the real showpiece: a prolonged prophecy against Tyre, the wealthy island fortress off the Phoenician coast. Tyre had mocked Jerusalem, and God took it personally. Ezekiel 26:3–4: "Behold, I am against thee, O Tyrus, and I will cause many nations to come up against thee, as the sea causeth his waves to come up. And they shall destroy the walls of Tyrus, and break down her towers: I will also scrape her dust from her, and make her like the top of a rock."

God named Nebuchadnezzar of Babylon as his instrument of vengeance. His forces will batter the city's walls with rams, torch the streets, and send horses stampeding through the rubble. Feeling unfulfilled as an actor and producer, God tries His hand at poetry in *A Funeral Song for Tyre* (Eze. 27:2–5):

> Now, thou son of man, take up a lamentation
> for Tyrus; O thou that art situated at the entry
> of the sea, which art a merchant of the people
> for many isles…O Tyrus, thou hast said, I am
> of perfect beauty. Thy borders are in the
> midst of the seas, thy builders have perfected
> thy beauty.

It all sounds strangely personal. God tells Ezekiel to inform the king of Tyre that being a slick businessman won't save him from the incoming hordes. The prophecy leaves no ambiguity: Tyre's destruction will be total. Eze. 28:19: "Thou shalt be a terror, and never shalt thou be any more."

Egypt is next on the hit list. God likens the pharaoh to a crocodile that will be hauled out of the Nile in fishing nets. Egypt had failed to help Jerusalem when Babylon invaded, and God is out for revenge. We're told the country will be laid low, turned into a desolate backwater under Nebuchadnezzar's heel.

But then comes a strange bit of news. Ezekiel 29:18: "Nebuchadnezzar king of Babylon caused his army to serve a great service against Tyrus…yet had no wages, nor his army, for Tyrus, for the service that he served against it." Translation: The siege didn't work. After all the battering and scraping, Babylon had come up empty-handed.

Ezekiel avoids commenting further on this failed prophecy and instead doubles down on Egypt: the crocodile will be dragged ashore, and the cedar tree will fall. The Egyptians will join the ghostly ranks of fallen nations in the underworld which include: Assyria, Elam, Edom, Meshech, Tubal, and other uncircumcised riffraff.

God then refocuses on Ezekiel and Israel. The prophet is appointed a "watchman" for his people. The moral logic gets fuzzy: a good man who strays will not be saved by his prior virtue, but a wicked man who reforms can be forgiven. Even

God seems to sense this isn't entirely fair, but judgment is judgment. Israel has sinned and will become a wasteland.

Then comes a glimmer of hope. In Chapter 34, God describes a shepherd tending his flock. He'll gather scattered sheep, bind the injured, fend off predators, and lead them to fresh pastures. The shepherd will also separate the good sheep from the bad. God then says in this story the shepherd is God and the sheep represent Israel. Thanks, Captain Obvious. Still, restoration is promised. Israel will abandon idols, see its fields flourish, and rebuild its cities. Enemies will fall. Jerusalem will rise.

Ezekiel devotes a significant amount of space to Tyre. The bulk of chapters 26–28 focus on the city's downfall, complete with divine lyrics and political warning. Tyre's arrogance, its location, and its success all make it a symbol ripe for divine vengeance.

Historically, there was a Babylonian siege of Tyre from 586 to 573 BCE. It dragged on for thirteen years and ended not in destruction, but in a negotiated settlement: the Tyrian king abdicated, and the city became a Babylonian vassal. The island portion of Tyre remained intact. Ezekiel's prophecies seem to have been written before the siege began and revised after it became clear that Tyre would be a tough nut to crack.

Tyre was ultimately conquered, but not by Nebuchadnezzar. In 332 BCE, Alexander the Great demanded the city's surrender. When rebuffed, he famously built a land bridge from the shore to the island—half a mile out—using mobile siege towers to protect his forces. After seven months, he captured the city with a combined land and sea assault, in one of the most extraordinary feats of ancient military engineering.

Some apologists claim Alexander's conquest fulfilled Ezekiel's prophecy. But that's a stretch. The Bible explicitly says Nebuchadnezzar would raze Tyre and that it would "never be any more." That didn't happen. Tyre survived for centuries. So unless God decided to outsource vengeance to Macedonia 250 years later, the prophecy rings hollow.

Ezekiel 37-48

Chapter 37 opens with the memorable story of the Valley of Dry Bones. God's spirit sweeps Ezekiel up and drops him in a desert strewn with skeletal remains. Ezekiel 37:3–4: "And he said unto me, Son of man, can these bones live? And I answered, O Lord God, thou knowest. Again he said unto me, Prophesy upon these bones, and say unto them, O ye dry bones, hear the word of the Lord."

Ezekiel does as instructed, and the bones begin to rattle and reassemble. Ligaments, muscles, and skin regrow. God tells Ezekiel He will breathe life into these bodies so that the dead may live again and return to the land of Israel.

Then comes a second visual aid. God instructs Ezekiel to take two sticks, one labeled "Kingdom of Judah," the other "Kingdom of Israel" and bind them together to symbolize the reunification of the divided kingdoms. Honestly, it's not a hard concept to grasp and didn't require props.

Next, we meet the mysterious and malevolent figure of Gog, ruler of Magog, a territory that includes Meshech and Tubal. Gog will form an alliance with Persia, Cush (likely Sudan), and Put (Libya). Strangely, it's God who orders this coalition to attack Israel, but then becomes enraged by the assault He orchestrated and annihilates Gog and his forces. Their corpses will lie unburied for seven months, serving as a feast for birds and scavengers. But after this bloody mess, Israel will be restored and assured of divine protection.

Then Ezekiel is taken on another visionary journey, this time by a glowing bronze man wielding a long linen tape measure. Unlike his earlier voyeuristic tour through Jerusalem's secret idol-filled passages, this one is like an extended biblical episode of *Fixer to Fabulous*. Tape Measure Man walks Ezekiel through the dimensions of a future Temple down to the cubit.

The descriptions are mind-numbing: the east gate, the outer courtyard, the north gate, the south gate, the inner courtyard, the composition of the altar and doors, etc. The structure is massive, with 10-foot-thick walls (one reed), gates measuring

84 feet across, and walls stretching 840 feet in length. Tape Measure Man tells Ezekiel he'd better be paying attention—there will be a quiz.

The stupefying detail continues, reminiscent of Leviticus. Sacrificial animals must be free of defects. Priests can't wear wool, must marry virgins or widows of other priests, and must keep their hair not too short, not too long. Also, uncircumcised men are barred from the temple (spare a thought for the poor soul assigned to check compliance at the door). Once again, we're reminded of the importance of honest weights and measures, a recurring bee in the bonnet for Old Testament writers. The rituals are revisited too: Passover, the Festival of Shelters, Sabbath sacrifices, and guidelines for keeping the Temple kitchens ritually pure.

Finally, Ezekiel lays out a new map of the Holy Land, assigning land to each of the twelve tribes. For example, the northern boundary for six of the tribes runs east from the Mediterranean Sea to Hethlon, through the Hamath Pass to Enon, and to the Damascus border. In a surprisingly progressive twist, Chapter 47 states that non-Israelites living in the land must be treated as full citizens, with equal property rights. Jerusalem's new name? "The Lord is There."

What are we to make of these visions and blueprints? Yogi Berra supposedly said, "Prediction is very difficult, especially about the future." That's certainly true of biblical prophecy. The dominant theme across Isaiah, Jeremiah, and Ezekiel is consistent: Israel will be beset by enemies, Jerusalem will fall, but eventually the nation will be reborn, like Ezekiel's dry bones, into a unified, independent Jewish state under its own king.

Modern Israel was reestablished in 1948—so that box gets a check, at least in part. But there's no king, just a rotating cast of prime ministers. More importantly, the prophets also claimed that once the Messiah came, peace would reign and war would cease. Safe to say that part never materialized. In fact, Jerusalem was under Muslim control for nearly a thousand years—punctuated by the Crusades—before the British took over after World War I. That long interlude didn't exactly scream "God is Here."

Most prophecies, frankly, are duds. The Babylonians didn't reduce Tyre to rubble. Egypt wasn't left desolate. Swords weren't beaten into plowshares. And there's a conspicuous absence of anything happening outside the ancient Near East. Wouldn't it have been impressive if Ezekiel foresaw a bicoastal superpower in North America? Or if Isaiah had predicted air travel, trips to the moon, or the rise of new world religions that would eventually dwarf Judaism?

DANIEL

Daniel 1-6

The Book of Daniel is a wildly inventive and at times entirely unbelievable book about the Jewish exile Daniel in Babylon. Although this would set the action of the book in the 600s BCE, most modern scholars believe it was written, or at least edited, as late as the 200s BCE.

The story starts with Daniel being taken into the court of Nebuchadnezzar, the King of Babylon, because of his noble birth, smarts and good looks. He's taught their language and given the new name Belteshazzar (not to be confused with Belshazzar, Nebuchadnezzar's son according to Daniel). Fun fact: Belshazzar was actually the son of later Babylonian ruler Nabonidus, who ruled 556-539 BCE, *not* Nebuchadnezzar.

Daniel's first test of resolve comes when he refuses the royal diet, insisting instead on a diet of vegetables and water. He proposes a trial: one group (Group A) eats like Babylonians,

166

the other (Group B) like observant Israelites, abstaining even from wine. After ten days, Group B appears healthier, so Daniel and his friends are allowed to stick to their preferred fare.

Daniel doesn't have to wait long for the spotlight. Nebuchadnezzar has a troubling dream and summons his wizards, magicians, sorcerers, and astrologers to interpret it. (Do we really need four HR titles for the same job description?)

There's a catch: the king doesn't just want the dream interpreted, he wants the dream recited back to him, too. Daniel 2:5: "The thing is gone from me: if ye will not make known unto me the dream, with the interpretation thereof, ye shall be cut in pieces, and your houses shall be made a dunghill." In other words, Nebuchadnezzar will dismember his advisors and turn their homes into latrines if they can't do the impossible. They explain, reasonably, that no one on earth can do this. The king orders the whole lot executed.

Daniel, despite having had nothing to do with the original exchange, is now on the chopping block. Fortunately, God reveals both the dream and its interpretation to him. Daniel petitions for an audience with the king and lays it all out: the dream involved a giant statue with a head of gold, chest and arms of silver, belly and thighs of bronze, and legs of iron, with feet of iron and clay. A stone smashes the feet, the statue crumbles into dust, and the stone grows to fill the whole world.

Daniel interprets: each metal represents a kingdom, with Nebuchadnezzar as the golden head and successive, inferior empires following. The stone is God's everlasting kingdom. Nebuchadnezzar, overwhelmed, bows to Daniel, promotes him, and gives him a key to the executive washroom. The king then builds a 90-foot-tall statue and demands everyone to worship it.

Daniel's three friends Shadrach, Meshach, and Abednego refuse. They're tossed into a blazing furnace, but emerge untouched, while a mysterious fourth figure walks among them

167

(angel? divine bodyguard?). Nebuchadnezzar, again stunned, promotes them and declares their God untouchable.

Next, the king dreams of a tree that reaches the heavens. Daniel breaks the bad news: the tree is Nebuchadnezzar, and he will be cut down and forced to live like a wild beast. Sure enough, Nebuchadnezzar ends up in the wilderness, grazing like cattle for seven years.

While Nebuchadnezzar is away, his son Belshazzar takes the throne and hosts a debauched party. During the feast, a disembodied hand like "Thing" in the *Adams Family* movies writes a cryptic message on the wall. The young king is baffled—he's never even heard of Daniel—but his mother has, and she brings him in. Daniel deciphers the writing: *"Mene, Mene, Tekel, Upharsin."* Translation: You've been weighed, found wanting, and your kingdom is forfeit to the Persians. That very night, Belshazzar is killed, and Darius seizes power.

Daniel is made a high-level administrator, and his competence provokes jealous rivals. They trick the new king into signing a law forbidding prayer to any god but himself. Daniel, in a bit of performative piety, keeps praying at his open window. Darius, bound by his own decree, reluctantly tosses him into a den of lions. But the next morning, Daniel is alive and well. The king rejoices, and then has Daniel's accusers, along with their wives and children, chucked to the lions instead.

The parallels between Daniel and the Joseph story are hard to miss. Both are Jewish captives who rise in a foreign court due to dream interpretation. In both stories, the ruler has a pair of dreams that require decoding. In Genesis, Joseph correctly interprets the fate of two fellow prisoners and then predicts seven years of plenty followed by seven years of famine. In Daniel, the second dream forecasts Nebuchadnezzar's humiliation and exile. Both stories feature the number seven— seven years of famine for Egypt, seven years of humiliation for Babylon—adding a mystical numerology to their parallel arcs. Joseph resists Potiphar's wife; Daniel abstains from wine and unclean food. But Daniel pulls off the more impressive trick:

he doesn't just interpret the dream; he tells the king what it was. Is the text implying that Daniel outshines Jacob's favorite son?

The fiery furnace and the lions' den stories showcase divine rescue for those who stay faithful, supernatural proofs of God's protection that many believers treat as literal events. But their dramatic flair also invites skepticism. Yes, lions were used for executions in the ancient world, most famously in Roman arenas, but such punishments were rare. Still, these stories offered powerful narrative ammunition for early Christians, who saw in Daniel a model of resistance and divine vindication amid persecution. The connection between Old Testament heroism and New Testament martyrdom practically writes itself.

One thing that doesn't improve across these stories is the decision-making of foreign kings. In Daniel, Nebuchadnezzar threatens mass execution over a dream, then bows to a Hebrew exile. Darius signs a death warrant for anyone who prays, forgetting that his favorite employee is famously devout. In Esther, the Persian king green-lights a genocide and is shocked when it turns out to include his own queen. In Nehemiah, the king lets his wine steward take a 12-year sabbatical to manage urban infrastructure.

Ancient monarchs didn't rise to power by being naïve pushovers or by signing every decree that came across their desk. So, either the Bible has no real grasp of imperial governance, or it's leaning into a trope: foreign kings as foolish, decadent, and easily manipulated, especially in contrast to wise, incorruptible Jewish exiles. If so, Daniel isn't just about faith and dreams, it's about identity and propaganda.

Daniel 7-12

The last six chapters are told from Daniel's point of view and include predictions of Alexander the Great's death, visions of successive empires, and the eventual restoration of God's kingdom. These visions have the same *Lucy in the Sky with*

169

Diamonds vibe as the opening of Ezekiel and the psychedelic chaos of Revelation.

Daniel's first vision in Chapter 7 is a doozie. Four beasts rise out of a stormy sea: the first is a winged lion that loses its wings and becomes human-like; the second is a bear gnawing on ribs; the third is a flying leopard with four wings; and the fourth a monstrous creature with iron teeth and ten horns. Yet another creature emerges, one with human eyes and a boastful mouth.

Daniel then seems to be in a large space, possibly with other observers—angels or humans—when thrones are suddenly set up, and an "Ancient of Days" character dressed in white robes takes a seat on a flaming, wheeled throne. Picture a *Lord of the Rings* meets *X-Men* mash-up. The fourth beast is destroyed, while the other three are allowed to linger a while longer. Then, in a dramatic flourish, a figure "like a son of man" appears in the clouds and is given everlasting dominion.

It's a climactic moment, but Daniel, apparently just as baffled as the rest of us, turns to one of the bystanders in the vision and asks, "What the actual fuck is going on?" He's given this cryptic explanation in Daniel 7:23: "The fourth beast shall be the fourth kingdom upon earth, which shall be different from all kingdoms, and shall devour the whole earth, and tread it down, and break it in pieces." Eventually, a new king will rise, overthrow the others, suppress religious traditions, and rule for three and a half years.

The Son of Man riding on the clouds is a stunning cinematic vision. When we first encountered that phrase in Ezekiel, it was merely God's way of addressing His prophet: "And he said unto me, Son of man, stand upon thy feet and I will speak to thee" (Eze. 2:1). Now in Daniel, the "Son of Man" has evolved into a new apocalyptic character. And, of course, the Son of Man will have a starring role in the New Testament, but let's not get ahead of ourselves.

In Daniel's next vision, he finds himself in Susa, capital of the Persian Empire, where he sees a ram with two horns, one longer than the other. The ram is then rammed—literally—by a lightning-fast goat with one prominent horn. The goat

170

tramples the ram, and its horn is broken, replaced by four others. Daniel is baffled, but like Hermione Granger after an obscure Divination lecture, the angel Gabriel steps in to explain what's going on. The goat is Greece, the ram is Persia and Media, and the four horns are the kingdoms that will rise from Alexander's shattered empire.

Next, Daniel receives another vision, this time with Gabriel again on hand to interpret. The message? That in seventy weeks—likely meant to represent seventy times seven years—God will set things right for His people. The Jews will return from exile, the Temple will be restored, and a messianic figure may appear to usher in a new era.

In Daniel 10:6, he's given a final vision of a radiant heavenly figure whose appearance is overwhelming: a man clothed in linen, with a belt of gold, face like lightning, eyes like fire, and voice like a roaring crowd. Daniel collapses in fear, and the figure explains he was delayed by a cosmic struggle with the "prince of Persia," aided only by the archangel Michael. Daniel is confused by all of this, and honestly, so am I.

In Chapter 12, the angel tells Daniel that Michael will reappear during a time of great distress. Many who died will rise again, some to everlasting life, others to shame and torment. Then in 12:4, the angel offers this parting shot: "But thou, O Daniel, shut up the words, and seal the book, even to the time of the end: many shall run to and fro, and knowledge shall be increased." In other words: Close the book, seal it, and stop trying to understand it. *Now* you tell us!

Some of Daniel's symbolism is straightforward, such as the ram with two horns being Persia and Media, the conquering goat as Alexander (he sometimes wore a goat's head emblem on his battle helmet) and the four new horns the kingdoms founded by Alexander's generals after his death. The "boastful" horn is Antiochus IV Epiphanes, the Seleucid ruler who desecrated the Jewish temple in 167 BCE.

Daniel's vision of the four beasts in Chapter 7 refers to the kingdoms of Babylon, Media, Persia, and Greece. This sequence reflects the geopolitical reality of the ancient Near

East, with Babylon as the dominant power, followed by the Medes, then the Persians (who absorbed the Medes), and finally the Greeks under Alexander. From his vantage point in the 200s BCE, Daniel could have easily identified these kingdoms, because they'd all come and gone by that time. This relatively late date for the completion of Daniel is justified given that he is aware of Epiphanes's Temple attack.

However, early Christians, eager to make Daniel's visions point to Jesus, shoehorned Rome into the lineup. To these revisionists, the kingdoms were Babylon, "Media-Persia," Greece, and Rome. Why? Because if the fourth kingdom is Rome, then the "stone that smashes the statue" or the "Son of Man coming in glory" can be interpreted as Christ establishing his eternal kingdom during the Roman Empire.

But Daniel never mentions Rome. And Persia had conquered Media on the road to becoming an ancient superpower. If you'd asked Darius III on the eve of his battles with Alexander if he was "Persian" or "Medo-Persian," he surely would have said Persian, or just the "King of Kings," and he would have resented any hint that the Medes were his equal. Even in Daniel's ram and goat story, it shows that the Persian horn is superior to the Median one. So, although it's not a *total* fiction for Christians to combine the Medes and Persians into a single kingdom, it's a contortionist reading of history.

Daniel's "prophecies" aren't so much predictions of the distant future as they are cryptic allegories of recent history, especially the rise and fragmentation of Alexander's empire. The apocalyptic dressing gives it drama and distance, but the content reads like someone retrofitting history into a divine timeline.

THE 12 PROPHETS

Hosea

By tradition, this collection of writings from unknown authors dates to the early to mid–700s BCE. The focus is on the Northern Kingdom's infidelity to God and the righteousness of God's judgment, along with the hope of mercy that comes with Israel's repentance. This region of the kingdom, Samaria, fell to Assyria in 721 BCE, so to the extent Hosea is prophetic, it's either envisioning events in the recent past or the immediate future.

We start with a rather uncomfortable comparison of Israel and God to the troubled marriage of Hosea and his unfaithful wife, Gomer. They have three children whom God has commanded them to name: Jezreel, Unloved, and Not My People. If Gomer does not change her ways, the Lord will show no mercy to her children, strip her, and make her barren. Her vines and figs will be ruined, but once she stops worshipping Baal, her covenant with God can be renewed.

Hosea is told not to give up and that he must still love his adulterous wife, just as God loves Israel. As the police report summarized, God only beat up Israel because he (sob) loved her so very much.

Although the metaphor of God and Israel as a marriage is new, the underlying themes of Hosea are getting stale: Israel has forsaken God, is worshiping idols, and is descending into promiscuity; it must be punished. Only then can its sins be forgiven and God and Israel be one big happy family, albeit one with lots of trauma to work through.

Anyway, Israel is troubled. Murders are up, people are using inaccurate scales, adultery is common, priests are just in it for the money, and idol worship has supplanted God. It's so bad that even God has a hard time with applying the appropriate punishment. Hosea 4:14: "I will not punish your daughters when they commit whoredom, nor your spouses when they commit adultery: for themselves are separated with whores, and they sacrifice with harlots: therefore the people that doth not understand shall fall." In other words, how can adultery be judged when Israel itself is a prostitute?

A war between Israel and Judah seems to be on the horizon, one in which Israel will ask for help from its powerful neighbor, Assyria, a move that God says he'll attack like a lion, like a leopard in wait. Hosea 6:1: "Come, and let us return unto the Lord: for he hath torn, and he will heal us; he hath smitten, and he will bind us up." In other words, the people will finally get the message that God (like alcohol) is the cause of and the cure for all their problems.

But before all is forgiven, Israel will have to suffer. It's time for the people to get what they deserve, for them to see their children hunted down and killed. They are a dried-up plant that can have no children, and even if they did, the Lord would kill them. Israel will have her babies dashed to the ground and pregnant women ripped open. Hosea then prays for Israel that God protect the land like an evergreen plant, like a beautiful olive tree.

174

In Hosea 8:7, we find a memorable verse directed to Israel for its idolatry (you may recall that under Jeroboam, the kingdom had constructed golden calves in Bethel and Dan): "For they have sown the wind, and they shall reap the whirlwind…"

This phrase, "They sowed the wind, and now they are going to reap the whirlwind," was famously employed by British Air Marshal Sir Arthur "Bomber" Harris in 1942 to justify British attacks on Germany: The Nazis had started it, so they deserved the rain of fire what was about to be unleashed on their cities.

The short conclusion in Hosea 14:9 seems likely to fall on deaf ears: "Who is wise, and he shall understand these things? Prudent, and he shall know them? For the ways of the Lord are right, and the just shall walk in them: but the transgressors shall fall therein." In other words, the wise will take the book to heart, but the foolish will ignore it. Isn't that always the case?

Joel

Like Hosea, the authorship of *Joel* is unknown, although it may have been written in the 5th or 4th century BCE. We begin with a plague of locusts that is in the process of devouring everything in its path, with teeth as sharp as those of lions. There is no grain or wine to offer the priests because it's gone, all gone. There are no defenses. There has never been a plague like it in the past, and there will never be one so big in the future. It feels like the American Dust Bowl of the 1930s.

However, there is still hope if the people pray and fast because God is merciful. Joel 2:13: "And rend your heart, and not your garments, and turn unto the Lord your God: for he is gracious and merciful, slow to anger, and of great kindness, and repenteth him of the evil." By now, we know God's judgment can be petty, excessive, and indiscriminate, but let's put that to the side, I guess.

Anyway, God will make it right in the end. There will be abundant grain and wine, and God will judge the foreigners who have caused harm to Israel in the Valley of Judgment.

Tyre, Sidon, and Philistia will have their children sold in slavery, Egypt will be a ruined waste, and Jerusalem will never be conquered again (let's put that one in the failed prophecy bucket…). There's an interesting twist on the prophecy from Isaiah in Joel 3:10: "Beat your plowshares into swords, and your pruninghooks into spears: let the weak say, I am strong." We now have a prophecy that swords will be beaten into plows (Isaiah) and that plows will be beaten into swords (Joel). Maybe Joel is just showing off by contradicting a more well-known prophet.

Amos

Amos seems to have been written earlier than Joel, maybe in the 8th century BCE, but he also foresees the doom of Israel's neighbors, starting with Philistia. Amos 1:7: "But I will send a fire on the wall of Gaza, which shall devour the palaces thereof." Tyre will be destroyed by fire; Edom by fire; Ammon by fire; Moab by fire, and Judah will be destroyed by…wait for it…fire.

But the case against Israel (the Northern Kingdom) gets special attention. Its people are refusing to help the poor and like an episode of *Real Housewives of Samaria*, its privileged women are making their husbands continually resupply them with wine. God's retribution will be to destroy Israel like Sodom and Gomorrah, to have its youth killed in battle, and to have locusts destroy its crops. God's judgment will come like righteous water, like a mighty stream.

But Israel's regeneration is also foreseen. The days are coming when grain grows faster than it can be harvested, and the mountains drip with sweet wine. God will bring his people back and plant them in the fertile land.

Shouldn't the 8th-century BCE Book of Amos precede, rather than follow, the 4th-century BCE Book of Joel? If the order of these two books were switched, Amos' prophecy of locusts would more clearly be realized in the actual plague in Joel. But how impressive is it to predict locusts in Palestine?

Obadiah

Obadiah was written sometime after the fall of Jerusalem in 586/87 BCE and foretells doom to the Edomites, who were happy to stand by and allow the destruction of Israel's capital. Because they robbed and killed the descendants of David, they will be destroyed and dishonored forever. Obad. 15: "For the day of the Lord is near upon all the heathen: as thou hast done, it shall be done unto thee: thy reward shall return upon thine own head." Edom will be taken over by Israel, which will rage like a fire against the descendants of Esau (in Genesis, Esau was Jacob's older brother and progenitor of the Edomites).

To Amos, Israel's crimes included idol worship but also not doing enough for the poor and downtrodden. This has not been a focus in the Bible so far, although it's becoming a more consistent message in the prophetic books, and of course, it will be an even more central message in the New Testament.

Jonah

God commands Jonah to go to the Assyrian capital, Nineveh (modern-day northern Iraq), and proclaim to its people that they are wicked and doomed. This sounds like a thankless task, so Jonah tries to escape by getting on a boat bound for Spain.

He quickly falls asleep below deck, but a violent storm is sent by God, threatening to break the ship apart. The captain has to wake up Jonah (he must have just consumed an edible), and the crew draws lots to determine who's to blame. Jonah's number is drawn, and he confesses to being a Hebrew who's on the run from God. The sailors end up chucking him overboard, and the sea then dies down. We then reach the part of the story that every kindergartner knows. Jonah 1:17: "Now

177

the Lord had prepared a great fish to swallow up Jonah. And Jonah was in the belly of the fish three days and three nights."

Inside the fish, Jonah has the time to compose a prayer: He'd been near death, wrapped in seaweed, but he remembered how useless idols were and how much God should be praised. God then ordered the fish to vomit out Jonah onto a beach.

Hopefully, after showering, Jonah made his way to Nineveh, a city so large it took three days to walk through and proclaimed that the city would be destroyed in 40 days. The people of Nineveh (of course) believed him, and the (unnamed) king of Nineveh ordered everyone to wear sackcloth and fast to avoid God's judgment, which would have made no sense to the Assyrian polytheists.

Anyway, God spares Nineveh and provides a vivid experience to help Jonah understand His decision. God creates a beautiful plant for Jonah to rest under but then has a worm destroy it (it must have been a rather large worm). God says if Jonah could feel sorry for the loss of the insignificant plant, imagine how bad He would have felt after killing an entire city. But if God was going to let Nineveh off the hook, why did he bother getting Jonah involved in the first place?

The decision does not sit well with Jonah, who feels foolish for having threatened Nineveh when, deep down, he knew God would end up showing mercy. Jonah created the tagline "God Always Chickens Out," but manufacturing GACO hats proved too expensive, and he abandoned the project.

A more natural home for the story of Jonah would be in the *Arabian Nights*, but since it's in the Bible, we must take it seriously, I guess. There are lengthy articles from religious websites that speculate about the type of fish or whale that swallowed Jonah. One guess is that the fish was a whale shark, but evidently, the gullet of this creature is not wide enough for a human to pass through. Another potential culprit is a sperm whale, which, at least in theory, could swallow a person. However, even Biblical literalists acknowledge that no one could live for three days in the digestive acid of a whale's belly, but they also point out that God is capable of supernatural intervention. But if we are playing that card, why didn't God just put Jonah on a magic flying carpet to Nineveh? Also, note that Jonah was dead to the world for three days, just like Jesus would later be.

Micah

The prophet Micah might have been a contemporary of Isaiah and Amos. Like Amos, Micah foresees doom, but it's targeted more (but not entirely) towards Judah rather than the Northern Kingdom. The Lord will melt the mountains and pour down the valleys like water and will turn Samaria into a ruin. Micah promises to demonstrate his sorrow by walking naked, howling like a jackal, and wailing like an ostrich, which would allow him to blend in nicely in downtown Los Angeles.

Micah is rebuffed by the locals, who doubt God and prefer the rosier predictions of their paid prophets. Judah's leaders are called out for their corruption, which will result in ruin. Micah 3:12: "Therefore shall Zion for your sake be plowed as a field, and Jerusalem shall become heaps, and the mountain of the house as the high places of the forest."

But there will also be a time to go on the offensive. Jerusalem must punish its enemies with the newfound strength of a bull with iron horns and bronze hoofs. A future leader will come from a small town that will become critical to the Christian faith. Micah 5:2: "But thou, Bethlehem Ephratah, though thou be little among the thousands of Judah, yet out of thee shall he come forth unto me that is to be the ruler of Israel."

Micah then presses his case against Israel: God does not want sacrifices or oils; He only wants the people to show Him love and humility. But God also hates people who use false scales and weights (please, can we give it a rest?) and the exploitation of the poor. The day will come when God punishes the people, and you won't be able to trust your family or friends. But Jerusalem will rise, and its people will return from Egypt and far-flung cities. God will not stay angry with Israel forever; He just requires love and devotion.

Micah covers ground similar to material in the earlier Book of Amos, focusing on the bad behavior, judgment, and ultimate renewal of Jerusalem. Missing from Micah is a laundry list of neighboring cities or regions that will be burned, starved, or sacked for their actions against Israel. One other thing I've noticed from later Bible prophets is that while they condemn idol worship, they don't feel compelled to revisit most of Moses' laws. In fact, they emphasize fair treatment for the poor and the need for leaders to act ethically far more than we found in Exodus or Numbers.

We know from the Book of Ruth that the House of David rose from Bethlehem, and with Micah, we know that this same city will give rise to a future ruler of Israel. This is obviously important for the New Testament, but let's not get ahead of ourselves.

Nahum

Remember the parable of God's mercy at the end of the Book of Jonah? In this story, God created and then destroyed a shade plant, which saddened Jonah. God points out that this small disappointment would pale in comparison to the guilt of exterminating 120,000 people in Nineveh. It was a story to illustrate how God's compassion and wisdom surpass Jonah's pettiness. God is great, wise, and, above all, merciful.

Well, fuck that, Nineveh is back on the kill list! God's anger has been provoked, and His judgment will flow against Nineveh like a rushing flood, and like dry thorns, it will burn. The destruction of Assyria will be absolute. Nah. 1:14: "And the Lord hath given a commandment concerning thee, that no more of thy name be sown: out of the house of thy gods will I cut off the graven image and the molten image: I will make thy grave; for thou art vile." Corpses will be piled high and like a seductive harlot who lures men to their doom, the Lord will strip Nineveh naked and cover the city with "abominable filth." I think the police might want to check for freshly dug graves in Nahum's basement.

Like Thebes before it, Nineveh will burn (Nah. 3:8-10). Its officials will fly away like locusts. Nahum closes with its final message to Assyria in Nah. 3:18: "Thy shepherds slumber, O king of Assyria: thy nobles shall dwell in the dust: thy people is scattered upon the mountains, and no man gathereth them."

Nineveh was a jewel of the ancient world, boasting a giant, ornate palace and lush crops fed by an extensive irrigation system. It was perhaps the largest city in the world at the time (Jonah's figure of 120,000 checks out). Assyrian power had ebbed and flowed for centuries, but in 612 BCE, an alliance of Babylonians, Medes, and Scythians toppled the regime for good, ushering in Babylonian domination.

In *Nahum*, the sacking of Egyptian Thebes had already occurred, so it's safe to date this story after 663 BCE when the Assyrian Empire destroyed the city. As with much of the Bible's history, it's not straightforward. Though Nahum describes events between 663 and 612 BCE, some scholars suggest it was composed centuries later, when dreams of national revenge were especially in vogue.

Habakkuk

Habakkuk seems to have been written near the end of the 7th century BCE after the Babylonians had overthrown Assyria and become the dominant regional power. The central question of this book is how God can allow these nasty and prideful foreigners to occupy Palestine. This is addressed using a prayer from Habakkuk, followed by God's response. How can God treat His people like a swarm of insects, to be dragged like fish? In Hab. 2:3, God urges patience for Israel's eventual liberation: "For the vision is yet for an appointed time, but at the end, it shall speak, and not lie: though it tarry, wait for it; because it will surely come, it will not tarry."

181

Israel's patience will be rewarded; its enemies will tremble and find no relief in their worship of idols. Habakkuk finishes with a prayer: God, give me the strength of a sure-footed deer who keeps its balance in the mountains.

Zephaniah

The book dates from the 7th century BCE and foresees the divine destruction of Jerusalem and neighboring areas. Zep. 1:2–3: "I will utterly consume all things from off the land, saith the Lord. I will consume man and beast; I will consume the fowls of the heaven, and the fishes of the sea, and the stumbling blocks with the wicked; and I will cut off man from off the land, saith the Lord."

Jerusalem will be destroyed so that there is no vestige of Baal among its people. God will take a lamp and walk the streets to find the self-satisfied who think they can escape judgment. Their gold won't save them, and their bodies will rot in the open. Zephaniah then prays for the city that it may come to its senses and humble itself before God.

Jerusalem's neighbors are going to get whacked, too. No one will be left in Gaza; Philistia is doomed; Moab and Ammon will go up in flames like Sodom and Gomorrah; the people of Sudan will be put to death; Assyria will be destroyed and taken over by owls. After all this destruction, the survivors in Jerusalem will be in a better place. They will be prosperous, secure, and no longer afraid.

The prophetic themes are recycling: Israel is sinning; God will punish it for its transgressions; Israel will repent; Israel's enemies will be destroyed; God's blessings will flow; and a glorious future awaits.

But is any other prophecy really feasible? Would anyone make or derive comfort from a prophecy like: Things are wonderful, our faith is strong, our neighbors are unthreatening, but our future is irredeemably bleak, and there's nothing we can do about it? Humans are, above all, storytellers, and the story we want to tell ourselves is that however messed up things are now, the future is shimmering with potential, so bright we'll need shades.

Haggai

Haggai begins by stating that it was written during the second year of the reign of Darius (ruler from 522–486 BCE), reflecting the message that the Lord sent to Haggai, and is directed to the people of Jerusalem and its governor, Zerubbabel. It's noteworthy that Haggai himself is not stated as the author, so his followers presumably wrote the book.

Haggai takes the leaders of Jerusalem to task for sitting idle instead of rebuilding the Temple, which had been destroyed during the Babylonian occupation from 586 to 539 BCE. Why should the people live in rebuilt homes yet allow the Temple to remain in disrepair? Hadn't they noticed that their grain fields and vineyards hadn't been productive? The lack of rain, he says, has been a penalty from God because the Temple hasn't been rebuilt.

The citizens listen to the prophet and begin work to fulfill God's vision to make the new Temple even greater than the original. Hag. 2:8–9: "The silver is mine, and the gold is mine…The glory of this latter house shall be greater than of the former, saith the Lord of hosts: and in this place will I give peace…"

The book concludes with the vision that the heavens and earth will shake and kingdoms will fall but that the governor, Zerubbabel, will be appointed by God as his faithful servant. Maybe Haggai's disciples wrote the book, but I wonder if Zerubbabel had the chance to make final edits.

Zechariah

Zechariah is really two books in one. The first chapters present visions related to the rebuilding of the Temple in the 520s

BCE, and the second half comprises a collection of later writings about a future messiah, a term that is often misunderstood.

In Judaism, the Messiah (*Mashiach*) is expected to be a future Jewish king from the line of David who will bring political and religious redemption to Israel, rebuild the Temple, restore national sovereignty, and usher in an era of peace and divine justice. He will be anointed with holy oil and will be a mortal, human leader, not a divine or supernatural being. Unlike in later Christian interpretations, the Jewish Messiah is not a savior of souls but a restorer of national and religious order on Earth.

Anyway, Zechariah says God is disappointed with the ancestors of Jerusalem and describes a series of visions. The first involves red, dappled, and white horses that inspect the world and report that it lies subdued before the Lord. The next vision is in Zech. 1:18–19: "Then lifted I up mine eyes, and saw, and behold four horns. And I said unto the angel that talked with me, What be these? And he answered me, These are the horns which have scattered Judah, Israel, and Jerusalem." The number four keeps coming up in prophecy, from Ezekiel to Daniel, and now Zechariah.

Other visions follow. A man with a measuring line appears (reminiscent of the Tape Measure Man in Ezekiel), a stone with seven sides is shown to High Priest Joshua, a gold lampstand appears, and a message is given to Zerubbabel to continue rebuilding the Temple. A list of thieves will be reported on a giant flying scroll, and an evil woman in a basket will be flown to Babylon by two other women with wings.

Chapters 7–8 continue the themes of earlier prophets: show mercy to one another, be kind to widows, orphans, and foreigners living in your country, and don't lie under oath. In Chapter 9, we get a recitation of neighboring countries that will be harshly dealt with: Syria will be destroyed; Tyre will burn; Gaza will suffer great pain; and the proud Philistines will be humbled.

Zech. 9:9–10 foresees a new king establishing peace across the region:

> Rejoice greatly, O daughter of Zion; shout, O
> daughter of Jerusalem: behold, thy King
> cometh unto thee: he is just, and having
> salvation; lowly, and riding upon an ass, and
> upon a colt the foal of an ass. And I will cut
> off the chariot from Ephraim, and the horse
> from Jerusalem, and the battle bow shall be
> cut off: and he shall speak peace unto the
> heathen: and his dominion shall be from sea
> even to sea, and from the river even to the
> ends of the earth.

This prophecy is about a future ruler, a Messiah, who will unite the nation and govern as an earthly king in peace. And the phrase "riding upon an ass, and upon a colt the foal of an ass" will confuse future Bible writers to no end: Is this king riding on one donkey, or two? And how the hell would you ride two at the same time?

Chapter 11 starts with a parable about a shepherd who breaks his staff into two parts—Favor and Union—and the warning that a worthless shepherd will be destroyed and his arm withered (a callback to Jeroboam's withered appendage in the Book of Kings). God will protect His people; He will terrify the enemy's horses and make their riders go crazy.

The book finishes with an apocalyptic vision. Zech. 14:2: "For I will gather all nations against Jerusalem to battle; and the city shall be taken, and the houses rifled, and the women ravished, and half of the city shall go forth into captivity, and the residue of the people shall not be cut off from the city." In other words, God will allow—will require—the demolition of Jerusalem. This sounds like what happened during the Babylonian occupation, but it's presented here as an event that will occur in the indeterminate future.

But God will make it right. He will cause fresh water to flow into the Dead Sea, bring a plague on the nations that make war on Jerusalem, and kill all their camels and donkeys.

Malachi

This short book seems to have been written after the Temple was rebuilt, sometime in the late fifth century BCE (circa 420–400 BCE). It's a mixture of preaching against religious backsliding and prophecy. Malachi observes that priests are no longer sacrificing the best animals and that they are marrying foreign women (this also bothered Ezra). God says He hates divorce, but it seems He's more concerned about His people no longer honoring Him rather than just Jerusalem's men having wandering eyes.

Judgment Day approaches, and a messenger will come like strong soap, like a purified fire, so that tithes will be paid, and those who give false testimony, cheat employees, and take advantage of widows will be judged. It's interesting to see that these are the high crimes Malachi is concerned about, not idol worship, coveting, or murder.

The day is coming when evil and pride will burn like straw, but if you obey God, you'll be as happy as a calf freed from its stall. *The Book of Malachi*, the final book of the Old Testament, ends with a hazy vision that seems both threatening and encouraging, one that will later be seen to predict Jesus as the new Elijah. Mal. 4:5–6: "Behold, I will send you Elijah the prophet before the coming of the great and dreadful day of the Lord: And he shall turn the heart of the fathers to the children, and the heart of the children to their fathers, lest I come and smite the earth with a curse." We think we understand this vision because of how New Testament Christians reinterpreted and leveraged it. But like the rest of the prophetic voices in the Bible, it's more of a kaleidoscope whose image mutates as it's exposed to new sources of light.

186

FINAL THOUGHTS: OLD TESTAMENT

The Old Testament is wild, wonderful, obscene, morally dubious, often incoherent, occasionally beautiful and thought-provoking. And yes, large portions are dull as paste. But I never detected anything that suggests a supernatural origin. What is it about the story of Moses and his descendants that allowed it to remain relevant long after the *Epic of Gilgamesh* faded into obscurity?

Nature of God

In the first chapter of Genesis, God is all-powerful, but by the next chapter, He seems unsure how to manage the humans He just created. He's quickly frustrated, eventually flooding the entire world and killing everything that breathes—except Noah and his floating zoo. Why? "Corruption of flesh" and "violence," whatever that means. But no sooner do humans repopulate the earth than they're back to their usual mayhem, and God is smiting them again.

God's presence is wildly inconsistent. He seems blind to the Israelites' suffering in Egypt for centuries until Moses finally shows up. He kills people for trivial reasons: complaining about food, or committing vaguely defined offenses. Er, for instance, is struck down without explanation. Then his brother Onan gets zapped for refusing to impregnate his brother's widow.

Though the God of the Pentateuch occasionally softens, divine judgment is still capricious and cruel. In Job, God lets Satan destroy an innocent man's life on a bet—and seems more amused than concerned. Some Bible books sidestep God entirely. Ecclesiastes shrugs that life is meaningless. Song of Solomon, meanwhile, borders on soft-core porn.

We are to believe that God was silent for the first 200,000 or so years of *Homo sapiens'* existence, then suddenly revealed Himself to a small band of Bronze Age nomads in the Levant.

The rest of the planet—Asia, the Americas, Africa beyond Egypt—isn't mentioned. God's singular obsession is with the Israelites, their liberation from Egypt, their wilderness years, and their conquest of Canaan. The fate of humanity beyond that narrow context doesn't seem to concern Him.

Good and Evil

The Ten Commandments loom large, but the Bible offers multiple versions (see Exodus 20, Exodus 34, Deuteronomy 5), and new laws pop up throughout the Torah. These sometimes expand upon or contradict earlier ones.

And they're underwhelming. Only six have clear moral content—don't murder, steal, lie, or commit adultery, for example—and even these are inconsistently applied. Adultery merits death, yet Jacob is tricked into sleeping with Leah instead of Rachel, which, by modern standards, is still adultery. God doesn't seem bothered. As for murder: Israelites are repeatedly ordered to kill men, women, and children during conquest, and God is fine with it. The commandment not to kill really means: Don't kill fellow Israelites under ordinary circumstances.

The 10th commandment, prohibiting coveting, criminalizes feelings. Ironically, Ecclesiastes admits envy is a major driver of human ambition. Other commandments veer into the bizarre: kill witches, avoid mixing fabrics, and never boil a goat in its mother's milk. Literalist Christians are oddly selective, ignoring the fabric ban, for example, while condemning homosexuality with gusto. One wonders if they protest too much.

Later prophets express concern for the poor and oppressed. Psalms, Isaiah, and Jeremiah all call for justice for widows, orphans, and foreigners. That may stem from a basic principle of reciprocity: Israelite identity was forged in exile, so they knew what it meant to be vulnerable. Fair weights and measures are also stressed, suggesting an interest in honest economic dealings, however primitive the system.

But let's not sugarcoat it. Women are treated as property. Dinah is raped, and her father debates whether retribution is even worth the trouble. Captive girls are forced into sexual slavery. Polygamy is normal. If a man dies, his widow is handed off to his brother like a piece of inherited livestock. Homosexuality is condemned as an abomination, but lesbianism goes entirely unmentioned—perhaps outside the authors' frame of imagination. Today's calls for "Biblical marriage" would mean one man and several submissive wives. Why so many women find this model appealing is beyond me.

The Afterlife

The Old Testament offers only a hazy notion of the afterlife. The dead go to Sheol, a shadowy underworld where good and bad alike reside. There's no reward or punishment, just silence and oblivion. Hints of resurrection emerge late, notably in Daniel 12:2: "Many of them that sleep in the dust shall awake, some to everlasting life, and some to shame and contempt."

Isaiah and Job offer vague gestures toward vindication after death, but these are hardly robust theologies. Ezekiel's Valley of Dry Bones is more about national renewal than personal afterlife. There's still no link between moral behavior and eternal reward. Heaven and hell as we now understand them are largely New Testament innovations. The God of the Old Testament is grounded in the now, rewarding obedience with land and cattle, and punishing disobedience with plagues or slaughter.

As Literature

The Bible gives us unforgettable stories: the Creation, the Flood, Isaac's near sacrifice, the walls of Jericho, Samson's strength, and David's slingshot. Their staying power lies partly in their sparseness; they invite reinterpretation. What kind of

189

fish swallowed Jonah? With whom did Jacob wrestle? What exactly was that burning bush?

Biblical language saturates our culture: "by the skin of your teeth" (Job), "a thorn in the flesh" (Numbers), "eat, drink, and be merry" (Ecclesiastes), "the writing on the wall" (Daniel), "let there be light" (Genesis).

But there are also plot holes and duplications. Abraham twice passes off Sarah as his sister; Isaac does the same. Lot is visited by divine beings and a mob threatens them—nearly identical to a later story in Judges. Some discrepancies are quietly revised—Chronicles omits the wildly implausible claim in Kings that 185,000 Assyrians died overnight. Yet Isaiah brings the number right back.

As Prophecy

Biblical prophecy has not aged well. Nebuchadnezzar did not conquer Tyre. Spears have not been beaten into plowshares. Some prophecies are impossibly cryptic ("a woman in a basket carried to Babylon by winged women"), others transparently postdated (the fall of Persia to Greece). Messianic texts are often recontextualized—Isaiah 7 says "young woman," not "virgin." And some prophecies are so generic—"there will be locusts in Palestine"—as to be laughable.

The only "prophesies" that seem to come true are the ones that were made and fulfilled within the same story. For example, in Genesis we are told Rebekah's elder child will serve the younger, which comes true after Jacob tricks Esau. But this seems more like a clever plot device than true prophesy.

Final Reflections

People often cherry-pick the uplifting parts and skip the tedium or horror. Joseph forgiving his brothers is touching, until you realize he and Pharaoh enslaved Egypt in the process. Mosaic victories read like epic triumphs until you understand they include rape and ethnic cleansing. The Sabbath wood-gatherer was stoned to death.

Some believers try to explain away the cruelty and contradiction, insisting the Bible is ultimately about love and justice. But the violence and strangeness are not detours. They're central. If we want students to understand the Bible, let's assign the whole thing. Let them see the poetry—but also the misogyny, magical thinking, and moral incoherence.

The Old Testament is primarily a narrative of God's covenant with Israel. Everything else is peripheral. God liberates the Israelites from Egypt (an event for which there is no clear archaeological support), leads them through the wilderness, and delivers them to Canaan after wiping out its inhabitants. Through the prophets, we are told that one day, Jerusalem will be restored, and a king will rule in righteousness. Thousands of years later, many still wait for that king, and for the peace and justice he's supposed to bring.

We now turn to the New Testament, beginning with the *Gospel of Matthew*. Four centuries have passed since the prophet Malachi closed the Old Testament. This intertestamental period—the span between the Hebrew Bible and the birth of Jesus—was marked by dramatic upheaval: the spread of Greek (Hellenistic) culture, the Maccabean rebellion, the rise and fall of a brief Jewish kingdom, and the eventual Roman occupation of Judea in 63 BCE.

This was an era of religious ferment, messianic hopes, and social unrest. Many individuals claimed divine visions, performed miracles, or warned of impending apocalypse. Most were quickly forgotten. But one traveling preacher—and the movement that formed around him—would go on to reshape the world.

James E. Clark

THE NEW TESTAMENT

"The New Testament is not a unified book with a single message. It is a collection of texts written by different authors at different times, in different contexts, with different perspectives—even about who Jesus was and what his mission meant."
Bart D. Ehrman, *Jesus, Interrupted*

MATTHEW

Matthew 1-2

Before we get into the text, let's outline the book's likely parentage. Although traditionally attributed to the Apostle Matthew, scholars consider the author anonymous. It's more accurate to think of this as a product of the "School of Matthew," if there was such a thing. *The Gospel of Matthew* was written sometime after *Mark*, following decades of oral tradition, and solidified into its current form around 80-90 CE, roughly 50 years after Jesus' death and nearly 90 after his birth.

Matthew is the first of the three Synoptic Gospels (Matthew, Mark, and Luke), which share similar narratives, structure, and wording. The Synoptics, along with John, comprise the Canonical Gospels. The material used to compose Matthew came from four sources:

1. **Mark** – Of Matthew's 1,071 verses, about 600 overlap with Mark.
2. **Q** – A hypothetical lost collection of Jesus' sayings used by both Matthew and Luke. Roughly 200 verses in Matthew are attributed to Q.
3. **M** – Another proposed lost source unique to Matthew.
4. **Creative license** – A likely contribution from the author himself.

Note: Q is short for *Quelle*, the German word for "source." It has nothing to do with the conspiracy theory involving Hillary Clinton and cannibalistic pedophile cabals.

To summarize: Matthew did not write Matthew, nor was it written by an eyewitness to the events described. The author might not have met anyone who knew Jesus. He had read the Old Testament, at least in Greek, and was keen to position Jesus as the fulfillment of prophecy, however tenuous the connection. A useful summary of mainstream scholarship on the dating of the Gospels can be found in Bart Ehrman's *Jesus, Interrupted* (see Further Reading).

None of this necessarily invalidates the text. Indeed, the character of Jesus shines through, at least the version imagined by Christian writers several generations after his death.

The Gospel opens with Jesus' genealogy, tracing his lineage from Abraham to David, then to Solomon, and finally to Joseph, husband of Mary. This likely explains why Matthew is placed first in the New Testament—it's the only Gospel that opens with a genealogy. Oddly, this lineage is traced through Joseph, even though he wasn't biologically involved in Jesus' conception. God, not Joseph, was the father. Mary's genealogy isn't mentioned; she was just a woman.

We then get the story of Jesus' conception. Matthew 1:18: "Now the birth of Jesus Christ was on this wise: When as his mother Mary was espoused to Joseph, before they came together, she was found with child of the Holy Ghost." Joseph, described as "a just man," planned to quietly break off the engagement. But an angel appeared in a dream, explained that Mary had been impregnated by the Holy Spirit, and told him to marry her and name the child Jesus. Joseph complied and did not have sex with her until after Jesus was born. The angel didn't command abstinence—it seems Joseph made that call on his own.

In Matthew 1:23, the angel says Jesus' birth fulfills a prophecy from Isaiah: "Behold, a virgin shall be with child and shall bring forth a son, and they shall call his name Emmanuel, which being interpreted is, God with us." But most modern translations of Isaiah 7:14 now say a "young woman" will conceive, not a virgin, making the prophecy irrelevant to the virgin birth narrative. And even if Mary were a virgin, so what? That doesn't make her child divine or validate anything he did as an adult.

Next, wise men (Magi) from the east—apparently following a star (so presumably traveling at night?)—arrive in Jerusalem and ask King Herod where to find the newborn "King of the Jews." Herod, alarmed, consults his advisers, who point to Bethlehem as the prophesied birthplace. He tells the Magi to report back so he too can "worship" the child. Spoiler: he has other plans.

The Magi, still guided by the star, find Mary and Joseph in Bethlehem and offer gifts: gold, frankincense, and myrrh. Warned in a dream not to return to Herod, they go back to their (unnamed) homeland. An angel then appears to Joseph, warning him to flee to Egypt with Mary and Jesus. Furious that he's been duped, Herod orders the massacre of all boys under two in and around Bethlehem—implying that Jesus may have been a toddler, not a newborn, when the Magi arrived.

After Herod's death, an angel tells Joseph it's safe to return. They settle in Nazareth. Matthew 2:23: "And he came and dwelt in a city called Nazareth: that it might be fulfilled which was spoken by the prophets, He shall be called a Nazarene." This time, Matthew doesn't bother to cite a real Old Testament passage to misrepresent—no such prophesy actually exists.

And there are more plot holes. Why did King Herod rely on foreign astrologers to find a child allegedly born in his kingdom? Why didn't he send spies or soldiers directly to Bethlehem? Why did he need a prophecy explained to him? And what does it even mean to follow a star? Why did the Magi need celestial GPS to find Jerusalem, which was a major metropolis and political center?

Matthew 3-7

In the second chapter of Matthew, we left Jesus as a young boy, newly settled in Nazareth with his mother Mary and adoptive father Joseph. We now jump decades forward. In Chapter 3, we meet John the Baptist, a wild-eyed end-times preacher who refuses to baptize the Pharisees and Sadducees.

Baptism for the forgiveness of sins isn't a concept found in the Old Testament. It seems to have emerged during the Second Temple period, somewhere between the third and first centuries BCE, possibly influenced by ritual purification practices and sectarian movements like the Essenes.

It's worth pausing to identify the Pharisees and Sadducees. Both were Jewish sects active during the Second Temple period. The Pharisees were popular among the middle classes, believed in angels, demons, and the resurrection of the dead, and had significant influence over synagogue life. The Sadducees were more Hellenized, denied supernatural beliefs like resurrection, and controlled the Temple establishment and priesthood. It's not entirely clear what John the Baptist had against either group. Perhaps they didn't share his apocalyptic urgency or simply refused to recognize him as a prophet.

In any case, Jesus appears at the Jordan River, where John baptizes him. This is a crucial scene because, traditionally, the greater baptizes the lesser. John acknowledges the awkwardness, saying, "I have need to be baptized of thee, and comest thou to me?" (Matt. 3:14). But Jesus insists, and as John proceeds, the heavens open, and the Spirit of God descends like a dove, declaring, "This is my beloved Son, in whom I am well pleased" (Matt. 3:17).

Immediately afterward, Jesus is led into the wilderness, where he fasts for 40 days and nights. The devil arrives for a three-part temptation duel: turn stones into bread; throw yourself from the temple parapet; and bow down to Satan. Jesus resists and rebukes him. After Satan flees, angels arrive to look after Jesus.

Soon after, Jesus hears that John has been arrested. He picks up John's message almost verbatim: "Repent: for the kingdom of Heaven is at hand" (Matt. 4:17). He begins assembling his inner circle, calling Simon Peter and his brother Andrew, then James and John, the sons of Zebedee. These fishermen are promised they'll become "fishers of men."

Jesus then begins performing healings and attracts large crowds from Galilee and beyond. While God in the Old Testament occasionally cured people, healing was never a central feature of his PR strategy. But miracle cures are increasingly vital to Jesus' ministry and the reason his disciples and followers start to imagine his power is greater than that of other prophets and miracle workers.

Jesus, now publicly recognized by John and affirmed by God, has begun preaching, healing, and building his movement. He's ready to take his message to a larger audience, and that brings us to one of the most influential speeches in Western history: the Sermon on the Mount.

Spanning chapters 5 through 7, the sermon opens with the Beatitudes—"Blessed are the poor in spirit: for theirs is the kingdom of Heaven" (Matt. 5:3)—setting a tone of humility and inner transformation. Jesus tells the crowd that they are the light of the world and insists he has come not to abolish the Mosaic Law but to fulfill it. "Till heaven and earth pass, one jot or one tittle shall in no wise pass from the law" (Matt. 5:18). So, when modern Christians claim that Jesus overturned the Old Testament law, it's fair to point them to this passage that emphatically does not say that.

Still, Jesus wastes no time in reinterpreting the Law. It's not enough to avoid murder; you also shouldn't insult or degrade others. It's better to resolve disputes than risk judgment. It's not just adultery that's forbidden, but even lustful thoughts. Divorce is also addressed: if you divorce your wife for any reason other than sexual immorality, you cause her, and her next partner, to commit adultery. Instead of "an eye for an eye," Jesus says to turn the other cheek. If someone forces you to go one mile, go two. And rather than love your neighbor and hate your enemies, Jesus commands you to love your enemies and pray for them.

He continues: don't make a show of your piety. When you give to the poor or pray, do it quietly. "But thou, when thou prayest, enter into thy closet...and pray to thy Father which is in secret" (Matt. 6:6). Then comes the Lord's Prayer (Matt. 6:9–13), which many, like myself, memorized in school—though we learned "trespasses" instead of "debts," which subtly changes the tone and arguably improves it.

The sermon continues with practical advice: You cannot serve both God and money. Don't judge others if you don't want to be judged. Don't cast your pearls before swine, meaning, don't offer gifts to those who won't value them. Before correcting others, deal with your own issues. Treat others as you would want to be treated—the Golden Rule. Watch out for false prophets, whose "rotten fruit" reveals their nature. And don't procrastinate. "Take no thought for the morrow: for the morrow shall take thought for the things of itself" (Matt. 6:34).

The sermon ends with a stark warning: whoever hears these teachings and ignores them is like a fool who builds his house on sand. When the storm comes, the house collapses, and "great was the fall of it" (Matt. 7:27). The chapter closes by noting that the crowd was astonished.

Ditto. Mic drop. This was radical, countercultural stuff. A bold, compassionate call to humility, personal responsibility, and moral courage. People are to be self-effacing, committed to others, and unwavering in their integrity before God. If

Moses or Aaron had delivered this sermon in the wilderness, the Israelites would probably have looked around in confusion and then started collecting stones. Honestly, I think the same might happen in some modern megachurches.

Which raises a difficult question: how do Jesus' words here square with much of contemporary American Christianity, with its emphasis on wealth, political tribalism, and disregard for the poor? Or for that matter, how do these teachings align with the Mosaic Law Jesus claims to uphold?

If you divorce a woman for anything other than adultery, does that really make her an adulteress, someone who should be stoned, per Deuteronomy? Is that what Jesus wants? Or is he deliberately stretching the Law to its ethical extreme, pushing his audience beyond the letter of the Law to its spiritual heart?

Matthew 8-12

After the remarkable Sermon on the Mount, the next few chapters feel like a hard landing. Jesus begins making the rounds, curing the sick with just a word or a touch of his garment. He heals a man with a skin disease, a centurion's servant, and Peter's mother-in-law. Then, while crossing the Sea of Galilee, a violent storm arises. Jesus is asleep and must be awakened before he rebukes the wind and calms the waters. (This echoes the Jonah story, where Jonah is also asleep on a storm-tossed boat and has to be awakened by the crew.)

Back on land, Jesus encounters two demon-possessed men who recognize him as a "Son of God" and ask to be cast into a nearby herd of pigs. Jesus obliges, and the demons enter the pigs, who promptly rush off a cliff and drown. Matthew 8:33–34: "And they that kept them fled, and went their ways into the city, and told everything... And behold, the whole city came out to meet Jesus: and when they saw him, they besought him that he would depart out of their coasts."

In other words, the locals didn't thank Jesus for the exorcism, they asked him to scram. He had just wiped out their pig herd and posed a threat to the local economy. Not everyone appreciates divine intervention when it ruins their livelihood.

Jesus next heals a paralytic and then meets a tax collector named Matthew, who becomes a disciple. It's worth noting that this scene complicates the tradition that the author of the Gospel was Matthew himself. If so, why doesn't the text say, "That tax collector was me"? The anonymity suggests otherwise.

Jesus continues his healing spree: he cures a woman with chronic bleeding, brings an unnamed girl back to life, gives sight to two blind men, and restores speech to a mute demoniac. These miracles serve to establish Jesus' authority, perhaps as a prophet, perhaps as a "Son of God" (as the demons had said), or as the enigmatic "Son of Man." In ancient Judea, many believed that charismatic prophets, priests, or zealots could cure diseases. Sadly, "faith healing" is still practiced today, often targeting the desperate, the poor, and the devout.

Was Jesus upping the ante by raising the dead? Maybe. But no one seems to think the resurrected girl is special, and she doesn't report anything from the afterlife. That's a missed opportunity. And if Jesus could raise one person, why not many? A mass resurrection would have certainly gotten the Romans' attention and maybe even a few scribes to record it. Honestly, the whole magical healing storyline doesn't do much for me.

Next, Jesus commissions his disciples. Their mission is to minister to the "lost sheep of Israel," curing diseases, casting out demons, even raising the dead, and proclaiming that the kingdom of heaven is near. They are told to travel light: no money, no bag, no extra clothes, not even a staff. Their only power is the authority granted by Jesus.

But it won't be easy. Matthew 10:22–23: "And ye shall be hated of all men for my name's sake: but he that endureth to the end shall be saved. But when they persecute you in this city, flee ye into another: for...ye shall not have gone over the cities of Israel, till the Son of man be come."

That phrase—Son of Man—again raises questions. In Ezekiel, "Son of man" is how God addresses the prophet. But Jesus seems to be using the phrase the way it had been used in Daniel, where a Son of Man arrives on a storm cloud to establish some sort of new order. Is Jesus the Son of Man, or is this character someone else? If it's Jesus, it'd be simpler for him just to say so.

While the Sermon on the Mount taught turning the other cheek, Jesus now shifts tone. Matthew 10:34–36: "Think not that I am come to send peace on earth: I came not to send peace, but a sword." Following Jesus, he says, will divide families. "A man's foes shall be they of his own household." It's not the feel-good message you get in Sunday School, but Jesus is laying it out plainly: this movement will cost you.

In Chapter 11, we return to John the Baptist, who is still in prison. Jesus praises him as the fulfillment of prophecy: "Among them that are born of women there hath not risen a greater than John the Baptist" (Matt. 11:11). (As an aside: "born of women"? We call them *mothers*, Jesus.)

But despite the miracles, the surrounding cities still refuse to repent. Jesus warns them they'll face judgment worse than Tyre, Sidon, or even Sodom.

That's a bit ironic, since Ezekiel prophesied Tyre's destruction by Nebuchadnezzar, but Tyre survived the Babylonian siege. So, Jesus is invoking a failed prophecy to warn about repentance. He'd just warned about false prophets earlier. That tension seems worth noting.

Chapter 12 opens with Jesus and his disciples plucking grain on the Sabbath. You'll recall that in Numbers, a man was stoned to death for gathering sticks on the Sabbath. Here, Jesus invokes common sense over rigid law: "I will have mercy, and not sacrifice." He reinforces this by healing a man's withered hand on the Sabbath—scandalous to the Pharisees, who begin plotting against him. But to be fair, they were following the law as they understood it, however cruel or outdated those laws might now seem.

Later, Jesus delivers a warning: Matthew 12:31: "All manner of sin and blasphemy shall be forgiven unto men: but the blasphemy against the Holy Ghost shall not be forgiven." This is in response to accusations that he casts out demons by satanic power. But the concept of the Holy Ghost (or Holy Spirit) hasn't really been explained. Why is this spirit so touchy?

Matthew 13-17

We start with a series of parables. A Sower scatters seeds and some are eaten by birds, some fall on rocky ground, and some among thorns, but a few land in fertile soil and grow into productive plants. When the disciples admit they don't get it, Jesus explains: the seed on the path is like someone who hears but doesn't understand; on the rock, it's someone with shallow faith; in the thorns, it's someone whose faith is choked by worldly concerns; and in the good soil, someone who hears and understands, yielding a fruitful harvest. Honestly, the disciples might've figured this out if they'd thought about it for a few minutes.

The seed parables continue with a poisonous weed called a tare (also known as darnel), mustard seeds that grow into trees, and a fishing net. The darnel is likened to the wicked at the end of the world. Matthew 13:40–42: "As therefore the tares are gathered and burned in the fire; so shall it be in the end of this world. The Son of Man shall send forth his angels, and they shall gather out of his kingdom all things that offend, and them which do iniquity; And shall cast them into a furnace of fire: there shall be wailing and gnashing of teeth." So much for subtlety.

Jesus then returns to his hometown, Nazareth, where he's met with skepticism. He remarks, "A prophet is not without honor, save in his own country, and in his own house" (Matt. 13:57). But let's linger here a moment. Matthew seems intent on emphasizing Jesus' Nazareth origins, perhaps to tie back to the mysterious prophecy mentioned in Chapter 2 (which, notably, doesn't seem to exist). Sure, Jesus was born in Bethlehem, but Matthew's Jesus is unmistakably a Nazarene.

Then comes a detour to Herod's palace, where things get Shakespearean. Herod's niece dances so seductively at a party that he offers her anything she wants. Taylor Swift tickets? A pony? No, she asks for John the Baptist's head on a platter. Herod, unable to say no to a determined teenager, obliges. Jesus takes the news hard, but there's no time to grieve—a crowd has assembled, and they need food. "We have but five loaves and two fishes," the disciples say. Jesus turns this into enough to feed five thousand, plus women and children (who, of course, aren't counted).

Later, while the disciples are out on a boat, they see a figure walking toward them across the water. It's Jesus. Peter joins him briefly before sinking when his faith falters. Back on the boat, the disciples finally say, "Thou art the Son of God" (Matt. 14:33). This might be the first time they use this phrase. But even now, Matthew seems intentionally ambiguous. Is Jesus a prophet? A man of God? The Son of God? Is "Son of Man" the same as "Christ," or are we supposed to track subtle distinctions? It's starting to feel like Matthew is figuring it out as he goes.

In Chapter 15, Jesus debates with the Pharisees about what's truly clean or unclean. The disciples don't wash their hands before eating (gross, but they didn't know about bacteria), and Jesus says that spiritual defilement comes not from what enters the mouth but from what comes out of it: murder, adultery, fornication, theft, perjury, slander. An interesting list, and noticeably free of idolatry and Sabbath violations, which obsessed God in the Old Testament.

Then comes the story of the Canaanite woman whose daughter is demon-possessed. She begs Jesus for help, and the disciples want to send her away. But Jesus heals her daughter anyway, despite the woman being a Gentile. We're meant to admire Jesus for broadening his outreach beyond Israel, but still, why is it so impressive to do good if you are the Son of God, Son of Man, whatever?

Back on the Galilean hillsides, Jesus heals many, and after three days, the crowd is hungry. This time, it's seven loaves and a few small fish, and the result is another miraculous buffet that feeds four thousand men, plus the ever-neglected women and children. At this point, Jesus' team seems bad at event planning, and Matthew is clearly into repetition: two sea miracles, two mass feedings, all involving inadequate supplies and stunned disciples.

Then Jesus asks the question that's been hovering in the air: "Whom do men say that I the Son of man am?" (Matt. 16:13). Peter answers, "Thou art the Christ, the Son of the living God" (Matt. 16:16). Jesus congratulates him and says Peter is the rock on which the church will be built. Then, oddly, Jesus warns the disciples not to tell anyone that he is the Christ (Matt. 16:20). Does that mean he is the Christ, but it's a secret? Or that he isn't, so don't spread misinformation? The ambiguity continues.

Jesus then predicts his own suffering and death, followed by resurrection. Peter protests, understandably, but Jesus snaps back: "Get thee behind me, Satan…for thou savourest not the things that be of God, but those that be of men" (Matt. 16:23). That feels harsh. Peter's a mortal, after all. Isn't expecting him to divine the cosmic plan a bit much?

To follow Jesus, you must renounce yourself and take up the cross. After all, "what is a man profited, if he shall gain the whole world, and lose his own soul?" (Matt. 16:26). Then Jesus ends with a provocative line: "There be some standing here, which shall not taste of death, till they see the Son of man coming in his kingdom" (Matt. 16:28). If Jesus is the Son of Man, he really could be clearer about it.

Jesus then leads the disciples into the mountains where they see him "transfigured" into a radiant being, soon joined by Moses and Elijah. A voice says in Matt. 17:5: "… This is my Beloved Son, in whom I am well pleased: hear ye him." The scene recalls both Moses' transcendent image when he

204

delivered the Commandments, and Jesus' own baptism where a dove descends and a voice affirms him.

Finally, tax collectors confront Jesus and Peter. Jesus seems to say he's exempt from taxes but tells Peter to go fishing. The first fish he catches has a coin in its mouth, which they use to pay the tax (hopefully after rinsing it off). There's probably some deep symbolism here, but it's hard to say what. What is clear is that Matthew is moving toward the climax: Jesus will suffer and die, and the kingdom of the Son of Man will arrive with urgency, violence, and imminence. Some of the current cast might still be alive when it happens.

Matthew 18-23

Who is the greatest in heaven? That's the question Jesus addresses as we start Chapter 18: "Verily I say unto you, Except ye be converted, and become as little children, ye shall not enter into the kingdom of heaven. Whosoever therefore shall humble himself as this little child, the same is greatest in the kingdom of heaven" (Matt. 18:3–4).

This is followed by practical instructions on conflict resolution: If your brother does wrong, approach him privately. If he still refuses to listen, bring along witnesses. If that fails, escalate it to the broader group. And if even that doesn't work, treat him like a gentile or a tax collector—which is ironic, given that Jesus frequently ate with both.

Peter then asks how often we're expected to forgive someone who wrongs us. Jesus responds in Matt. 18:22, "Not seven times, but seventy times seven." (Some translations say seventy-seven.) Either way, the point is clear: forgiveness should be limitless. This line deliberately echoes Genesis 4:23–24, where Lamech tells his wives: "I have slain a man to my wounding, and a young man to my hurt. If Cain shall be avenged sevenfold, truly Lamech seventy and sevenfold."

In other words, Jesus flips the script: where Genesis glorifies escalating revenge, Jesus demands radical forgiveness. Also, just how many people did Lamech kill, one or two? The verse is vague. The parallel structure—"a man for wounding me, a young man for striking me"—is classic Hebrew poetry and, as usual, leaves room for interpretation.

Many Christians today describe themselves as "New Testament people," preferring Jesus' teachings to the more brutal laws of the Old Testament. But Matthew won't let us off that easily. The Gospel constantly references Hebrew Scripture, both to validate Jesus' teachings and to frame him as the fulfillment of prophecy. Even in the Sermon on the Mount, where Jesus offers a striking ethical vision, Matthew carefully roots it in Torah. And let's not forget: Christians claim Jesus and God are one and the same. If that's true, then the angry God of Exodus is still part of the divine package. You don't get to be a New Testament person without also owning the Old.

Next, Jesus tells a parable about forgiveness: A servant's massive debt is forgiven by his master, but that same servant refuses to forgive a minor debt owed to him and is punished for it. The message? God expects your forgiveness to others to mirror his forgiveness of you.

Then comes a shift in the law regarding divorce. In Matt. 19:9, Jesus says: "Whosoever shall put away his wife, except it be for fornication, and shall marry another, committeth adultery." This goes beyond Mosaic Law, which allowed divorce for various reasons if a certificate was given (Deut. 24:1). Earlier, in Matt. 5, Jesus had already raised the bar by saying that anyone who marries a divorced woman commits adultery, a crime under the Law punishable by death. Now he tightens it further: even the husband who initiates the divorce is guilty of adultery if he remarries, unless his wife had been sexually unfaithful. The disciples, understandably rattled, ask whether marriage is even worth it under such strict terms.

Jesus pivots to eunuchs: "There are some eunuchs who were born that way, some made eunuchs by others, and some who made themselves eunuchs for the kingdom of heaven's sake. He that is able to receive it, let him receive it" (Matt. 19:12). It's a cryptic answer to a direct question. Is he discouraging marriage? Advocating celibacy? Acknowledging gender nonconformity? Whatever the intent, it's a curious detour in a conversation about divorce.

Jesus continues his critique of wealth, dropping another famous line in Matt. 19:24: "It is easier for a camel to go through the eye of a needle than for a rich man to enter the kingdom of God." Much ink has been spilled trying to soften this: perhaps the "needle" refers to a narrow gate in Jerusalem? But Jesus doesn't hedge. The message is clear: wealth is a spiritual obstacle. How modern megachurch pastors square this with their private jets and palatial estates remains a mystery.

Peter reminds Jesus that the disciples gave up everything to follow him. Jesus replies that they'll be rewarded with eternal life and seats of honor, adding: "Many that are first shall be last, and the last shall be first" (Matt. 19:30). Wait, there's a hierarchy in heaven? Even in the afterlife, are we stuck with org charts?

Skipping ahead, Jesus prepares to enter Jerusalem, setting up the final act of Matthew's Gospel. His disciples are sent to fetch (i.e., commandeer) a donkey and a colt. Matt. 21:7 says: "And brought the ass, and the colt, and put on them their clothes, and they set him thereon."

This may sound like Jesus is riding two animals at once, and that's because of Matthew's rigid adherence to prophecy, specifically Zechariah 9:9, which speaks of a king entering Jerusalem "riding upon an ass, and upon a colt the foal of an ass." But Zechariah was using parallelism, not pluralism. He meant one animal. Matthew, possibly misunderstanding the poetry, includes two.

So, how exactly did Jesus ride them? One leg on each? Sitting on one while dragging the other? In a 17th-century fresco in Genoa by the Carlone brothers, Jesus rides one donkey while the other awkwardly peeks out from behind. His flowing robe conceals the logistics. This is what happens when Biblical literalism collides with ancient metaphor.

After arriving, Jesus famously flips the tables of the money changers in the Temple and then curses a fig tree for not bearing fruit. He also offers a now-iconic quip about taxes: "Render unto Caesar the things which are Caesar's, and unto God the things that are God's."

When the Sadducees try to trip him up with a legalistic resurrection scenario—asking which husband a widowed woman would belong to in the afterlife—Jesus replies that in heaven, people will be "as the angels of God" (Matt. 22:30). It's a clever dodge, but it clashes with the common belief that we'll be reunited with loved ones in something like our earthly form.

Asked what the greatest commandment is, Jesus answers in Matt. 22:37–39: "Thou shalt love the Lord thy God with all thy heart…and…love thy neighbor as thyself." This might sound like a theological pivot, as if he's replacing the Commandments, but he's really distilling all 613 of them into two guiding principles. As in Matthew 5, he affirms the Law while adding his own spin, walking a tightrope between tradition and innovation.

Finally, as Chapter 23 closes, Jesus hints at his fate, quoting Psalm 118:26: "Blessed is he that cometh in the name of the Lord," framing his arrival as yet another fulfillment of prophecy and foreshadowing the crucifixion.

Matthew 24-28

As Chapter 24 begins, we know where the story is headed. Leaving the Temple, Jesus tells the disciples that not a single stone will be left standing. They ask him, "When shall these things be? And what shall be the sign of thy coming, and of the end of the world?" (Matt. 24:3). This feels like the first time it's clearly implied that Jesus is the Christ, the Son of Man, who will return at the end of days—though, as we'll see, he continues to dodge opportunities to say this outright.

Matthew was written after 70 CE, when the Romans destroyed the Second Temple, so it's not surprising that Jesus is portrayed predicting this event because it had already happened.

Jesus tells the disciples that there will be signs of the end: "wars and rumors of wars...famines...pestilences...and earthquakes" (Matt. 24:6–8). Bible prophecy continues to disappoint. At what point in human history have those things not been happening?

Previously, we were told that the arrival of the Son of Man would be sudden and violent—now Jesus elaborates. It will come like lightning. If you're on the roof, don't go back inside. If you're in the field, don't return for your cloak. Then: "The sun [shall] be darkened, and the moon shall not give her light" (note: the moon doesn't emit light), "and the stars shall fall from heaven...and they shall see the Son of man coming in the clouds of heaven with power and great glory" (Matt. 24:29–30).

Jesus uses parables to emphasize how fast things will go pear-shaped. Stay awake, because you don't know when your master will return. Have oil in your lamp. Invest your money wisely so the Son of Man won't toss you into the outer darkness. When all is said and done, the Son of Man will sit on his throne with angels at his side and separate the sheep from the goats. Those who fed the hungry, gave drink to the thirsty, clothed the naked, and visited prisoners will be welcomed. As Jesus puts it, "Truly I tell you, whatever you did for one of the least of these brothers and sisters of mine, you did for me" (Matt. 25:40.). It's a powerful moral: God will judge not only your actions, but also your inaction.

Two days before Passover, the priests begin scheming a show trial for Jesus, using the holiday as convenient cover. Judas Iscariot agrees to betray Jesus for thirty silver coins and then joins him and the other disciples for their final meal together.

During this Last Supper, Jesus says one of them will betray him and each denies it. Then Jesus takes bread and wine:

"Take, eat; this is my body." And with the cup: "Drink ye all of it; For this is my blood of the new testament, which is shed for the remission of sins" (Matt. 26:26–28). This ritual, known as the Eucharist (from the Greek *eucharistia*, "thanksgiving"), is a symbolic meal commemorating Jesus' sacrifice, still central to Christian worship.

Jesus tells them they'll meet again in Galilee after his death. Peter insists he'll never abandon him, but Jesus replies: "Before the cock crow, thou shalt deny me thrice" (Matt. 26:34). In Gethsemane, Jesus prays while Peter and the two sons of Zebedee keep falling asleep. Judas then arrives with a group of armed men. He identifies Jesus with a kiss, and though one disciple draws a sword and cuts off a man's ear, Jesus is taken into custody.

During his trial, the high priest Caiaphas asks Jesus if he is the Christ, the Son of God. Jesus answers, "Thou hast said: nevertheless I say unto you, Hereafter shall ye see the Son of man sitting on the right hand of power, and coming in the clouds of heaven" (Matt. 26:64). It's a strange phrasing, with the first part seeming to deflect, while the second to affirm. Caiaphas tears his robes and declares Jesus must die. Others spit on him and strike him. Meanwhile, Peter, who has followed at a distance, denies knowing Jesus three times before the rooster crows. Realizing what he's done, Peter weeps bitterly.

Jesus is handed over to the Roman governor, Pontius Pilate. Judas, filled with regret, tries to return the thirty pieces of silver. The priests refuse to take it back into the temple treasury—it's "blood money," unfit for sacred use—but they don't exactly turn it away. Instead, they use it to buy a potter's field as a burial place for foreigners, which becomes known as the Field of Blood. Matthew links this to Old Testament prophecy, especially Zechariah's vision of thirty pieces of silver (Zech. 11:12–13), though that passage has nothing to do with betrayal.

This episode begins what Christians call the Passion—the final period of Jesus' life, from his arrest to his crucifixion, named for the Latin *passio* ("suffering"). The Passion narratives are meant to highlight both Jesus' physical torment and his willing submission to God's plan, though the details vary from Gospel to Gospel.

Pilate asks Jesus if he is the King of the Jews. Jesus gives another cryptic answer: "Thou sayest" (Matt. 27:11). Pilate then offers the crowd a choice: pardon Jesus or the "notorious" Barabbas. They choose Barabbas. Pilate washes his hands of it and orders Jesus to be crucified.

It's worth noting that Roman governors didn't typically bend to mob pressure. Pilate had the legal power to execute and likely wouldn't have performed this pantomime of public consultation. Also, no external historical source mentions a tradition of Passover pardons, so this may well be a literary invention.

Jesus is mocked, beaten, given a crown of thorns, and made to carry his cross to Golgotha. He's offered gall (a painkiller) but refuses. Above him is posted the sign: This is Jesus, King of the Jews to further ridicule him. Even the two thieves crucified beside him mock him. After nine hours, he cries out: "My God, my God, why hast thou forsaken me?" (Matt. 27:46), a direct quote from Psalm 22.

Then Jesus dies. The Temple veil, which separated the Holy of Holies, is torn in two. There's an earthquake, and according to Matt. 27:52–53: "The graves were opened; and many bodies of the saints which slept arose, And came out of the graves after his resurrection, and went into the holy city, and appeared unto many." What happened to them afterward after that? Did they go home? Did anyone record the miracle of the walking dead? Matthew suggests the tombs opened at Jesus' death, but the saints didn't walk around until after the Resurrection. So were they just lying exposed in their tombs for three days?

Matthew offers few details on the crucifixion itself. Surprisingly, there are few ancient descriptions of the actual practice, likely because it was so well-understood at the time. Archaeological finds, from England to Venice to Jerusalem, confirm that crucifixion was real and brutal. Nails through the

211

heel or hands were used, though some victims may have simply been tied to a cross and left to die slowly. Romans reserved this punishment for non-citizens, particularly rebels and criminals.

Rather than leaving Jesus' body exposed, as was the norm, Matthew says Joseph of Arimathea got Pilate's permission to bury him in a rock-hewn tomb. Was this possible? Yes. Was it likely? Not really. The Romans rarely made exceptions. The priests persuade Pilate to post guards at the tomb to prevent the disciples from stealing the body and claiming a resurrection. But Mary Magdalene and another Mary (not Jesus' mother) show up after an earthquake and see an angel who tells them, "He is not here." The guards faint. Jesus appears to the women and tells them to inform the others he will meet them in Galilee.

The priests bribe the guards to say the disciples stole the body. Matthew adds, "This saying is commonly reported among the Jews until this day" (Matt. 28:15)—a dig at the Jewish community that preferred Barabbas, mocked Jesus, and covered up his resurrection. This framing, regrettably, laid the groundwork for centuries of antisemitism.

The Gospel ends with the eleven disciples meeting Jesus in Galilee. Some doubt, but all worship him. Jesus tells them to go forth and make disciples of all nations. That's it. No Ascension, no fireworks. A surprisingly low-key conclusion to what's supposed to be the climax of history.

We'll see what the other Gospels have to say about the return of the Son of Man. In Matthew, it was supposed to be violent, imminent, and unmistakable, happening before some of the disciples had died. It's been 2,000 years. At what point does this prophecy get filed under "failed," or will each new generation keep kicking the apocalyptic can down the road, finding every war, plague, or earthquake to be yet another sign?

MARK

Mark 1-7

The *Gospel of Mark*, though second in the canonical order, is widely regarded as the first to be written, likely between 65 and 75 CE, roughly 30 to 40 years after Jesus' death. Traditionally attributed to Mark the Evangelist (c. 12–68 CE), a companion of the Apostle Peter, its authorship is now considered anonymous by most scholars. Matthew and Luke draw heavily from Mark, often word for word, while also incorporating material from the hypothetical "Q" source, as well as unique content labeled "M" (for Matthew) and "L" (for Luke), which were not used by or available to Mark. Interestingly, until the 19th century, many assumed Mark was merely an abbreviated version of Matthew.

There's a strong case that the "historical Jesus," or at least the one early Christians believed in, is most plainly visible in Mark. It is the earliest Gospel and the least embellished, though still filled with supernatural stories of healing and exorcism.

In Matthew, Jesus is born of a virgin, lives in Bethlehem, flees to Egypt, and finally settles in Nazareth. Mark skips all of this and begins with Jesus' baptism by John the Baptist. Is Mark signaling theological discomfort with the virgin birth narrative, or did Matthew and Luke have access to sources Mark didn't? In any case, Mark 1:11 reads: "And there came a voice from heaven, saying, Thou art my beloved Son, in whom I am well pleased." This closely echoes Matthew, but there's a key difference. In Matthew, John protests that Jesus should be the one baptizing him. In Mark, John simply performs the baptism, and then the dove descends. No hesitation.

Jesus then begins his Galilean ministry. Like John, he proclaims that the kingdom of God is near and urges people to repent. He recruits disciples and performs a series of miracles: casting out a demon, healing Simon's mother-in-law, and others. It's at this point in Matthew where we get the remarkable Sermon on the Mount, arguably the highlight of the Bible so far. It doesn't appear in Mark at all—either a glaring omission or a later literary creation by Matthew.

More miracles follow. Jesus heals someone with a severe skin disease, restores a paralytic, eats with tax collectors, and allows his disciples to pluck grain on the Sabbath. Interestingly, the tax collector is named differently: Matthew in Matthew, Levi in Mark.

Jesus also teaches in parables, including the Sower of seeds. Some seeds thrive; others don't. As in Matthew, the disciples are baffled and need an explanation. Jesus calms a storm while asleep in a boat and casts demons into a herd of pigs, who then charge into a lake. One demon tells Jesus its name in Mark 5:9: "My name is Legion, for we are many." Mark adds that there were 2,000 pigs, an oddly specific and suspiciously large number. In Matthew, the number of pigs is unspecified—just a "herd"—possibly to make the story more believable. In both accounts, the locals are furious about the pigs' destruction and ask Jesus to leave. Whether it was a herd or 2,000, the economic loss is staggering, and Jesus offers no compensation. It's a rarely acknowledged detail: Jesus stole someone's livelihood.

Jesus also raises a girl from the dead. In Matthew, she's unnamed; in Mark, we learn she is Jairus's daughter. But she says nothing about what she saw, or didn't see, on the other side. Jesus then sends out his disciples, giving them authority over unclean spirits (though not, as in Matthew, over death itself). They are told to take no bread, no bag, *just a staff.* But in Matthew, they are instructed to take nothing, *not even a staff.* So which is it, bring a staff or not? Believe it or not, this discrepancy has fueled centuries of apologetic debate. Augustine of Hippo (354–430 CE) famously argued that the difference was between a physical and a spiritual staff and provided an early example of how biblical literalism can contort even brilliant minds into pretzels.

Next, Mark reports the beheading of John the Baptist, which causes Jesus to withdraw. A crowd gathers, and Jesus miraculously feeds them with five loaves and two fish. Then he walks on water to the disciples' boat. Notably, in Matthew, Peter also walks on water. Not so in Mark, a telling omission. It's easy to imagine Matthew adding this detail to elevate Peter, whom Jesus later calls the rock upon which the church will be built (Matt. 16:18).

Chapter 7 circles back to purity laws. The Pharisees are appalled that the disciples eat without washing. Jesus replies: "There is nothing from without a man, that entering into him can defile him: but the things which come out of him, those are they that defile the man" (Mk. 7:15). The disciples still don't get it, so Jesus elaborates: "For from within, out of the heart of men, proceed evil thoughts, adulteries, fornications, murders... All these evil things come from within, and defile the man" (Mk. 7:21–23).

Mark 8-14

We begin Chapter 8 with Jesus and the disciples traveling outside of Galilee, where Jesus performs more miracles and continues his moral teachings. He cures a Gentile, heals a deaf man, and for the second time multiplies loaves and fish to feed a crowd. Jesus then asks the disciples, "Whom do men say that I am?" (Mk. 8:27), to which Peter replies that he is the Christ. Jesus, as in Matthew, tells them not to speak a word of this to anyone.

Mark then describes Jesus at the transfiguration, where he's joined by Moses and Elijah. Jesus tells the stunned disciples they are to tell no one about this dramatic scene "until after the Son of man had risen from the dead" (Matt. 9:9). He also banishes a demon from an epileptic boy, something the disciples were unable to do because they lacked sufficient faith. These scenes appear in similar form in Matthew.

But Mark differs from Matthew on divorce. In the Sermon on the Mount, Matthew's Jesus says that if you divorce your wife, except in the case of infidelity, both she and her future husband commit adultery. In Mark, Jesus is even stricter: "Whoever shall put away his wife, and marry another, committeth adultery against her. And if a woman shall put away her husband, and be married to another, she committeth adultery" (Mk. 10:11–12). In other words, Matthew appears to allow divorce for infidelity, but Mark says no exceptions. And since Mark was the first Gospel, what we're actually seeing is a later softening of the law regarding divorce.

Still, the gist is clear: once you marry, you can't get divorced, except perhaps for adultery, which in biblical law warranted the death penalty. The Old Testament harshly forbade homosexuality and even seemed to permit abortion in cases of suspected infidelity (see Numbers 5). The New Testament, at least so far, says nothing about abortion or homosexuality, but has a lot to say about divorce. Why, then, do modern evangelicals focus so fiercely on gay sex and abortion, which

216

Jesus never mentions, while largely ignoring his explicit stance on divorce?

The narrative then continues with stories that also appear in Matthew: Jesus blesses the children, tells the rich young man to give up his wealth if he wants eternal life, and says it's easier for a camel to pass through the eye of a needle than for a rich man to enter the kingdom of God. He heals a blind man, and then he enters Jerusalem. In Mark 10:18, Jesus has the following to say: "Why callest thou me good? There is none good but one, that is God." That's an interesting thing for him to say. Is Jesus "good?" *He* doesn't seem convinced.

Jesus then enters Jerusalem riding a single donkey—not a donkey and a colt (as Matthew bizarrely has it). The next day, outside Bethany, Jesus is hungry and approaches a fig tree. It's out of season and has no fruit, so Jesus curses it: "No man eat fruit of thee hereafter forever" (Mk. 11:14). It's unclear what lesson we're supposed to draw here. The tree wasn't doing anything wrong; it was simply out of season.

Anyway, Jesus clears the Temple of money changers, explains that Caesar is owed what is Caesar's, and answers the Pharisees' tricky question about the afterlife of a woman who had married multiple brothers (serially, not simultaneously). Jesus dodges by saying that in the afterlife, people will be like angels—i.e., not married. It's the same evasion as in Matthew.

One story unique to Mark is that of the Widow's Mite (Mk. 12:41–44). Jesus praises a poor woman for donating a tiny coin, saying she gave more than the rich because she gave all she had. It's a touching story, perhaps, but one that's also been used to justify guilt-tripping the poor into giving beyond their means.

In Chapter 13, Jesus predicts wars and rumors of wars, followed by the dramatic arrival of the Son of Man and the stars falling from the sky. He then tries to tie in the parable of the fig tree with a time prophecy: "When her branch is yet tender… ye know that summer is near…This generation shall not pass, till all these things be done" (Mk. 13:28–30). The tortured fig tree analogy aside, Jesus is clear—just as in

Matthew—that the end times will be sudden, violent, and imminent, to occur before the current generation dies out.

We then get the familiar Passion narrative: Judas agrees to betray Jesus, the Last Supper is held, and the Eucharist is introduced. Jesus is arrested at Gethsemane. But Mark includes a strange detail not found in Matthew: after Jesus is arrested, a young man following him is seized, and he runs away naked, leaving his linen cloth behind (Mk. 14:51–52). He is never identified, never mentioned before or after. I am not making this up.

Jesus appears before the Sanhedrin—though Caiaphas is not named—and when asked if he is the Son of God, he confirms it, knowing this amounts to blasphemy. He is handed over to Pilate, who asks if he's the King of the Jews. Jesus responds cryptically: "Thou sayest it" (Mk. 15:3). Mark includes the same dubious story as Matthew, where Pilate offers to release either Jesus or Barabbas (spelled Barnabas in some manuscripts). In Mark, Barabbas is called a murderer and insurrectionist. The idea that Pilate would pardon and release an insurrectionist seems far-fetched. This was first century Roman-occupied Judea, not modern America, after all.

In the end, the crowd demands Jesus' crucifixion. He is mocked, crowned with thorns, and led to die. After six hours, Jesus cries, "My God, my God, why hast thou forsaken me?" (Mk. 15:34) and dies. In Mark, as in Matthew, the bandits crucified alongside Jesus mock him. Mark, unlike Matthew, does not record the dead rising and wandering around Jerusalem.

As in Matthew, Joseph of Arimathea asks Pilate for Jesus' body. But in Mark, there are no guards placed at the tomb. Mary Magdalene and Mary the mother of James visit the tomb and find it open. A young man in a white robe (possibly an angel) tells them Jesus has risen and instructs them to tell the disciples to meet him in Galilee. But Mark's Gospel ends abruptly: "They said nothing to any man; for they were afraid" (Mk. 16:8). If the women said nothing to anyone, how did anyone find out?

As you may recall, Matthew includes a more elaborate ending, complete with an angel, Jesus himself, and marching orders for the disciples. The original Gospel of Mark, however, ends at 16:8. Later manuscripts add verses 9–20, the so-called Long Ending, where Jesus appears to Mary Magdalene, to two unnamed disciples, and finally to the eleven, some of whom still doubt. He tells them to go preach, promises believers will speak in tongues and handle snakes, and then ascends to heaven. The tone is abrupt; Jesus is there, and then he's not.

You can see how Matthew embellishes and retools the theological points made in Mark to better align with Old Testament prophecy and to inject more drama and divine agency. Mark doesn't mention Jesus' birth, whereas Matthew retrofits a virgin birth in Bethlehem and a move to Nazareth to fulfill (nonexistent) prophecy. Matthew includes the ethical tour de force of the Sermon on the Mount, absent from Mark. He adds supernatural signs at Jesus' death, like an earthquake, a torn curtain, and zombies.

Mark, more than Matthew, presents Jesus through action, not theology. And in its original form, Mark ends with no resurrection appearance and no ascension. But on other key points, there's little daylight between the first two Gospels: Jesus was some sort of divine being; he miraculously healed the sick and raised the dead; he taught a radical love for others; he clashed with the religious and political authorities; and he was crucified. Both Gospels predict that the Son of Man will return violently and soon to establish God's rule on Earth.

<u>LUKE</u>

Luke 1-2

The *Gospel of Luke* is the third of the New Testament's four canonical Gospels and, like Matthew, was written several decades after Mark—likely between 85 and 95 CE, or close to 70 years after Jesus' death and a full century after his birth. Luke draws from several sources: the Gospel of Mark, the hypothetical Q source (a lost collection of Jesus' sayings used by both Matthew and Luke), and L, a source unique to this Gospel. As with the other Gospels, the author is anonymous, though tradition attributes the work to Luke the Evangelist—purportedly born between 1 and 16 CE and dying between 84 and 100 CE—possibly a companion of Paul. Scholars widely agree that the same author wrote both Luke and Acts, but more on that later.

It's worth emphasizing that Luke's writer almost certainly never met Jesus, and perhaps not anyone who had. We often think of the Bible as a fixed document handed down fully formed, but it wasn't. Even if Luke was composed around 100 CE, we don't know how much the text changed before the earliest manuscript fragments from the second to fourth centuries. That's a long window for transcription errors, reinterpretations, and the steady evolution of Christian dogma. Also worth noting are the sources Luke didn't use: Roman records, eyewitness interviews, or non-Christian texts.

That's not surprising. There simply are no non-Christian sources on Jesus from the first century. This absence doesn't necessarily disprove his existence or ministry, but it certainly doesn't help the case. A report from a Roman centurion confirming Matthew's account of zombies wandering Jerusalem would have gone a long way: *Sir, there's something happening at the Temple you should see…*

Luke opens with a distinctive prologue, presenting the Gospel as a carefully organized account of Jesus' life, written "from the beginning." It's addressed to someone named Theophilus, who may be a real patron or simply a symbolic nod to "lovers of God."

The narrative begins with a story not found in Matthew or Mark: the conception of John the Baptist. The elderly Zechariah and his barren wife Elizabeth are told by an angel that they'll have a son. Zechariah is skeptical, so God strikes him mute for his lack of faith—a bit of divine overkill, perhaps. Unable to speak, he makes the universal gesture for "Let's have sex," and Elizabeth becomes pregnant. The story echoes the Genesis tale of Abraham and Sarah, another geriatric couple granted a miraculous pregnancy.

Meanwhile, the angel Gabriel visits the Virgin Mary, has her sign an Intimacy Consent Form, and she becomes supernaturally pregnant. Unlike in Matthew, Gabriel clearly identifies the child as the "Son of God," heir to the House of David, and "Son of the Most High." He also lets it slip that Mary's cousin Elizabeth is pregnant, prompting Mary to visit her. Upon hearing Mary's voice, Elizabeth's baby leaps in the womb, perhaps thrilled at the thought of being a second fiddle to Jesus before being beheaded by a crazed Swiftie. Elizabeth instantly understands that Mary is also pregnant and the significance of the moment: "Blessed art thou among women, and blessed is the fruit of thy womb" (Lk. 1:42). (Side note: Is Fruit of the Loom a tongue-in-cheek spin on fruit of thy womb?) John is born, and on the eighth day, during his circumcision, Zechariah regains his voice, just in time to override tradition and name the child John. He then gives a prophetic speech connecting his son to Isaiah's words about a voice preparing the way for the Lord.

Meanwhile, Mary is nearing the end of her pregnancy. You may recall that in Matthew, Jesus is born in Bethlehem, already living there with Joseph and Mary. After a visit from Eastern Magi and a narrowly avoided massacre, the family flees to Egypt and eventually ends up in Nazareth.

Luke tells a different story: Joseph and Mary already live in Nazareth but are forced to travel to Bethlehem because "there went out a decree from Caesar Augustus, that all the world should be taxed" (Lk. 2:1). Joseph, being of Davidic lineage, has to return to his ancestral town. Luke says this occurred while Quirinius was governor of Syria; but Quirinius didn't assume that post until 6 CE, long after Herod's death. Mary gives birth in a manger because there's no room at the inn. Angels appear to shepherds in the countryside announcing the Savior's birth, and they rush to worship him.

It's easy to overemphasize minor Gospel contradictions, like Jesus riding both a colt and a donkey in Matthew, versus just a colt in Mark. The contradictions between the birth narratives in Matthew and Luke, however, are more serious and irreconcilable. In Matthew, Jesus appears to be around two years old when the family flees Bethlehem for Egypt. In Luke, he's born in Bethlehem during a census, and the family returns directly to Nazareth afterward.

The census itself is a problem. There *was* a census under Quirinius in 6 CE, but it was a regional registration limited to Judea, following the annexation of Herod Archelaus's territory. It applied only to residents of Judea, not Galilee, and there's no evidence it required people to return to ancestral towns—a logistical absurdity. Would Augustus really crash the economy just to count heads? And how would you know where your ancestors came from? I'm descended from folks in Ireland, England, Germany, and North Africa, plus the U.S. Midwest. Where is my "ancestral" home?

Returning to Luke's story, we fast-forward to Jesus at age 12. After a Passover trip to Jerusalem, Jesus stays behind while his parents begin their journey home. In full panic mode and hoping Child Protective Services hadn't been alerted, they return and find him calmly engaging in theological debates at the Temple. The boy's alright—and already showing signs of the character who will both charm and frustrate people for the rest of the Gospel.

Luke 3-8

We time travel again. At the end of Chapter 2, Jesus was twelve; now he's thirty. John the Baptist is preaching that the end is near: "And now also the axe is laid unto the root of the trees: every tree therefore which bringeth not forth good fruit is hewn down, and cast into the fire" (Lk. 3:9). How can you avoid being caught in the coming conflagration? According to John, by sharing what you have and not taking bribes (he's oddly insistent on this point). John's message is resonating, and some people wonder if he might be the long-awaited Christ. He quickly shuts this down: "...but one mightier than I cometh, the latchet of whose shoes I am not worthy to unloose..." (Lk. 3:16).

John is then thrown in jail by Herod for criticizing Herod's relationship with his brother's wife, Herodias. Oddly, it is after John's imprisonment that Jesus is baptized. In Mark, Jesus is clearly baptized by John. In Matthew, John reluctantly baptizes Jesus, only after admitting that Jesus ought to be baptizing him. But in Luke, John is already in jail, so Jesus is baptized by...someone. This suggests a literary evolution: as Jesus' divine status is gradually heightened in the Gospel tradition, the image of him submitting to John's baptism becomes more awkward. It will be interesting to see how the later Gospel of John handles this scene.

Next comes a genealogy of Jesus, tracing his (adoptive) father Joseph's lineage all the way back to Adam. It's impressively detailed, but theologically awkward. If Jesus was born of a virgin, why does Joseph's ancestry matter? Are we supposed to care about the royal bloodline of a man who, by all accounts, contributed no DNA? The text never explains. Instead, it just keeps listing names, back through time, until we reach a strange threshold—one where theology blurs into myth, and we're only a breath away from the moment Luke drops the script entirely and hears the voice of God rumble from the heavens: "Luke...I am your father."

We then move to the familiar temptation-in-the-wilderness story, nearly identical to Matthew's version. The devil tempts Jesus with food, power, and spectacle; Jesus bats him away with scripture.

Jesus begins his ministry in Nazareth, reading from Isaiah 61 in the synagogue. He announces that the prophecy is fulfilled through him: he has come to bring good news to the poor, free the captives, heal the blind, and liberate the oppressed. His audience is initially amazed, but then furious, apparently offended that Jesus would suggest these blessings apply to outsiders. They try to hurl him off a cliff, but Jesus calmly walks through the crowd unharmed. This story isn't in Matthew, and in Mark, the crowd is merely skeptical, not murderous. Luke's version adds drama, and the cliff scene certainly heightens the narrative tension. Still, it's a curious claim: Isaiah 61 refers to the return from Babylonian exile and the rebuilding of Jerusalem, not to a first-century Galilean handyman.

Jesus then begins his Galilean ministry with a flurry of miracles, echoing Matthew and Mark: he casts out demons, heals Simon's mother-in-law, cures a paralytic, and starts collecting disciples. He dines with tax collectors and sinners at Levi's house, lets his followers pick grain on the Sabbath, and heals a man with a withered hand. Then: "And he came down with them, and stood in the plain, and the company of his disciples, and a great multitude of people…" (Lk. 6:17). This is where Jesus delivers a shortened version of the Sermon on the Mount, except here, it's on a plain.

Luke's "Sermon on the Plain" is a condensed remix of Matthew's more eloquent version. Maybe Luke wasn't as impressed with the speech, or maybe he was working from an earlier source. There are also some theological differences: Matthew 5:3 says, "Blessed are the poor in spirit, for theirs is the kingdom of heaven," but Luke 6:20 has Jesus say, "Blessed be ye poor: for yours is the kingdom of God." Dropping "in spirit" shifts the focus from spiritual humility to literal economic poverty. Luke tends to emphasize social justice more than the other Gospels.

More miracles follow. A Roman centurion asks Jesus to heal his servant and shows such confidence in Jesus' authority that Jesus doesn't even have to visit—the servant is healed remotely. Jesus is impressed, declaring the centurion's faith superior to anything found in Israel. Then, in a story unique to Luke, Jesus encounters a funeral procession in Nain. Moved by the grief of a widow, he raises her dead son by simply saying, "Young man, I say unto thee, Arise" (Lk. 7:14). This is a noticeable upgrade from earlier prophets like Elijah and Elisha, who had to perform physical rituals, including lying on corpses and kissing them to achieve the same result. Jesus just speaks, and boom—resurrection.

Word spreads and even reaches John the Baptist in prison. Confused, John sends messengers to ask if Jesus really is "the one to come." Jesus responds by citing his deeds: healing the sick, raising the dead, preaching to the poor. But this raises a question: why is John uncertain? Didn't his mother, Elizabeth, know Mary and the miraculous circumstances around Jesus' birth? Are we to believe that none of this came up in conversation during the last thirty years?

At a Pharisee's house, a sinful woman anoints Jesus' feet with expensive perfume, washes them with her tears, and dries them with her hair. Couldn't she have splurged for a towel?

The Pharisee is shocked, but Jesus praises the woman's love and humility. He says her many sins are forgiven, teaching that those forgiven much, love much—a powerful, if emotionally manipulative, message.

Jesus continues teaching with parables. He tells the one about the Sower scattering seed on different types of soil and the disciples once again don't get it. Jesus has to explain it to them in detail. Maybe he should've used a parable about fish instead of seeds.

Then Jesus calms a storm at sea and performs the dramatic exorcism of a man possessed by many demons. The demons beg to be sent into a nearby herd of pigs, which promptly stampede into a lake and drown. In Mark, the herd numbers 2,000, but Luke and Matthew wisely avoid specifics, calling it merely "a large herd." In Mark and Matthew, the townspeople ask Jesus to leave—he just wiped out their livestock—but in Luke, the locals also seem unnerved by the display of supernatural power.

Chapter 8 ends with Jesus raising Jairus's daughter from the dead. In both Mark and Luke, Jesus tells the family not to tell anyone what happened. Matthew omits this request. Why the secrecy? It's hard to say, maybe to avoid drawing attention too early, or perhaps because public knowledge of divine power would short-circuit the whole faith-through-belief dynamic. Still, it's inconsistent: Jesus performs public miracles all the time yet selectively demands silence.

Luke 9-13

We kick off Chapter 9 with Jesus giving the disciples their ministerial marching orders: they are to have authority over demons and to cure diseases. He instructs them to "take nothing for your journey, neither staves, nor scrip, neither bread, neither money; neither have two coats apiece" (Lk. 9:3). This is similar to the account in Matthew (no bag, tunic, sandals, or staff), but it differs from Mark, where Jesus explicitly allows them to take a staff. File under: Gospel inconsistencies.

Meanwhile, Herod is perplexed by rumors that John the Baptist has come back from the dead. That makes two of us. Luke omits the vivid story found in Mark and Matthew about John's beheading and the delivery of his severed head to Herodias. Did Luke find the tale too salacious? Or did he just skip it for space?

Jesus then leads the disciples to the mountains to pray where the transfiguration occurs. While the core elements are consistent with the accounts in Matthew and Mark, including Jesus' radiant transformation, the presence of Moses and Elijah, and the divine voice, Luke adds that the two figures speak with Jesus about his coming "departure" in Jerusalem, giving the scene more narrative momentum.

Next, Jesus feeds a crowd of 5,000 with five loaves and two fish, cures an epileptic demoniac, and prophesies the coming death of the "Son of Man." As in Mark and Matthew, he believes End Times are near. Luke 9:27: "There be some standing here, which shall not taste of death, till they see the kingdom of God."

We then begin the long road to Jerusalem. Jesus sends out advance parties, either 70 or 72 disciples, depending on which manuscript you're reading. This detail mirrors Numbers 11:16–25, where Moses appoints 70 elders. Once again, the Old Testament background is essential to understanding the New.

A lawyer (in Matthew, it's a Pharisee) asks Jesus which commandment is greatest. Jesus replies with a familiar summary: love God and love your neighbor. Luke follows this with the famous parable of the Good Samaritan—exclusive to this Gospel. A man traveling from Jerusalem to Jericho is attacked and left for dead. A priest and a Levite pass him by, but a Samaritan (a member of a despised ethnic and religious group) tends his wounds, takes him to an inn, and promises the innkeeper: "Take care of him; and whatsoever thou spendest more, when I come again, I will repay thee" (Lk.

10:35). The story expands on Jesus' command to love one's neighbor by redefining who counts as one.

We're then introduced to sisters Martha and Mary. Mary sits captivated by Jesus' teachings while Martha works and complains that Mary isn't helping. Jesus sides with Mary, saying she's chosen what matters. This likely inspired Margaret Atwood's *The Handmaid's Tale*, where "Marthas" are relegated to domestic labor in Gilead.

Jesus then gives the Lord's Prayer, but it's a shorter and less poetic version than the one found in Matthew's Sermon on the Mount. Next, Jesus drives out demons and delivers the memorable line: "Every kingdom divided against itself is brought to desolation; and a house divided against a house falleth" (Lk. 11:17). This line appears in Mark and Matthew as well, but it gained new life in Abraham Lincoln's 1858 "House Divided" speech: "A house divided against itself cannot stand. I believe this government cannot endure permanently half slave and half free."

Jesus is then invited to dine with a Pharisee, who's scandalized that Jesus doesn't wash before eating. In Mark and Matthew, it's the disciples who skip the ritual washing. Luke changes it to Jesus himself and shortens the scene, omitting the longer debate over clean and unclean laws.

Later, Jesus tells his followers to sell their possessions and give to the poor. It's one of his clearest and most ignored moral directives.

Another standout line follows in Lk. 12:48: "For unto whomsoever much is given, of him shall be much required." John F. Kennedy famously echoed and improved upon this sentiment in a 1961 address to the Massachusetts General Court: "For of those to whom much is given, much is required." He went on to say that history would judge our public service based on courage, judgment, integrity, and dedication.

Jesus then clarifies he's not here for peace and love alone: "Suppose ye that I am come to give peace on earth? I tell you, Nay; but rather division: For from henceforth there shall be five in one house divided, three against two, and two against three" (Lk. 12:51– 52). Wait, wasn't it just last chapter when Jesus said that any house divided against itself will fall? Now he's saying he came to divide families. Evidently, the apocalypse trumps family values.

In Chapter 13, we get more parables: the mustard seed, the yeast, and the barren fig tree. Notably, in this version, the fig tree is spared, not cursed—unlike in Matthew and Mark, where Jesus condemns a fruitless fig tree out of apparent spite.

Finally, Jesus acknowledges the looming threat: when warned that Herod wants him dead, he responds, "Go ye, and tell that fox, Behold, I cast out devils, and I do cures today and tomorrow, and the third day I shall be perfected...for it cannot be that a prophet perish out of Jerusalem" (Lk. 13:32–33). Jesus knows the script and where it must end.

Luke 14-19

Jesus continues to speak in parables, emphasizing humility and care for the least among us. He teaches, for instance, that when invited to a party, it's better to take the lowest seat than assume a place of honor. Likewise, he advises throwing a feast not for the wealthy, but for the poor and dispossessed. So far, so good.

But then we hit some of Jesus' more provocative (and problematic) statements. In Luke 14:26, he says: "If any man come to me, and hate not his father, and mother, and wife, and children, and brethren, and sisters, yea, and his own life also, he cannot be my disciple." Earlier, in Luke 12:51–53, Jesus had already warned: "Do you think I came to bring peace on earth? No, I tell you, but division. From now on, there will be five in one family divided against each other, three against two and two against three." Similar sentiments appear in Mark.

Perhaps these unsettling messages reflect the steep cost of following Jesus. Or maybe he's employing hyperbole to emphasize that loyalty to him must surpass all other commitments, without literally advocating for familial estrangement. Some suggest that the word translated as "hate" might be better understood as "love less," or that his call for family disruption is softened by parables highlighting compassion for children and the vulnerable. Still, if we take Jesus at his word, he's demanding a radical reassessment of traditional family values, placing allegiance to him above all else, even above one's own life. How many Christians today actually live by that standard?

From here, Jesus pivots to themes of joy and redemption. He compares God's delight in a repentant sinner to a shepherd finding a lost sheep or a woman recovering a lost coin. This leads to the famous parable of the prodigal (spendthrift) son. A wayward son squanders his inheritance on wine and women, then returns home in repentance. His father welcomes him back with open arms and a feast. Meanwhile, the dutiful son, who has worked loyally all along, grumbles at the lack of recognition. The father replies: "It was meet that we should make merry, and be glad: for this thy brother was dead, and is alive again; and was lost, and is found" (Lk. 15:32). While the parable emphasizes forgiveness and grace, it leaves open questions: Did the prodigal son truly change? And why does the loyal son receive no tangible reward?

Jesus follows with more teachings: that one cannot serve both God and money, that the law of Moses remains in effect, and that divorce and remarriage are tantamount to adultery. He echoes Moses' severity by affirming the death penalty for adultery yet remains silent on issues like abortion and homosexuality.

Luke also introduces striking imagery of eternal punishment. In the parable of the rich man and Lazarus, both men die: Lazarus is comforted in Abraham's embrace while the rich man suffers torment in Hades. The rich man begs for someone to warn his brothers, but Abraham replies: "If they hear not Moses and the prophets, neither will they be persuaded, though one rose from the dead" (Lk. 16:31). Here, Jesus reinforces a familiar theme: the moral failing wasn't wealth itself, but the neglect of the poor.

As Luke's narrative builds toward its climax, Jesus warns that the arrival of the Son of Man will be swift and unexpected, like the flood in Noah's time or the destruction of Sodom. He repeats the famous line that it's easier for a camel to pass through the eye of a needle than for a rich man to enter heaven. A unique Lukan story follows: that of Zacchaeus, a tax collector who pledges to give half his wealth to the poor. Jesus responds: "This day is salvation come to this house, forasmuch as he also is a son of Abraham. For the Son of man is come to seek and to save that which was lost" (Lk. 19:9–10). Notably, Zacchaeus isn't required to give up everything, only enough to show genuine transformation, a more attainable standard than some of Jesus' earlier, harsher demands.

Finally, Luke turns to Jesus' entry into Jerusalem. We'll soon see whether he rides a colt (as in Mark) or both a colt and a foal at the same time (as in Matthew). Just prior to this, we encounter the parable of the talents. A nobleman entrusts three servants with money before departing. When he returns, two have multiplied their share; the third, afraid of failure, has done nothing. The nobleman scolds the unproductive servant and declares: "But those mine enemies, which would not that I should reign over them, bring hither, and slay them before me" (Lk. 19:27). This parable underscores the upheaval Jesus brings—disrupting families, challenging norms, and, metaphorically or not, wielding a sword. And if Jesus isn't the nobleman in this story, who is?

Luke 20-24

Jesus enters Jerusalem on a single colt (not two) and is greeted by an exultant crowd singing, "Blessed be the King that cometh in the name of the Lord" (Lk. 19:38). Some Pharisees urge him to silence the crowd, but he replies that if they were silent, the very stones would shout.

Afterward, Jesus tells the parable of the wicked tenants, also found in Mark and Matthew. In the story, a landowner plants a vineyard, equips it, and leases it to tenants before leaving on a journey. When harvest time arrives, he sends servants to collect his share, but the tenants beat, insult, and kill them. More servants meet the same fate. Finally, the landowner sends his son, assuming they will respect him. They kill him too, hoping to seize his inheritance.

Jesus concludes the parable with a rhetorical question: "What will the owner of the vineyard do?" He answers: "The owner will destroy the tenants and give the vineyard to others." The symbolism is clear: God as the landowner, Israel as the vineyard, the prophets as the servants, the religious leaders as the tenants, and Jesus as the son. The religious authorities are incensed when they realize Jesus is calling them the wicked tenants.

Jesus also expels the money changers from the temple and delivers the line about rendering unto Caesar what is Caesar's, and unto God what is God's. The idea of paying taxes to a secular authority wasn't exactly revolutionary but imagine how different history might have been had the early Christian writers instructed believers to pay taxes only to the Church. Without this early separation of church and state, would Western capitalism or pluralistic democracy have emerged?

The Pharisees continue trying to trap Jesus with legal riddles. They present a hypothetical woman whose husband dies and who subsequently marries each of his brothers. "Whose wife will she be in heaven?" they ask. Jesus replies that in the resurrection people will be like angels, an answer consistent with the ambiguous and evasive responses in Mark and Matthew. Like the rest of us, Jesus can't seem to paint a compelling picture of heaven.

Jesus then prophesies the fall of Jerusalem, foreseeing it surrounded by armies—a passage often interpreted as a prediction of the Roman destruction of the Temple in 70 CE. But considering Luke was likely written between 80 and 100 CE, this "prophecy" is more hindsight than foresight.

Luke also includes the story of the poor widow who donates two small coins, praising her for giving all she had. This touching detail also appears in Mark but is absent from Matthew.

Chapter 21 then shifts to apocalyptic imagery: "And there shall be signs in the sun, and in the moon, and in the stars; and upon the earth distress of nations... Men's hearts failing them for fear... And then shall they see the Son of man coming in a cloud with power and great glory" (Lk. 21:25–27). As in the other Gospels, the End Times are always just around the corner.

In Chapter 22, Judas agrees to betray Jesus. The disciples share the Last Supper, during which Jesus institutes the Eucharist and foretells Peter's denial and eventual repentance. At the Mount of Olives, Jesus prays: "Father...if thou be willing, remove this cup from me: nevertheless not my will, but thine, be done" (Lk. 22:42). He's arrested by an armed group, identified by Judas' kiss, and brought before the Sanhedrin.

Luke adds a twist not found in Mark or Matthew: Pilate sends Jesus to Herod Antipas. Herod, who had earlier executed John the Baptist, is intrigued but ends up mocking Jesus and sending him back. While it's theoretically possible that Pilate, the Roman governor, deferred to Herod (the tetrarch of Galilee), it feels more like a literary flourish, possibly to highlight Herod's ongoing guilt over John's death or to spread the blame for Jesus' execution.

Before the crucifixion comes the scourging. The oft-cited "39 lashes" comes from Deuteronomy 25:3, but while all four Gospels say Jesus was whipped, none specify the number. The Romans, however, were not bound by Jewish limits and used whips embedded with metal or bone, inflicting horrific damage.

Jesus is then crucified between two others. One, the so-called "Penitent Thief," says: "We receive the due reward of our deeds: but this man hath done nothing amiss." Jesus replies: "Verily I say unto thee, Today shalt thou be with me in paradise" (Lk. 23:41–43). This story is often used to illustrate the power of last-minute repentance. But it raises difficult theological questions. If a murderer and cannibal like Jeffrey

Dahmer can secure eternal paradise with a deathbed conversion, while someone like Gandhi—who lived virtuously but wasn't Christian—faces eternal torment, what does that say about divine justice?

Jesus dies and is buried by Joseph of Arimathea. On the third day, Mary Magdalene, Joanna, and Mary (mother of James) visit the tomb and find it empty. Two men in dazzling clothes, presumably angels, though Luke doesn't say so, announce: "He is not here, but is risen" (Lk. 24:6). They tell the women to report this to the disciples. In contrast, Mark's (longer ending) says the women were too afraid to tell anyone, and Matthew includes an appearance by Jesus himself alongside an angel.

In Luke, Peter rushes to the tomb and finds it empty. Later, two followers encounter a stranger on the road to Emmaus and realize, after a long conversation, that it's Jesus. This story mirrors the two unnamed figures in the long ending of Mark, but Luke fleshes it out with more detail. When the men return to tell the disciples, Jesus appears again, this time in their midst. Initially mistaken for a ghost, he invites them to touch his wounds and even eats grilled fish to prove he's real. Finally, Jesus leads them outside Bethany, raises his hands in blessing, and is "carried up into heaven" (Lk. 24:51).

Luke opens with a prologue promising an orderly account of Jesus' life. In that sense, he delivers. His Gospel is smoother and more structured than Mark's, but sometimes at the cost of energy and emotional depth. His nativity story diverges sharply from Matthew's, yet most believers have combined the two into a seamless, but fabricated, hybrid. Luke also tones down Matthew's dramatic Sermon on the Mount into a more pedestrian "Sermon on the Plain," but adds signature parables such as the Prodigal Son and the Good Samaritan.

Like the other Synoptics, Luke insists that the Son of Man will return before some of the disciples die, a prophecy that has aged poorly.

JOHN

John 1-4

The *Gospel According to John* opens with a memorable line: "In the beginning was the Word, and the Word was with God, and the Word was God." Written between 90 and 110 CE, it was almost certainly the last of the four canonical Gospels to be composed. Like the others, it's anonymous, though traditionally attributed to John the Apostle, the "disciple whom Jesus loved."

The author appears to have been aware of earlier Gospels, especially Mark and Luke, and, like the Synoptics, drew on the Old Testament. Still, John quotes the Hebrew scriptures far less often—14 times, compared to 27 in Mark, 54 in Matthew, and 24 in Luke. What becomes clear very quickly is that John is no simple retelling. This Gospel represents a major theological and stylistic departure from Matthew, Mark, and Luke. Rather than focusing on Jesus' deeds and sayings, John emphasizes his divine nature from the outset. That said, John does contribute some new and colorful miracle stories.

The Gospel begins with a poetic prologue proclaiming that the divine Word became flesh and insisting, "No man hath seen God at any time; the only begotten Son, which is in the bosom of the Father, he hath declared him" (John 1:18). But the Old Testament disagrees. In Exodus 24:9–11, Moses and seventy elders of Israel "gazed on God and then ate and drank." Also, in Genesis, Adam and Eve stroll and converse with God in the garden. Does that not count because it was before the Fall of Man? Either John is ignoring these episodes, or he's redefining "seeing God" to mean something else.

He continues: "For the law was given by Moses, but grace and truth came by Jesus Christ" (John 1:17). This isn't the first appearance of the term "Jesus Christ" in the New Testament, but it's used far more confidently here. In the Synoptic Gospels, even the disciples often seemed unsure about who Jesus really was. Not so in John. Jesus' identity as the Christ— *Christos* in Greek, meaning "anointed one" or "Messiah"—is made unmistakably clear from the start.

Next comes John the Baptist, who immediately recognizes Jesus as "the Lamb of God, which taketh away the sin of the world" (John 1:29). It's as if he's being interviewed by the Gospel writer. In verse 32, John declares: "I saw the Spirit descending from heaven like a dove, and it abode upon him." In Mark, John baptizes Jesus. In Matthew, he initially protests but ultimately complies. In Luke, Jesus is baptized, but John is already in jail when it happens. And now in John, the Baptist doesn't describe the baptism itself, just the descending dove. The story has evolved, and the pattern is revealing. Jesus' divine nature is growing more prominent, while John the Baptist's role is being downplayed.

Is there a theological cover-up underway? Some of John's followers thought he was the Messiah, and his fiery, apocalyptic teachings bear more than a passing resemblance to Jesus' own later prophecies about the coming of the Son of Man. We know from Matthew and Mark that Jesus was deeply affected by John's death, and, crucially, that John baptized Jesus. Was Jesus originally one of John's disciples who then inherited and transformed his movement? It's an uncomfortable question that John dodges.

John's narrative continues as Jesus begins assembling followers, including Andrew, Simon Peter, Philip, and Nathanael (a figure unique to this Gospel). Soon after, Jesus attends a wedding in Cana where the hosts run out of wine. Like so many biblical scenes, it involves poor event planning. Jesus tells the servants to fill the jars with water, which miraculously becomes wine. Guests are impressed, commenting that the host "hast kept the good wine until now" (John 2:10).

Then comes a chronological curveball: Jesus heads to Jerusalem for Passover and flips the tables of the money changers in the Temple. But wait, didn't that happen at the end of his ministry in the Synoptics, shortly before his arrest? In John, it happens near the beginning. Did Jesus visit Jerusalem twice and cleanse the Temple both times? Or is this a storytelling choice to front-load the drama?

Jesus then has a late-night conversation with Nicodemus, a Pharisee and member of the Sanhedrin. This dialogue introduces the concept of being "born again," and culminates in the Bible's most heavily advertised verse, John 3:16. When Nicodemus says it's obvious Jesus comes from God, Jesus replies: "Except a man be born again, he cannot see the kingdom of God" (John 3:3). Nicodemus, understandably confused, asks how someone can reenter the womb.

Here, a linguistic footnote becomes central. In Greek, the word anōthen can mean either "again" or "from above." Nicodemus takes it literally—"again"—while Jesus intends the spiritual meaning—"from above." But in Aramaic, the language Jesus actually spoke, this wordplay doesn't work; there's no such double meaning. This strongly suggests the dialogue was crafted by a Greek-speaking author aiming to impress a Hellenistic audience with layered spiritual metaphor.

237

If you are interested in this or other wordplays in the New Testament, refer to the Further Reading section, particularly Bart Ehrman's works such as *Jesus: Apocalyptic Prophet of the New Millenium*.

Then comes another doctrinal speed bump. John 3:13 claims, "No man hath ascended up to heaven, but he that came down from heaven, even the Son of Man which is in heaven." But that contradicts 2 Kings 2:11, where the prophet Elijah is taken to heaven in a chariot of fire. Did the author forget? Or is John here redefining "heaven" in a more exclusive theological sense?

The conversation with Nicodemus builds to the famous climax of John 3:16: "For God so loved the world, that he gave his only begotten Son, that whosoever believeth in him should not perish, but have everlasting life." This verse declares that belief, not behavior, is now the sole condition for eternal life. That marks a sharp departure from earlier Jewish teachings centered on law, justice, and good works. It even stands in contrast to the Synoptic Gospels, where ethical behavior and acts of mercy are central themes.

But what exactly does "begotten" mean? If we're being literal, you don't *beget* someone without sex being involved. So, is this meant metaphorically, or are we expected to believe God sired a child? Sired Himself, with Him as His father?

Jesus then begins baptizing near the Jordan, prompting John the Baptist's followers to complain. But John reassures them: Jesus, not he, is the Christ. The narrative then shifts to Samaria, where Jesus speaks with a woman at a well about "living water." Their conversation touches on theology, prophecy, and revelation. When the woman says, "I know that Messiah cometh," Jesus replies, "I that speak unto thee am he" (John 4:25–26)—another moment of explicit self-identification that the Synoptics mostly avoid.

Chapter 4 ends with Jesus reviving a royal official's son, a resurrection story found only in John. At this point, it's hard to keep track of all the dead coming back to life. But if the Gospel writers weren't too worried about reconciling their many tales of the newly undead, I won't feel guilty for losing count either.

John 5-11

In the middle chapters of John, Jesus continues to ramp up his claims of divinity, performs dramatic miracles, makes cryptic analogies about blood and flesh, and increasingly attracts hostility from the Jewish establishment. One flashpoint comes when Jesus heals a blind man on the Sabbath, an act that enrages the local authorities, especially after he explains himself by saying: "The Son can do nothing of himself, but what he seeth the Father do... For the Father loveth the Son..." (John 5:19–20). This appears to be another way of claiming divine status, or at least perfect alignment with God's will—ideas which, to monotheistic ears, would have sounded blasphemous.

Soon after, Jesus crosses the Sea of Galilee, where he feeds a large crowd by multiplying loaves and fish and then walks on water. These scenes also appear in Mark and Matthew, where they follow the execution of John the Baptist. Interestingly, John's Gospel never mentions John the Baptist's death, perhaps part of an editorial strategy to downplay his influence.

At the synagogue in Capernaum, Jesus makes one of his most jarring declarations: "I am the bread of life: he that cometh to me shall never hunger" (John 6:35), and later, "Except ye eat the flesh of the Son of man, and drink his blood, ye have no life in you" (John 6:53). This speech's cannibalistic overtones cause some disciples to walk away. Even the inner circle seems disturbed. Once again, Jesus equates himself with the "Son of man," reinforcing the idea that he and this apocalyptic figure are one and the same.

With tensions rising, Jesus retreats to Galilee. Notably, John now freely uses the term "the Jews" to describe his opponents—despite Jesus himself being a Jew, as the other Gospels acknowledge. This usage, which appears throughout

John, suggests an emerging split between Jesus' followers and the broader Jewish community, perhaps even before the crucifixion. Jesus insists that he's being targeted simply for healing on the Sabbath, to which the crowd responds: "Thou hast a devil: who goeth about to kill thee?" (John 7:20). Are they denying the threat, or is Jesus overstating it?

Messianic doubts persist. Some wonder if Jesus can really be the Messiah, since prophecy says he must come from Bethlehem, not Galilee. Matthew and Luke both try to resolve this with conflicting nativity narratives placing Jesus' birth in Bethlehem. Yet in John, nobody seems aware of these tales, which raises a question: did Jesus himself know the details of his supposed miraculous birth or his precocious Temple debates at age twelve (from Luke)? If so, he never mentions them.

In one well-known scene, the Pharisees bring Jesus an adulterous woman, reminding him that the Law prescribes stoning. Jesus replies: "He that is without sin among you, let him first cast a stone at her" (John 8:7). The accusers melt away, and Jesus tells her to sin no more. By declining to enforce Mosaic Law, Jesus once again positions himself above it— superior even to Moses and the prophets.

Tensions escalate. Jesus tells the Pharisees: "Ye are from beneath; I am from above...if ye believe not that I am he, ye shall die in your sins" (John 8:23–24). When he later compares himself to Abraham, the crowd again threatens to stone him, and Jesus skedaddles. He heals another blind man and uses the moment to rebuke the Pharisees for their spiritual blindness. Crowds continue to ask if he is the Messiah, and Jesus answers with his own rhetorical question: "Say ye of him...'Thou blasphemest'; because I said, I am the Son of God?" (John 10:36). Again, the response seems to be leading to violence, and again Jesus evades arrest.

Jesus then returns to Bethany, where he reunites with Martha and Mary (introduced in Luke), whose brother Lazarus has died and begun to decay. Jesus dramatically brings Lazarus back to life. Yet, as with other resurrection stories in the Bible, we hear nothing from the revived man himself, which seems like a missed opportunity.

News of this miracle spreads quickly. The high priest Caiaphas concludes that Jesus is too dangerous to be allowed to live and that it's better for one man to die than for the whole nation to suffer—a turning point that sets the stage for Jesus' final days.

John 12-21

Chapter 12 begins with a dinner attended by Jesus, the sisters Martha and Mary, the freshly resurrected Lazarus (who had presumably stopped decaying), and soon-to-be turncoat Judas. Mary anoints Jesus' feet with expensive perfume, which sets off Judas, who remarks that the 300 denarii could have been better spent on the poor (honestly, Judas had a point). In John, this meeting takes place six days before Passover, but in Mark 14:1 and Matthew 26:6 it's two days, and Lazarus wasn't present.

Meanwhile, the Pharisees, alarmed that Lazarus' return from the dead might help Jesus win over the Jewish public, conspire to kill Lazarus, a subplot that's never mentioned again.

The next day, Jesus enters Jerusalem riding a donkey: "As it is written, Fear not, daughter of Zion: behold, thy King cometh, sitting on an ass's colt" (John 12:14–15). The Old Testament reference is from Zechariah 9:9: "Rejoice greatly, O Daughter of Zion...behold, thy King cometh...lowly, and riding upon an ass, and upon a colt the foal of an ass." The next verse, though rarely quoted in Christian sermons, adds that this king will banish chariots and war-horses from Ephraim and bring peace from sea to sea. So: Did Jesus ride a donkey? Sure. Was he the peace-establishing king Zechariah envisioned? No. If Jesus riding a donkey is all it takes to fulfill that prophecy, we're working with a pretty low prophetic bar.

Jesus then foretells his death, saying: "He that loveth his life shall lose it; and he that hateth his life in this world shall keep it unto life eternal" (John 12:25). The crowd, understandably

241

puzzled, points out that the Messiah was supposed to remain forever. Jesus replies enigmatically, "Yet a little while is the light with you" (John 12:35), and departs.

In the next chapter, Jesus washes his disciples' feet. "He laid aside his garments; and took a towel, and girded himself. After that he poureth water into a basin, and began to wash the disciples' feet, and to wipe them with the towel wherewith he was girded" (John 13:4–5). Couldn't he have splurged for a second towel? One wonders about the logistics. He then delivers his "new commandment": "That ye love one another; as I have loved you, that ye also love one another" (John 13:34). What follows is a lengthy farewell speech and prayer.

To Thomas, Jesus declares: "I am the way, the truth, and the life: no man cometh unto the Father, but by me. If ye had known me, ye should have known my Father also" (John 14:6–7). He likens himself to the "true vine," with God as the vinedresser, warns that the world will hate his followers, and promises they will see him—then not see him—and then see him again. Interpret as you will.

This is a good moment to highlight a key difference between John and the Synoptic Gospels. In Matthew 16:28, Jesus says, "Verily I say unto you, There be some standing here, which shall not taste of death, till they see the Son of Man coming in his kingdom." Mark 9:1 and Luke 9:27 contain the same promise. The message is clear: the end was imminent, within a generation. But John, written as late as 110 CE, is conspicuously silent about the timing of the Son of Man's return. By then, all those standing there were long dead.

The familiar events of the arrest, crucifixion, and resurrection follow, but with some striking differences. Judas is arrested in this version but doesn't identify Jesus. Instead, Jesus steps forward and declares himself to the arresting party. It's a more dramatic and courageous moment than being betrayed with a kiss. Interestingly, Jesus is first brought not to Caiaphas, but to Annas, Caiaphas' father-in-law, before being handed over for trial. Jesus then goes to Pilate, whose portrayal changes across the Gospels. In Mark, Pilate is indifferent but gives in to the crowd. In Matthew, he's reluctant, even symbolically washing his hands to show he isn't responsible. Luke has Pilate finding no guilt in Jesus and sending him to Herod, who also declines to convict. In John, Pilate questions Jesus, seems intrigued by him, and repeatedly declares him innocent, yet ultimately folds under political pressure. By John 19:16, Pilate essentially turns Jesus over to the Jews to be crucified, rather than his own soldiers. There's a troubling arc here: the further the Gospel is from the events, the more blame shifts from Rome to "the Jews."

Another unique Johannine touch: Jesus' mother, Mary, is present at the crucifixion. That's a notable revision—she's absent in the earlier accounts. Has her inclusion here been shaped by rising Marian devotion in the late first century? Possibly. Also missing from John is the Penitent Thief (Luke's sympathetic criminal on a neighboring cross). Instead, Roman soldiers break the legs of the two thieves (to hasten death), but seeing Jesus already dead, they pierce his side with a spear. Water and blood spill out, a moment added by John to fulfill prophecy. But again, the cited verses (Zechariah 12:10, Psalm 34:20) don't seem especially messianic in context.

After Jesus dies, Joseph of Arimathea collects the body, and here John adds another helper: Nicodemus, who earlier spoke to Jesus in secret. Mary Magdalene visits the tomb, finds it empty, and sees two angels, then Jesus himself. She reports this to the disciples. Jesus later appears to them and then to Thomas, who famously doubts until he sees the wounds. The final chapter shows Jesus appearing yet again, cooking and eating fish with some disciples.

And then...no ascension. John doesn't describe Jesus rising into heaven. In fact, despite its theological importance, the ascension gets surprisingly little narrative attention in any of the Gospels. One wonders if the authors didn't know how to stage that final, magical exit and decided not to try.

In the Synoptic Gospels, the disciples and Jesus are sometimes coy or unsure about Jesus' nature. Not so in John, where Jesus is presented as God Himself, or at least some sort of equal. Yet this still presents a muddled picture. If God is Jesus, did He impregnate Mary to give birth to Himself? If Jesus is God, did He have to die to save us from His vengeance?

ACTS OF THE APOSTLES

Acts 1-7

The *Acts of the Apostles*, traditionally attributed to Luke (although the authorship of both Luke and Acts remains anonymous), serves as the second volume of the Gospel of Luke. The shared style, structure, and themes of these texts, along with the opening of Acts referencing the earlier work, support the view that they were written by the same person.

The dating of Acts is an ongoing scholarly debate. An earlier date in the 60s CE is suggested by the absence of references to events such as the destruction of the Temple in 70 CE or the deaths of key figures like Paul (around 64–68 CE). A later date, possibly into the early second century, is argued based on theological and literary developments that align with broader trends in early Christian thought. The uncertainty reflects the challenges of reconstructing the historical context. If Luke was completed around 90 CE, Acts was likely written shortly thereafter. The earliest complete manuscripts of Acts date to the 3rd and 4th centuries CE.

Acts emphasizes several key themes: the role of the Holy Spirit, the spread of the Gospel beyond Jewish communities, and the formation of a diverse yet increasingly unified Christian identity. The narrative follows major figures like Peter and Paul as they navigate theological, cultural, and political challenges to build a growing faith community.

The book begins with the same salutation to "Theophilus" that opened Luke. Acts states that after the Passion, Jesus appeared to the disciples for forty days (a detail not mentioned in Luke), and was then taken up into heaven by a cloud. This is the fifth biblical account of the ascension, and like the others, it is curiously lacking in vivid detail or drama for such a supposedly monumental event.

The disciples then elect Matthias to replace Judas, and we're given a graphic account of Judas' demise: "Now this man purchased a field with the reward of iniquity; and falling headlong, he burst asunder in the midst, and all his bowels gushed out…insomuch as that field is called…Aceldama, that is to say, The field of blood" (Acts 1:18–19). This contradicts the version in Matthew (Mark and Luke are silent), where Judas, overcome with remorse, returns the thirty pieces of silver and hangs himself. Perhaps hanging was seen as too dignified, and Acts needed a more gruesome ending, but it's hard to reconcile these accounts. If Judas hanged himself, how did he also fall headfirst and burst open?

Next, the disciples celebrate Pentecost—fifty days after Passover—when a violent wind sweeps over them and they begin speaking in a multitude of languages. The story appears designed to emphasize the universality of the Gospel. Importantly, this "speaking in tongues" refers to real, intelligible languages, not the ecstatic glossolalia associated with modern charismatic movements.

The disciples quickly begin attracting converts. Peter and John heal a lame man near the Temple, suggesting they have inherited Jesus' miraculous powers. This doesn't sit well with the Sadducees, who command them to stop, but Peter and John stand their ground and testify to the resurrection of Jesus. The early Christians also band together for support: "They were of one heart and of one soul…and had all things in common" (Acts 4:32). This seems like a practical response to hardship but also reads like socialism, a concept many Christians reject until they benefit from it.

We then encounter the strange story of Ananias and Sapphira, a wealthy couple who promise to donate the proceeds from a land sale to the disciples but secretly withhold some of it. When confronted, both drop dead at Peter's feet, striking fear into the community. Apparently, Peter now possesses the power not only to heal people but to kill them.

Peter and the apostles continue performing miracles and preaching the resurrection. They are jailed, but an angel frees them. Brought before the Sanhedrin, they face condemnation until the Pharisee Gamaliel intervenes. He advises caution: "Refrain from these men, and let them alone…lest haply ye be found even to fight against God" (Acts 5:38–39). The apostles are flogged anyway and ordered to keep quiet.

A new character, Stephen, is appointed as a leader. He's a fiery speaker who draws attention from the authorities. Summoned before the Sanhedrin, he delivers a long speech reviewing the story of Moses and denouncing his audience: "Ye stiffnecked and uncircumcised in heart and ears, ye do always resist the Holy Ghost: as your fathers did, so do ye" (Acts 7:51). Unsurprisingly, this doesn't go over well. The crowd stones him to death (why are there always so many rocks lying around?), while a young man named Saul—soon to be Paul—looks on approvingly.

Acts 8-15

Fresh from the stoning of Stephen, Saul continues his campaign of persecuting Christians, causing many to scatter. But Philip and Peter press on, performing miracles and seeking new converts. Philip casts out demons, heals paralytics, and cures the lame. He also baptizes an Ethiopian eunuch—an important early moment in Christianity's expansion beyond Jewish boundaries. Peter converts Simon the Magician (though whether Simon truly believed or just wanted magical power is left ambiguous), and then we arrive at one of the most transformational stories of the early Church.

Saul is traveling from Jerusalem to Damascus when a light from heaven suddenly shines, knocking him to the ground and temporarily blinding him. Possibly concussed, he hears a voice: "Saul, Saul, why persecutest thou me?" (Acts 9:4). It's Jesus speaking from beyond the grave. Saul is told to go into the city and await further instructions, which come from a disciple named Ananias. Saul remains blinded for three days— symbolic, perhaps, of Jesus' own three-day death and resurrection. Is Saul now setting himself up as a quasi-divine figure? He converts, becomes a Christian, and travels to Jerusalem. Barnabas vouches for him, but the other disciples remain understandably suspicious; some Greek-speaking Jews even plot to kill him.

Meanwhile, Peter cures a paralytic and raises a woman named Tabitha from the dead in Joppa (modern-day Jaffa): "Tabitha, arise" (Acts 9:40). She sits up, as if summoned from a nap rather than the grave. Peter then visits a Roman centurion and has a vision that will fundamentally shape the Christian understanding of compliance with the Law and the universality of their emerging religion. But before we get to that, let's consider the foundational role miracle cures played in the early Church's self-presentation.

The success of early evangelism isn't based primarily on the beauty of Jesus' ethical message; it's based on the claim that he was resurrected and that his followers wield supernatural power. To establish apostolic authority, you had to perform signs and wonders—raising the dead, curing the sick, casting out demons. Jesus did all of these, plus a few extras like walking on water and turning water into wine. In Matthew 10:8, Jesus commanded his disciples: "Heal the sick, cleanse the lepers, raise the dead, cast out devils." During Jesus' ministry, the disciples didn't always live up to that charge, but after the resurrection, they're making up for lost time. Philip expels demons. Peter raises the dead and, in one memorable case, causes a couple to drop dead for withholding a donation.

Back to Peter. While visiting a newly converted centurion, Peter falls into a trance and sees "heaven opened, and a certain vessel descending unto him, as it had been a great sheet knit at the four corners, and let down to the earth: Wherein were all manner of four-footed beasts...and there came a voice... Rise, Peter; kill, and eat" (Acts 10:11–13). With one word— "Eat!" —Peter seems to be saying it's no longer necessary to follow the dozens of dietary laws in the Old Testament. If only he could have conjured a similar one-word command for believers to more freely express their sexuality we might have avoided centuries of unnecessary and dangerous restrictions on love and marriage.

Revising the Law is no small matter, yet Peter (and Saul) seem to understand that its restrictions could impede growth. The Old Testament model of religious expansion was by conquest, intermarriage, or population growth. However, at least for now, the Gospel would be spread through conversion of Jews and Gentiles alike, a point Peter reinforces when he returns to Jerusalem.

After declaring that even the uncircumcised can be saved, he's arrested, but an angel springs him from jail. Herod has the guards executed, and then he himself is struck down, "eaten by worms," possibly a vivid description of a fatal parasitic or gastrointestinal condition.

Meanwhile, Saul and Barnabas set out from Antioch (in Syria), traveling to Cyprus and then to Perga in Pamphylia (modern southwestern Turkey). In Cyprus, they encounter Bar-Jesus, a magician who opposes their message. Saul, now also called Paul, rebukes him and strikes him blind. That's right: just as Paul was blinded by divine revelation, now he can blind others with the force of his words.

Their mission continues in both Jewish and Gentile communities, and Paul performs another miracle by healing a cripple. In Iconium, Paul is stoned, yet somehow survives, and manages to limp back to Antioch. Was it a full-on execution attempt, or did someone just lob a rock at him and Paul turned it into a near-death encounter? Either way, he squeezes every drop of PR value out of the incident before moving on to the next major theological controversy: circumcision.

The prevailing view was that new converts to Christianity had to undergo circumcision, as Jewish law required. But this requirement, unsurprisingly, posed a painful obstacle to attracting male Gentile converts. Meanwhile, women's roles in this expanding movement are mostly mentioned in passing, if at all. Peter argues for lowering the barriers to entry, and then James (possibly Jesus' brother) proposes a compromise: no circumcision required, if converts avoid idolatry, blood consumption, and sexual immorality.

With that theological hurdle cleared, Paul begins planning his second missionary journey, aiming to spread the Good News across the wider Mediterranean world.

Acts 16-20

Paul's second missionary journey, described in Acts 15:36–18:22, spans roughly three years, beginning around 49 CE in Antioch. From there, Paul travels through Syria and Cilicia, then on to Derbe and Lystra, where he recruits Timothy. He continues through Phrygia and Galatia and, prompted by a vision, crosses into Macedonia. There, he preaches in cities like Philippi, Thessalonica, and Berea. Paul eventually makes his way to Athens, where he delivers his famous sermon before the Areopagus, and then to Corinth. After a brief stop in Ephesus, he circles back to Antioch, completing the trip.

In Philippi (Macedonia), Paul and his companion Silas exorcise a spirit from a slave girl, incurring the wrath of local profiteers who had been making money off her fortune-telling.

The resulting uproar lands them beaten and jailed. That night, they pray and sing hymns—surely a hit with the other inmates—when an earthquake strikes: "And immediately all the doors were opened, and every one's bands were loosed" (Acts 16:26). Strikingly, Paul and Silas don't flee. Instead, the stunned jailer takes them into his home, nurses their wounds, and becomes a convert. Once it's revealed they are Roman citizens, the magistrates allow them to go free. In Matthew, an earthquake heralded Jesus' death; now in Acts, one liberates Paul. Someone's clearly feeling their oats.

Thessalonica proves less welcoming—Paul is driven out—but in Athens, things begin on a more promising note. He delivers a speech against idolatry and quotes approvingly from Greek poetry: "For we are also his offspring" (Acts 17:28). Eventually, Paul winds up in Corinth. Later, in Gallio, Jewish leaders try to prosecute him, but the Roman proconsul dismisses the case as an internal religious squabble: not his circus, not his monkey.

Paul's third missionary journey, dated to around 53–57 CE, is more pastoral than exploratory. He revisits many of the churches he helped establish, spending a significant stretch in Ephesus, and traveling through Macedonia and Greece. This period focuses on teaching and organizing, while laying the groundwork for his eventual trip to Jerusalem.

Along the way, Paul attracts a zealous new ally: Apollos, a passionate preacher of Jesus as the Messiah. In Ephesus, Paul founds a church and becomes something of a miracle celebrity. His power is so potent that even handkerchiefs he had touched are said to heal sickness and expel demons (modern televangelists still run that playbook, for a small "suggested donation"). In one scene, a Jewish exorcist tries invoking Paul's authority, only for the demon to reply: "Jesus I know, and Paul I know; but who are ye?" (Acts 19:15), before launching from its host and violently attacking the would-be healer and his friends.

Paul leaves Ephesus, but not before provoking a near-riot. The local silversmiths, who make shrines to the goddess

Artemis, fear that Paul's anti-idol message could tank their business. Later, while in Macedonia, Paul's verbosity proves hazardous. During one of his famously long sermons, a young man named Eutychus nods off, falls from a third-story window, and dies: "And there sat in a window a certain young man named Eutychus...and was taken up dead" (Acts 20:9). Paul revives him, embraces him, and presumably continues preaching, hopefully with more snack breaks.

By this point, Paul is the dominant missionary figure in Acts. In fact, Acts mentions Paul about 150 times, compared to 70 mentions of Jesus—a reflection of Paul's rising stature in the evolution of Christianity. Has the movement found its Brigham Young?

Paul's Greatest Hits (so far):
1. **Blinding Elymas the Sorcerer (Acts 13:6–12):** Paul strikes Elymas blind for opposing the Gospel, leading the Roman proconsul to believe.
2. **Healing a Crippled Man in Lystra (Acts 14:8–10):** Paul cures a man lame from birth, prompting the crowd to mistake him for a god.
3. **Casting Out a Spirit of Divination (Acts 16:16–18):** Paul exorcises a spirit from a slave girl, effectively ending her promising career as an oracle.
4. **Earthquake in Prison (Acts 16:25–34):** A quake frees Paul and Silas from jail and converts their jailer.
5. **Filling Disciples with the Holy Spirit (Acts 19:1–7):** Paul lays hands on twelve men in Ephesus, who begin speaking in tongues and prophesying.
6. **Extraordinary Miracles in Ephesus (Acts 19:11–12):** Healing power is transferred even through Paul's handkerchiefs and aprons.
7. **Raising Eutychus from the Dead (Acts 20:9–12):** Paul brings back to life a listener who dozed off and died during one of his marathon sermons.

Acts 21-27

The last chapters of Acts follow Paul's legal travails with the Jews—a religious dispute that eventually drags the Roman justice system, however reluctantly, into the mess. Paul arrives in Jerusalem and is almost immediately accused of undermining the Law of Moses by tolerating Jews who no longer follow traditions like circumcision. While he's at the Temple, a mob surrounds him, and a Roman tribune has to step in to prevent bloodshed. (A tribune was roughly equivalent to a modern battalion commander.) Paul is arrested but allowed to speak from custody. He delivers a polished defense, affirming his Jewish roots and recounting his vision on the road to Damascus. But when the Romans prep him for flogging, Paul quietly mentions that he's a Roman citizen—and everything changes. In Roman-occupied Judea, unlike modern America, falsely arresting and abusing a citizen wasn't just an administrative mistake you could whitewash. It was the kind of screw-up that could cost you your post, your honor, and maybe even your neck.

Later, Paul appears before the Sanhedrin, which falls into chaos with tension between the Pharisees (who believe in resurrection) and the Sadducees (who do not). There's a plot to kill Paul by luring him into returning to the Temple to be ambushed, but Paul is shunted off to Caesarea and its Roman governor, Felix. Paul remains imprisoned for several years before appealing his case to Caesar. Note that this is another incident where a prison can't hold him. In Philippi, he'd been freed by an earthquake that also loosened his chains (as earthquakes do, I guess), but this time, he is able to secure at least temporary freedom by using the Roman legal system.

The next stop is King Agrippa, Rome's client king over territories outside of Judea, including parts of modern-day Lebanon and Syria. Paul makes his case: "I was not disobedient unto the heavenly vision: But shewed first unto them of Damascus, and at Jerusalem, and throughout all the coasts of Judea, and then to the Gentiles, that they should repent and

253

turn to God, and do works meet for repentance" (Acts 26:19–20). Agrippa is impressed and says that had Paul not asked for Caesar's review of the matter, he could have been released immediately.

Paul then finds himself on a perilous journey across the sea, bound for Rome and a confrontation with the emperor. His ship runs aground off Malta, and the passengers make their way onto land. While gathering firewood, Paul is bitten by a "viper" that clings to his hand. The locals, expecting him to swell up and die, are amazed when he simply shakes it off into the fire. Convinced he's a god (Paul might have been thinking the same thing), they offer him hospitality. Modern herpetologists note there are no dangerous snakes native to Malta, so Paul may have been bitten by a harmless or mildly venomous snake—either way, he made the most of the misunderstanding. He also cures the island's chief official of a fever, rounding out his personal miracle tally to nine.

Finally, Paul arrives in Rome and is available for trial in front of Caesar (presumably Emperor Nero), but he never actually appears before him. Instead, Paul "dwelt two whole years in his own hired house, and received all that came in unto him, Preaching the kingdom of God, and teaching those things which concern the Lord Jesus Christ, with all confidence, no man forbidding him" (Acts 28:30–31).

Does Paul's experience with Roman justice make sense? It's hard to see how a dispute about Jewish religious practice would warrant much attention from Felix or Agrippa, much less Nero. No one wants to kick problems "upstairs" unless there are compelling reasons to do so. Agrippa was a king, so why would he be afraid to act in a local matter? Nero had an empire to (badly) manage, so he would not have wanted to be engaged unless it was critically important. Under the system known as *cognitio extraordinaria*, which developed during the Imperial period starting with Augustus, the emperor or his representatives could directly oversee trials; however, this was not a common practice.

There are no non-biblical records of any of this, despite historical accounts from the time by Tacitus, Suetonius, and Cassius Dio. It's impossible to say Paul didn't appear before Agrippa or have an appointment scheduled with Nero, but it seems unlikely. It does seem credible, however, that Paul encountered conflict with the Jewish establishment and continued his evangelism, ending up in Rome, where he appears to have an extended and reasonably comfortable stay, although possibly under house arrest.

So ends Acts, not with martyrdom or a thunderclap from heaven, but with Paul preaching in a rented Roman flat. For a faith born with a bang, the Book of Acts closes with an oddly bureaucratic whimper.

THE LETTERS OF PAUL

If the Old Testament belonged to Moses and the Gospels to Jesus, the balance of the New Testament is Paul's. The Apostle Paul is traditionally believed to have died around 64–68 CE during the reign of Emperor Nero; however, there is no conclusive evidence. Perhaps, like Jesus, he died at the hands of Rome, or he fled and later died of natural causes. However, it seems unlikely that he'd have stopped his evangelism if he'd survived Nero's anti-Christian purges after the burning of Rome in 64 CE.

The Bible presents Paul's letters from the longest to the shortest in length, an editorial decision made as early as the fourth century. Perhaps this makes it easier to navigate, but it might also suggest that the early church was uncertain about which letters were authentic and when they were written.

We now have a much more reliable (but not bulletproof) understanding that suggests that of the 14 letters attributed to Paul, only seven are almost certainly written by him and six are highly suspect. One, Hebrews, was probably written after his death. But is this a distinction without a difference? Our modern conception of religious texts is that only God can change them, and He has not shown any such interest. So, if an author pretending to be Paul in 1 Timothy instructs women to learn in silence and forbids them from having authority over men, does it matter if these are really Paul's beliefs? The Bible is inerrant, right?

The following is an approximate chronology of Paul's trips and related letters.

First Missionary Journey (c. 47–48 CE):
• Paul, along with Barnabas, traveled through Cyprus and parts of Asia Minor. No letters are attributed to this journey.

Second Missionary Journey (c. 49–52 CE):
• **1 Thessalonians (c. 50 CE):** Written during Paul's time in Corinth. This is his earliest letter, addressing new believers in Thessalonica.
• **2 Thessalonians (date debated):** Addressing concerns about Christ's return, though its authenticity is questioned due to stylistic differences.

Third Missionary Journey (c. 53–57 CE):
• **Galatians (c. 53–56 CE):** Likely written during the early part of the journey, this letter defends the doctrine of justification by faith.
• **1 Corinthians (c. 54 CE) and 2 Corinthians (c. 55 CE):** Sent to the church in Corinth from Ephesus, these letters address divisions, moral issues, and misunderstandings about resurrection.
• **Romans (c. 57 CE):** Written from Corinth, Romans explains sin, grace, and salvation.
• **Philippians (c. 61–63 CE):** Conveys gratitude and joy, focusing on Christ-centered unity and humility.

In Rome (c. 60–68 CE):

- **Philemon (c. 60–62 CE):** A personal letter appealing for the reconciliation of Onesimus, a runaway slave, with his master, Philemon.

- **Colossians and Ephesians (c. 60–62 CE):** These letters, disputed in authorship, focus on the cosmic role of Christ and unity within the church.

Final Years and Later Writings (c. 62–68 CE):

- **The Pastoral Epistles (1 Timothy, 2 Timothy, Titus):** Reflect concerns about church leadership and structure. These are widely considered inauthentic.

- **Hebrews (c. 60–90 CE):** Has traditionally been grouped with Paul's writings, but it might have been written up to several decades after his death.

Let's start our review according to *chronology* rather than the order in which the letters are presented in the Bible.

1 and 2 Thessalonians

1 Thessalonians is a letter from Paul to the young Christian community in Thessalonica, which he had helped establish but had to leave abruptly due to opposition. This strain is referenced in 1 Thess. 2:4 when he says, "God, which tryeth our hearts." Despite his anxiety over their situation, Paul is surprisingly upbeat: "For ye are our glory" (1 Thess. 2:20), he tells them. He also refers to a visit Timothy had made to the community, during which Timothy reported that they were holding up well under pressure.

Paul urges the Thessalonian Christians to control their sexual desires, though he doesn't go into specifics. He then pivots to a message of reassurance about the Lord's return. In 1 Thess. 4:16–17, he offers one of the earliest and most vivid descriptions of what later theology would call the "rapture":

> For the Lord himself shall descend from
> heaven with a shout, with the voice of the
> archangel, and with the trumpet of God: and
> the dead in Christ shall rise first:
> Then we which are alive and remain shall be
> caught up together with them in the clouds, to
> meet the Lord in the air: and so shall we ever
> be with the Lord.

No one will see this event coming in advance; Paul says it will happen like "a thief in the night" (1 Thess. 5:2). While Paul doesn't use the "Son of Man" language found in Mark, Matthew, and Luke, the idea is similar: sudden, divine intervention—and soon. Paul seems to believe this could very well happen within the lifetime of his audience.

2 Thessalonians, possibly written later (and probably not by Paul), describes the return of the Lord in far more apocalyptic terms. Gone is the imagery of believers rising majestically into the clouds. Instead, 2 Thess. 1:7–10 envisions a fiery reckoning:

> When the Lord Jesus shall be revealed from
> heaven with his mighty angels,
> In flaming fire taking vengeance on them that
> know not God, and that obey not the gospel
> of our Lord Jesus Christ:
> Who shall be punished with everlasting
> destruction from the presence of the Lord,
> and from the glory of his power;
> When he shall come to be glorified in his
> saints, and to be admired in all them that
> believe...

There is also mention of a "wicked one" or "man of sin," a kind of proto-Antichrist figure, who will wreak havoc before being "consumed with the spirit of [the Lord's] mouth" and destroyed "with the brightness of his coming" (2 Thess. 2:8).

Given the severity of what's to come, Paul (or the author) stresses urgency: "Pray for us, that the word of the Lord may have free course, and be glorified, even as it is with you." (2 Thess. 3:1)

The letter ends with a call to discipline and productive behavior. The author reminds them, "if any would not work, neither should he eat" (2 Thess. 3:10), and warns against associating with people who reject apostolic teaching. This verse has found surprising staying power in American politics. Republican lawmakers have cited it when arguing that Medicare or SNAP recipients should be required to work to receive benefits, often quoting it verbatim.

What these "family values" politicians don't quote, however, is Acts 4:32–35, which describes the early Christian community's commitment to resource-sharing and collective ownership. No one claimed private possessions, and everything was held in common. It's an example of how citing the Bible as a moral blueprint can be more about selective endorsement than principle. If you want to support the poor, the Bible has verses for you. If you want to deny aid to the poor, the Bible has verses for that too.

Surely, we can agree that in a civilized society, work should be encouraged but also that children should never go hungry.

Galatians

Galatians is a short, fiery epistle written circa 53 CE that addresses critical theological debates in early Christianity. It was directed to the churches in Galatia, near modern-day Ankara, Turkey. Paul starts as a cranky-pants: "I marvel that ye are so soon removed from him that called you into the grace of Christ unto another gospel: Which is not another; but there be some that trouble you, and would pervert the gospel of Christ" (Gal. 1:6–7). This "different gospel" was propagated by Judaizers, teachers who insisted that Gentile converts to Christianity must adhere to Jewish customs, particularly circumcision and other Mosaic laws, to achieve salvation.

Paul vehemently opposes this teaching, as it undermines the core message of the Gospel, a point he makes in Galatians 2:16: "Knowing that the works of the law do not justify a man, but by the faith of Jesus Christ." This represents a radical shift from traditional Jewish teachings in the Old Testament, which hold that the Law is not only the foundation for appropriate moral behavior but must be followed to act in accordance with God's will. The underlying issue is whether the followers of Christ are Jews or are something new. Paul is increasingly in the "new" camp.

A well-known verse is Gal. 3:28: "There is neither Jew nor Greek, there is neither bond nor free, there is neither male nor female: for ye are all one in Christ Jesus." Paul is making a powerful case for the universality of Christ, one that is accessible to all people, regardless of their sex, social status, or existing religious practice. He is not rejecting slavery as an institution, only suggesting that slaves could also be Christians. Paul was not a pushover, so I must believe that if he had wanted to advocate for the end of slavery, he would have done so.

By the end of Galatians, Paul has worked through some of his frustration and is more encouraging. The Law is not the be-all and end-all; it's the Spirit that's important. If you have the Spirit, you'll avoid sins like idol worship, orgies, sorcery, impurity, bad temper, and quarrels (this last one might be a dig at some of the people of Galatia). He reiterates his message in Gal. 6:13, speaking of the Judaizers: "For neither they themselves who are circumcised keep the law; but desire to have you circumcised, that they may glory in your flesh." In other words, not only is being circumcised unnecessary but you can also be circumcised and not follow Moses' laws, making it a form of painful virtue signaling.

Paul's teaching that Christ is accessible to Jews, Gentiles, men, women, slaves, and freemen enabled him to extend his message to a broad audience, presenting the new faith as universally inclusive and appealing to the widest range of potential followers. Paul is a true believer and an impressive

261

leader and organizer. He's also turning out to be a savvy marketer.

1 Corinthians

The Apostle Paul wrote the *First Epistle to the Corinthians*, although Sosthenes, whom Paul mentions in his introduction, seems to have been a co-author or scribe. The letter was addressed to the Christian church in Corinth, a bustling Greek city known for its trade, art, philosophy and notorious immorality.

Paul begins by building on themes found in 1 Thessalonians, particularly that God has revealed Himself through the Spirit. He writes, "For the Jews require a sign, and the Greeks seek after wisdom: But we preach Christ crucified…" (1 Cor. 1:22–23). Later, he adds: "Let no man deceive himself. If any man among you seemeth to be wise in this world, let him become a fool, that he may be wise" (1 Cor. 3:18). I think Paul is saying you shouldn't put all your eggs in the wisdom basket, that sometimes insight comes only through blind, even illogical submission. But this is also a tortured defense of faith. Outside of religion, is there any institution that demands we suspend our powers of discernment and submit wholly to its revealed truths?

Paul then addresses an issue that apparently needed clarification: is incest okay? Fortunately, Paul's answer is "no." He follows this with an extended meditation on marriage that spans chapters 6 through 8. Paul is careful to note when he's speaking for himself rather than conveying divine command, although with Paul's ego there's not always much daylight between the two. On relationships, he writes: "All things are lawful unto me, but all things are not expedient" (1 Cor. 6:12), which might be his way of saying, "What happens in Corinth stays in Corinth." But only up to a point.

Paul says the body is a temple and warns against uniting oneself with a prostitute. "It is good for a man not to touch a woman," he says in 1 Cor. 7:1, which I take to mean that celibacy is fine. He follows this with the unremarkable observation that marriage is generally beneficial and divorce undesirable. He also notes that if an unbelieving spouse leaves a believing partner, the believer is free to remarry, a practical accommodation that, in a different setting, might have caused literalist Jews to start looking for stones to throw.

Then comes a surprisingly progressive moment: "The wife hath not the power of her own body, but the husband: and likewise also the husband hath not the power of his own body, but the wife" (1 Cor. 7:4). In other words, sexual obligation goes both ways. This is a strikingly egalitarian sentiment for its time. In the Old Testament, marriage was often a transaction between a bride's father and the groom, designed to unite families and ensure economic continuity. Plural marriage—one man, many wives—was common. Paul breaks with these customs and offers a more mutual, arguably modern, view of marriage. Yeah, Paul!

Paul's own marital status is ambiguous, which might explain his comfort with the unmarried life. "I say therefore to the unmarried and widows, It is good for them if they abide even as I" (1 Cor. 7:8). Was Paul widowed? Divorced? Gay? We don't know, and he doesn't say. But it's clear Paul isn't pressuring anyone to marry, that is unless you're too horny to function. In 1 Cor. 7:9, he writes: "But if they cannot contain, let them marry: for it is better to marry than to burn," implying that marriage is a safety valve for lust rather than a holy ideal. It's another practical concession but not a glowing endorsement of the institution.

Later, Paul reminds the Corinthians to avoid idol worship and throws in a grim history lesson: God killed 23,000 Israelites in a single day (although in Numbers, the figure is 24,000) and also unleashed venomous snakes on them. This serpent reference may be a rhetorical flex, alluding to Paul's own immunity to a "viper" bite on Malta. He then writes: "God is faithful, who will not suffer you to be tempted above that ye are able…" (1 Cor. 10:13). I've always found the Christian use of this verse troubling. Were victims of the Holocaust "tested" within their ability to endure?

Despite a few egalitarian notes, Paul shows his patriarchal hand in 1 Cor. 11:6: "For if the woman be not covered, let her also be shorn." He insists that woman reflects the glory of man (because, per Genesis, she came from man), and in church, women must remain silent: "If they will learn anything, let them ask their husbands at home: for it is a shame for women to speak in the church" (1 Cor. 14:35). This sexist command is often dismissed by Christians who point out that it's Paul, not Jesus saying it. But if Paul can be ignored here, why take anything else he says seriously?

You'll recall from Acts that on the Day of Pentecost, the apostles were filled with the Holy Spirit and began to speak in actual foreign languages. In Corinth, however, people were "speaking in tongues" that no one could understand. Paul acknowledges this phenomenon—he even boasts, "I thank my God, I speak with tongues more than ye all"—but then adds: "Yet in the church, I had rather speak five words with my understanding…than ten thousand words in an unknown tongue" (1 Cor. 14:18–19). He's nudging them away from ecstatic babble without alienating them.

Then comes one of the Bible's literary high points: Chapter 13. Allow me to quote it in full, as it remains one of the most beautiful meditations on love ever written:

> Though I speak with the tongues of men and of angels and have not charity, I am become as sounding brass or a tinkling cymbal.
> And though I have the gift of prophecy, and understand all mysteries and all knowledge; and though I have all faith, so that I could remove mountains and have not charity, I am nothing.
> And though I bestow all my goods to feed the poor, and though I give my body to be

burned, and have not charity, it profiteth
me nothing.

Charity suffereth long, and is kind; charity
envieth not; charity vaunteth not itself, is
not puffed up,

Doth not behave itself unseemly, seeketh not
her own, is not easily provoked, thinketh
no evil;

Rejoiceth not in iniquity, but rejoiceth in the
truth;

Beareth all things, believeth all things, hopeth
all things, endureth all things.

Charity never faileth: but whether there be
prophecies, they shall fail; whether there
be tongues, they shall cease; whether there
be knowledge, it shall vanish away.

For we know in part, and we prophesy in part.

But when that which is perfect is come, then
that which is in part shall be done away.

When I was a child, I spoke as a child, I
understood as a child, and I thought as a
child, but when I became a man, I put
away childish things.

For now, we see through a glass, darkly; but
then face to face: now I know in part; but
then shall I know even as also I am
known.

And now abideth faith, hope, charity, these
three; but the greatest of these is charity.

I want to give credit where it's due, but this section feels
more like Sosthenes than Paul. It lacks the argumentative tone
of the rest of the letter and has poetic clarity and warmth that
is otherwise missing.

Paul then turns to the resurrection. He claims that Jesus
appeared after his death to "the twelve" and then to more than
500 people. The "twelve"? That seems sloppy, as Judas was
already gone by then. And as for the 500, who were they? Why

is there no corroborating detail? No names? No locations? For many Christians, this vague reference counts as evidence of the resurrection. But would these same believers accept the thousands who claimed to see the Virgin Mary in the sky over Fátima in 1917?

Jesus preached that salvation involved keeping commandments, following his moral teachings, repenting, and preparing for the coming Kingdom. Paul shifts the focus. For him, the resurrection becomes central—more important than ethics or commandments. He also, like Jesus, believed the Kingdom was coming soon. Maybe that explains his lukewarm endorsement of marriage: why start a family if the world is ending?

Paul adds that we will receive new bodies after the resurrection: "There is a natural body, and there is a spiritual body" (1 Cor. 15:44). The physical body is perishable; the spiritual body is eternal. Interestingly, Paul, who hedged when discussing sex and marriage ("this is just me speaking..."), offers no such caveat here. He defines the Christian vision of the afterlife without checking in with the boss.

2 Corinthians

The Apostle Paul wrote *2 Corinthians* in Macedonia around 55–56 CE, about a year after his first letter to the Corinthians. 1 Corinthians featured lyrical passages ("faith, hope, and love"), laid out sexist rules on worship (women are to be silent in church), and reshaped Christian ideas of the afterlife, distinguishing the earthly body from the spiritual one destined for heaven. 2 Corinthians is often praised by believers as a deep meditation on suffering, reconciliation, and the power of divine grace. To me, it feels more like a remix than a revelation and is less striking than Paul's first letter.

For a moment of modern biblical comedy, then-presidential candidate Donald Trump famously cited 2 Corinthians 3:17 during a speech at Liberty University on January 18, 2016: "Two Corinthians, right? 3:17, that's the whole ball game.

'Where the Spirit of the Lord is, there is liberty.'" His mispronunciation—"Two Corinthians" instead of "Second Corinthians"—became an instant meme, highlighting his shaky grasp of Scripture. Still, many in the Liberty audience applauded, not just the verse but Trump's broader messages: hardline immigration policies, support for guns, dismissive comments about Martin Luther King Jr.'s "small" crowd sizes, and his promise that under his leadership, the "war on Christmas" would be over.

Back to Paul. Much of 2 Corinthians reads like the reiteration of earlier themes. He says things like, "Our sufficiency is of God" (2 Cor. 3:5), "For we preach not ourselves, but Christ Jesus the Lord; and ourselves your servants for Jesus' sake" (2 Cor. 4:5), and "let us cleanse ourselves from all filthiness of the flesh and spirit, perfecting holiness in the fear of God" (2 Cor. 7:1). This seems like familiar stuff.

Still, some interesting ideas surface. In 2 Cor. 12:7–9, Paul mentions his famous "thorn in the flesh," though whether it's physical or spiritual remains unclear. He says he pleaded with God to remove it, but God's response was: "My grace is sufficient for thee: for my strength is made perfect in weakness." Translation: your pain stays, but you'll find divine strength in enduring it.

Paul also seems keenly aware of criticism coming from some Corinthian believers. He admits he is ambitious but insists it's in service of the Lord. He wants recognition for all he's suffered, clearly expecting a bit of respect in return. He ticks off a list of his hardships: "in labors more abundant, in stripes above measure, in prisons more frequent, in deaths oft. Of the Jews five times received I forty stripes save one. Thrice was I beaten with rods, once was I stoned, thrice I suffered shipwreck…" (2 Cor. 11:23–25). It's part spiritual résumé, part martyr's flex.

There's also a call for financial generosity. Paul writes, "He which soweth sparingly shall reap also sparingly; and he which soweth bountifully shall reap also bountifully" (2 Cor. 9:6). In other words: give to the church, and you'll get divine dividends. Paul argues that giving is both a moral obligation and a spiritual investment—what one believer contributes helps make up for what another lacks. These quasi-socialist sentiments are echoed elsewhere in the New Testament.

Paul closes on a warmer note, urging unity and peace: "Be perfect, be of good comfort, be of one mind, live in peace; and the God of love and peace shall be with you. Greet one another with an holy kiss. All the saints salute you" (2 Cor. 13:11–13). A fittingly affectionate farewell for a letter that, while less revolutionary than its predecessor, still offers moments of vulnerability, persuasion, and Paul's signature mix of theology and self-defense.

Romans

Paul's *Letter to the Romans*, was likely composed around 56–57 CE, during Paul's stay in Corinth, and addressed to the Christian community in Rome. The primary purpose of Romans was to articulate the Gospel message, unify Jewish and Gentile believers, and address divisions within the church. Paul's letter serves as a theological treatise, exploring themes such as sin, salvation, grace, faith, and righteousness. Paul also revisits the topic of love, which he (or Sosthenes) had so beautifully expressed in 1 Corinthians.

Paul kicks it off with a condemnation of homosexuality. In Romans 1:26–27, he discusses "unnatural" practices, specifically mentioning both women and men engaging in behaviors that go against what he considers the natural order established by God. Paul writes that women "exchanged natural sexual relations for unnatural ones," and men "abandoned natural relations with women and were inflamed with lust for one another." In the Old Testament, male homosexuality was punishable by death, and lesbianism seemed to get a hall pass, yet Jesus was silent on the topic, so Paul is creating a new Christian morality (or at least documenting prevailing Jewish attitudes).

Paul then revisits themes from his earlier letters, notably Galatians, when he argues for the universality of the Christian faith: There is no value in circumcision without adherence to the Spirit. The word circumcision is mentioned at least 15 times in Romans. In Rom. 3:23–24, Paul provides a summary of his entire thesis: "For all have sinned, and come short of the glory of God; Being justified freely by his grace through the redemption that is in Christ Jesus."

Another important theological point follows in Rom. 5:1–2: "Therefore being justified by faith, we have peace with God through our Lord Jesus Christ: By whom also we have access by faith into this grace wherein we stand, and rejoice in the hope of the glory of God." In other words, "works" are not going to get you saved, you must have faith in God. I don't think Paul is saying works are unimportant to the faithful, but these contributions will flow from faith rather than substitute for it. The implication is that if you have to pick one, it's better to have faith than to produce useful work. This is not a surprising sentiment when you consider the early Christian belief that Judgment Day would be right around the corner.

Paul says in Rom. 5:12–13: "Wherefore, as by one man sin entered into the world, and death by sin; and so death passed upon all men, for that all have sinned: until the law sin was in the world: but sin is not imputed when there is no law." Clearly, Paul felt the need to put Christian morality in the context of Adam and Eve's sin, with Christ providing redemption, but this seems forced. Don't we all have a moral compass without having to believe in talking snakes? Paul lacks confidence in people's innate ability to act ethically: "For the good that I would I do not: but the evil which I would not, that I do" (Rom. 7:19). Did Moses really need to tell the Israelites that murder was wrong or did they already know that long before he descended Mount Sinai with the Commandments?

Another well-known verse is in Rom. 8:31: "If God be for us, who can be against us?" Paul is not saying that the Christian life will not be without temptation, trials, or setbacks, only that God's grace can overcome these. Paul also expands on some

269

of Jesus' most notable teachings: we all have different gifts; don't pay back evil with evil; obey governing authorities; after all, they have been installed by God; love, rather than the Mosaic Law, is the ultimate commandment; don't judge (unless the person you're judging is gay, then you are free to judge away); be considerate of your neighbors.

Although the Book of Romans probably predated the Gospels, Paul clearly accessed some of the same oral (or written) traditions that informed them. When Paul speaks of respecting the government, I think he's channeling Jesus' admonition to give unto Caesar what is Caesar's, with its order to both pay taxes to the state and tithes to the Church. Paul asserts that God establishes government authority and, therefore, deserves honor. Really? Did God endorse Hitler (many Protestants and Catholics believed He did), or is Paul speaking in a more general sense?

Paul finishes Romans with words of encouragement for the Roman church: "The God of peace shall bruise Satan under your feet shortly. The grace of our Lord Jesus Christ be with you" (Rom. 16:20).

Philippians

As in other epistles, Paul acknowledges a co-author, in this case, Timothy. The date of this short letter to the Christian church in Philippi (Macedonia) is disputed, although some sources confidently say it was during a period of imprisonment in Rome. The letter could have been written in Ephesus between 52 and 55 CE, Caesarea between 57 and 59, or Rome around 62; take your pick. The epistle might also have originally been multiple separate letters that were later combined. Why didn't Paul date his letters?

Regardless, it's hard to see the value of the letter unless you are deeply invested in Paul's understanding of Christ. Paul's writings share a similar style, as is evident in *Philippians*. He is earnest, often self-deprecating, sometimes frosty when his motives are questioned, and he reconciles nearly every verse with Old Testament passages. In the approximately 150 words from Phil. 12–18, which deals with salvation, there are at least 16 references to other books of the Bible. You can see why 18th-century Scottish historian Sir David Dalrymple is credited with saying that practically the entire New Testament could be reconstructed using only the Old Testament.

Paul starts off by thanking his audience, as he does in all his letters, and then tells the Philippians: "For to me to live is Christ, and to die is gain. But if I live in the flesh, this is the fruit of my labor: yet what I shall choose I wot not" (Phil. 1:21–22). He wants to be dead and with Christ but is tied to the earth to be useful to his ministry. He goes on: "Fulfil ye my joy, that ye be likeminded, having the same love, being of one accord, of one mind" (Phil. 2:2), all necessary features for a new church trying to take hold in foreign soil.

Paul uses the imagery of a race several times, starting in Phil. 2:16: "...I may rejoice in the day of Christ, that I have not run in vain, neither labored in vain." He adds in Phil. 3:14: "I press toward the mark for the prize of the high calling of God in Christ Jesus," as he looks forward to salvation. It's hard not to see some fatalism creep into his writing; in a race, there's always a finish line. But he ends with the sense of hope: "I can do all things through Christ which strengtheneth me" (Phil. 4:13).

Philemon

Philemon was composed around 57–62 CE, while Paul was in prison at Caesarea Maritima (Roman Judea) or from Rome during his confinement, and addressed to Philemon, possibly a bishop in Colossae (modern-day Turkey). After Paul's salutation, he gets to his request to Philemon. It appears that Onesimus, a runaway slave, was imprisoned with Paul or had somehow come to his attention and converted to Christianity. Paul says to Philemon: "Whom I have sent again: thou therefore receive him, that is, mine own bowels: Whom I would have retained with me, that in thy stead he might have ministered unto me in the bonds of the gospel" (Phm. 12–13). I really wish I had not used the KJV for that quote. Paul also promises to pay for any damage Onesimus might have caused as he fled (perhaps he'd stolen some money on the way out the door).

Paul is putting his confidence in Philemon to do the right thing, perhaps pardoning Onesimus, even freeing him, or at least not killing him, which would have been his right. Paul is making his request personal and emphatic: "Having confidence in thy obedience I wrote unto thee, knowing that thou wilt also do more than I say" (Phm. 21). Paul is asking for Onesimus to be received back by Philemon as a Christian brother, but Paul doesn't specifically ask for Philemon to free the slave, only to treat him with restraint.

Christians sometimes celebrate Paul's letter because it advocates for compassion towards a slave. Critics point out that Paul didn't specifically request Onesimus' freedom and avoided any criticism of the institution of slavery. However, I think Paul's request was well-crafted. Paul might have been the most prominent Christian alive, so he was putting his prestige on the line with the request, which Philemon would have understood.

The fact that this epistle was included in the Bible probably means that Paul's request was granted. It seems unrealistic to have expected Paul to have attacked slavery head-on. Insisting that he act like an ancient Frederick Douglass is an unrealistic expectation. Paul's purpose was to secure the freedom of, or at least avoid capital punishment for, his friend and convert Onesimus. A broader critique of slavery was unnecessary and could have been counterproductive. Perhaps Paul was neither the fervent abolitionist his defenders claim nor as timid as his critics suggest.

Colossians

Paul is traditionally credited with writing Colossians, likely around 60–62 CE during his first imprisonment in Rome.

However, many Bible scholars now question Paul's authorship, citing linguistic differences and a more developed Christology than what we find in the undisputed Pauline letters.

To my untrained eye, 2 Thessalonians didn't seem like it was written by Paul; Colossians, by contrast, felt more convincing. It mirrors the format, tone, and rhetorical structure of his earlier letters. But does it matter if Paul wrote it or not? It's in the Bible and so deeply embedded in Christian doctrine that its authorship has become almost irrelevant.

The Colossians were members of the Christian community in Colossae, a small city in the Roman province of Asia, located in modern-day Turkey. After a perfunctory greeting, Paul (or whoever) reiterates a familiar theme: that goodness flows from God. He opens with this blessing: "...being fruitful in every good work, and increasing in the knowledge of God" (Col. 1:10). He then offers a prayer of thanks to God and "his dear Son: In whom we have redemption through his blood, even the forgiveness of sins" (Col. 1:13–14).

But Paul then pivots, suggesting the Colossians were veering off course and needed a corrective nudge from Paul, God's ever-humble servant. He also presents himself as a willing martyr for their benefit: "Who now rejoice in my sufferings for you, and fill up that which is behind of the afflictions of Christ in my flesh for his body's sake, which is the church" (Col. 1:24). He promises that hidden gems of "wisdom and knowledge" are available if they remain firm in faith. In Col. 2:10–13, we get a dense theological passage structured as a cascading parallelism:

> And ye are complete in him, which is the head
> of all principality and power:
> In whom also ye are circumcised with the
> circumcision made without hands, in putting
> off the body of the sins of the flesh by the
> circumcision of Christ:
> Buried with him in baptism, wherein also ye
> are risen with him through the faith of the

> operation of God, who hath raised him from
> the dead.
> And you, being dead in your sins and the
> uncircumcision of your flesh, hath he
> quickened together with him, having forgiven
> you all trespasses.

The imagery evokes a strangely intimate bodily relationship with Christ, perhaps a departure from how Paul or the Gospel writers typically framed salvation.

Anyway, don't sweat the small stuff, like your physical existence: "Set your affection on things above, not on things on the earth. For ye are dead, and your life is hid with Christ in God" (Col. 3:2–3). This kind of cosmic detachment seems bizarre, especially in an era when most people were farmers and would starve if they didn't work. Taken literally, Paul's advice could be fatal.

He does return to a more uplifting message familiar from his other letters: "Where there is neither Greek nor Jew, circumcision nor uncircumcision, Barbarian, Scythian, bond nor free: but Christ is all, and in all" (Col. 3:11). That's the kind of egalitarian sentiment that helped Christianity spread.

But then comes the jarring household code, including the infamous verse: "Servants, obey in all things your masters according to the flesh; not with eyeservice, as men-pleasers; but in singleness of heart, fearing God" (Col. 3:22). In other words: Don't just work because you have to, do it as an act of religious devotion. Boo, Paul!

It's easy to see how this was weaponized by slaveholders in the American South to justify the brutal subjugation of African Americans. Modern translations soften the language, rendering part of this as "not only when their eye is on you," a phrase that echoes Gilead's creepy greeting "under His eye" in *The Handmaid's Tale*.

The letter closes with an update on Onesimus, the slave Paul had earlier urged Philemon to treat kindly. Onesimus is now evidently free and is being sent to assist the Colossians on their spiritual journey. He was freed, yeah, Paul! However, the message remains clear: slaves are property; if the master wants to free one, great. If not, slaves are to serve with full devotion to both their earthly and heavenly lords.

Ephesians

According to tradition, the Apostle Paul wrote Ephesians while imprisoned in Rome, around 62 CE. It was addressed to the Christians in Ephesus, a major city in the Roman province of Asia, modern-day Turkey. Ephesus was a wealthy and influential hub, known for its thriving commerce, rich culture, and religious diversity. It was also home to the Temple of Artemis, one of the Seven Wonders of the Ancient World.

Ephesians shares many similarities with Colossians, and it's unclear which was written first. Both were traditionally credited to Paul, yet neither seems to have actually been written by him. They read as convincing forgeries (to me, anyway), echoing Paul's tone, structure, and cadences. Both letters emphasize the universality of faith, promote ethical behavior, endorse slavery, and see no conflict in these positions.

The letter begins with a long poetic reflection on salvation, followed by the declaration: "For by grace are ye saved through faith; and that not of yourselves: it is the gift of God: Not of works, lest any man should boast" (Eph. 2:8–9). This is a foundational claim. He's saying that works—actions, including keeping the Commandments—won't save you. Your only hope is the grace of God, received as a gift. Keep in mind that Jesus said you need to keep the Commandments forever. Paul (or ghostwriter) begs to differ. The text continues, describing the "mystery" of Christ as something revealed through the prophets, accessible to Gentiles, rich in divine wisdom, and furthered by the noble sufferings of Paul himself.

Paul then offers moral exhortations: Be truthful, avoid sin, don't let the sun go down on your anger, stop stealing, be generous, avoid idolatry, don't tell dirty jokes, and don't drink too much wine. (A visit to the Comedy Club is clearly off the table.)

Chapter 4 shifts to a call for unity. Paul encourages each believer to choose a vocation that brings joy and purpose. Then comes a cryptic theological comment: "Now that he ascended what is it but that he also descended first into the lower parts of the earth?" (Eph. 4:9). Is this the source of the idea that Jesus visited Hell? Possibly. The verse might be there to suggest that if Jesus can journey to hell and back, Christians should develop spiritual resilience. Still, the original citation for this is Psalm 68:18, where it's about the Exodus, not a future Messiah.

The letter concludes with some of the most controversial material in the New Testament: "Wives, submit yourselves unto your own husbands, as unto the Lord. For the husband is the head of the wife, even as Christ is the head of the church... Therefore, as the church is subject unto Christ, so let the wives be to their own husbands in everything" (Eph. 5:22–24).

The author softens this (slightly) by adding: "Husbands, love your wives, even as Christ also loved the church, and gave himself for it" (Eph. 5:25). But the hierarchy is clear: God at the top, then men, then women, then children. This order is reinforced elsewhere. In 1 Corinthians 14:34, Paul says: "Let your women keep silence in the churches: for it is not permitted unto them to speak...they are commanded to be under obedience." And in 1 Corinthians 11:3: "The head of every man is Christ, and the head of the woman is the man, and the head of Christ is God."

Women are near the bottom rung. But slaves are lower still. They are told to "be obedient to them that are your masters according to the flesh, with fear and trembling, in singleness of your heart, as unto Christ" (Eph. 6:5), and to serve "with good will doing service, as to the Lord, and not to men" (Eph. 6:7). Maybe in the next life both master and slave will be rewarded, but here on earth, slaves are told to accept their lot and submit.

Paul finishes by urging the Ephesians to "take unto you the whole armor of God" (Eph. 6:13) to guard against evil and spiritual darkness. But you must wonder: would the author of Ephesians have willingly submitted as a slave, or would he have donned God's armor and fought back?

And for that matter, how can modern women read Paul's letters and overlook the Bible's hostility to their gender and human potential?

1 Timothy, 2 Timothy, and Titus

These three epistles—*1 Timothy, 2 Timothy, and Titus*—are often grouped together as Paul's "pastoral letters" because they're addressed not to entire congregations, but to individual church leaders. 1 and 2 Timothy were directed to a young pastor in Ephesus, and Titus to one in Crete. According to tradition, Paul wrote these letters near the end of his life, sometime between 63–67 CE. But most modern scholars agree they were penned by someone else, likely between the late first and mid-second century—meaning they may have been written up to 80 years after Paul's death.

Even a casual reader can sense the difference: the vocabulary, tone, and theological focus diverge sharply from Paul's earlier letters. The brash urgency, the anxious charisma, even Paul's ego are all dialed way down. Apparently, their authenticity was questioned even in the early church, but they were canonized anyway. Scholarly challenges resumed in earnest during the Enlightenment. As with other pseudonymous Pauline letters, many believers today remain unaware or unconcerned about who wrote them. After all, Moses didn't write Deuteronomy, but most Christians aren't losing sleep over that.

1 Timothy opens with a warning against "myths and endless genealogies" (1 Tim. 1:4)—a curious complaint, considering how much of the Old Testament consists of exactly that. Paul (I'll use the convention that he's the author) says the law exists not for the righteous but for sinners: the lawless and

disobedient, the ungodly, murderers, whoremongers, men that defile themselves with mankind (1 Tim. 1:9–10).

Paul also wastes no time laying into women in 1 Tim. 2:9–14: "Women should adorn themselves in modest apparel...not with braided hair or gold or pearls... Let the woman learn in silence with all subjection. But I suffer not a woman to teach... For Adam was first formed, then Eve. And Adam was not deceived, but the woman being deceived was in the transgression."

So much for gender equality. He then outlines the ideal traits for deacons and bishops, who should be temperate, dignified, and monogamous. Paul warns against false teachers, urges deference to elders, and gets weirdly judgmental about widows. Younger widows, he claims, "wax wanton (*get frisky*) against Christ" and remarry, thus incurring "damnation" (1 Tim. 5:11–12).

On slavery: "Let as many servants as are under the yoke count their own masters worthy of all honour, that the name of God and his doctrine be not blasphemed" (1 Tim. 6:1). So much for liberation theology. The wealthy are told to be generous and "rich in good works" (1 Tim. 6:18), a much softer standard than Jesus' "camel through the eye of a needle" line, but at least it's something.

2 Timothy begins with the exhortation to accept the gift of Christ and to trust that "the Lord give thee understanding in all things" (2 Tim. 2:7). Not exactly a hallmark Pauline zinger, but it does carry that epistolary flair. The letter continues with practical advice: "Flee also youthful lusts: but follow righteousness, faith, charity, peace..." (2 Tim. 2:22). Then it shifts to apocalyptic warning.

In the "last days," we're told: "Perilous times shall come. For men shall be lovers of their own selves, covetous, boasters, disobedient to parents, unholy, fierce, lovers of pleasures more than lovers of God" (2 Tim. 3:1–4).

Frankly, this is boilerplate doom-mongering. Has there ever been a time when that didn't describe humanity? Yet 2,000 years later, we're still waiting for the end. The traditional

Christian view envisions a cataclysm—a sudden, dramatic finale to history. But maybe it won't end with a bang. Maybe it'll be a slow fade: ecological collapse, anti-intellectualism, the death of civic virtue, a rise in cynicism and apathy. Not a fiery judgment, but a quiet extinction born of indifference

Moving on to Titus: Church leaders, as "God's stewards," must be self-controlled, hospitable, and upright. False teachers are to be silenced, for they corrupt "whole households…for filthy lucre's sake" (Titus 1:11). These people "profess that they know God; but in works they deny him, being abominable…reprobate" (Titus 1:16). Harsh words. And yet, what do you do when such people command deep loyalty within the congregation, or are devoted voters?

Titus continues with moral instructions. Old men should be dignified and sensible. Older women must love their husbands and be good examples. Slaves are once again told to honor their masters. Younger men are urged to be "sober-minded" (Titus 2:6), an easy ask, I'm sure. Paul tells Titus to urge obedience, avoid slander, and not get tangled up in "foolish questions and genealogies" (Titus 3:9). Again, the genealogies. The final command is sharp: "A man that is a heretic after the first and second admonition reject; Knowing that he that is such is subverted, and sinneth, being condemned of himself" (Titus 3:10–11).

This all sounds pious and reasonable, but we shouldn't ignore the uncomfortable fact: these letters are forgeries. Their anonymous authors assumed Paul's identity, borrowed his clout, and wrote in his name. It's a kind of ancient identity theft. Even today, many Bibles gloss over this, presenting all thirteen Pauline letters as if they came straight from the Apostle's pen. That's not just misleading, it's dishonest.

Hebrews

The *Letter to the Hebrews*, traditionally dated between 60 and 90 CE, is another example of a work once attributed to Paul but now recognized as anonymous. Scholars cite the absence of

Paul's usual greeting, differences in the original Greek, and distinct theological themes as evidence that he was not the author. These doubts were noted as early as the 3rd century by Eusebius. The King James Bible nonetheless attributes Hebrews to Paul, illustrating how, as with many biblical texts, authorship has often been misassigned.

Some argue Hebrews must have been written before 70 CE, as it makes no reference to the destruction of the Temple—an omission that would be striking in a letter so focused on Jewish ritual and priesthood.

Unlike the Pastoral Epistles, which focus on church leadership, or Paul's authentic letters, which try to unify Jews and Gentiles, Hebrews addresses Jewish Christians who may be wavering in their faith. The letter emphasizes the fulfillment of Old Testament prophecy in Christ and his superiority over past prophets and priests.

Drawing (actually, cherry-picking) from the Psalms, Hebrews 1:5–8 portrays Christ as uniquely divine: "Thou art my Son, this day have I begotten thee." Of the angels, God says, "Who maketh his angels spirits, and his ministers a flame of fire." Yet Hebrews acknowledges that the significance of Christ's exalted role is not yet fully realized. As Heb. 2:8–9 states: "For in that he put all in subjection under him, he left nothing that is not put under him. But now we see not yet all things put under him." This is a striking concession: Christ may reign in theory, but the world still suffers. Like Jesus, believers must also endure suffering, at least for now.

In Heb. 4:13, the author exhorts readers not to lose confidence: "Neither is there any creature that is not manifest in his sight: but all things are naked and opened unto the eyes of him with whom we have to do." Just as Moses led the Israelites out of Egypt and wandered for forty years, so too must Christians remain faithful during uncertainty, trusting that vindication will come.

Christ, Hebrews argues, surpasses even Melchizedek, the mysterious king-priest who appears briefly in Genesis 14:18–20. Melchizedek blesses Abram (later Abraham) after battle, and Abram gives him a tenth of the spoils. But Christ's priesthood, unlike Melchizedek's or the Levitical order, is eternal, based on "the power of an endless life" (Heb. 7:16). Jesus represents a new covenant, one that replaces the old. His blood sacrifice supersedes the rituals and animal offerings once performed in the tabernacle. Moses gave the Law, but Christ controls Heaven. Mosaic sacrifices may have temporarily addressed sin, but Christ washes it away permanently. This is a radical departure from the teachings of Jesus, who said Moses' laws were to be kept forever.

Hebrews 10:19–20 summarizes several chapters: "Having therefore, brethren, boldness to enter into the holiest by the blood of Jesus, by a new and living way, which he hath consecrated for us, through the veil, that is to say, his flesh." This reimagines the Old Testament sanctuary—with its literal veil and sacrificial blood—as a metaphor for Christ's body and crucifixion, now the sole entryway to salvation.

Let's pause. Death by crucifixion was horrific, but it wasn't rare. After the Spartacus revolt (Third Servile War, 73–71 BCE), Roman general Crassus crucified some 6,000 rebel slaves along the Appian Way as a public deterrent. Centuries earlier, after capturing Tyre in 332 BCE, Alexander the Great had 2,000 men crucified. Thousands died this way—slow, excruciating deaths, with no hope of resurrection.

Jesus endured that same punishment. But unlike others, He did so with the assurance that His suffering was temporary, His resurrection guaranteed, His heavenly throne reserved. So which sacrifice carries greater weight? A nameless slave fighting for freedom, with no promise of reward? Or Jesus, whose suffering, while real, came with foreknowledge of victory? Isn't the soldier who lays down his life for others, without divine assurance, engaged in a more profound act of selflessness?

But back to our text. After encouraging belief, it warns of the dire cost of not believing. Like Moses threatening death to the unfaithful, Hebrews offers this: "It is a fearful thing to fall into the hands of the living God" (Heb. 10:31). Keep the faith, not just for salvation, but to follow the examples of heroes past: Enoch, who "was translated that he should not see death; and was not found, because God had translated him" (Heb. 11:5); Noah, who "being warned of God of things not seen as yet, moved with fear, [and] prepared an ark to the saving of his house" (Heb. 11:7); and Abraham, who "went out, not knowing whither he went," trusting that God would lead him to the promised inheritance (Heb. 11:8). Earthly fathers discipline us for a short time; God, for eternal good. In other words, expect short-term pain for long-term gain, and don't forget: if you stop believing, God's "consuming fire" awaits, "For our God is a consuming fire" (Heb. 12:29).

The letter ends on a surprisingly tender note: "Be not forgetful to entertain strangers: for thereby some have entertained angels unawares" (Heb.13:2). The call to treat strangers with compassion runs through the Bible. For example, Leviticus 19:34 says: "The stranger that dwelleth with you shall be unto you as one born among you…for ye were strangers in the land of Egypt." God may have ordered genocides, plagues, and stonings, but here at least, He speaks with moral clarity. Kindness to the outsider, the immigrant, the unknown guest: that's a biblical command worth dusting off.

LETTERS TO ALL CHRISTIANS

The last seven epistles in the Bible are universal, in other words, addressed to Christians at large. As with Paul's letters, they are usually printed in the Bible from longest to shortest. As with some of the Pauline letters, authorship and dating are problematic. This collection reflects a transitional moment in early Christianity. Jesus didn't return as promised. Infighting emerged and outside persecution mounted. The letters are less about spreading the Gospel and more about holding the line, guarding against apostasy, outsiders, sexual freedom, and theological drift.

The first and probably best-known is *The Letter of James*. James identifies himself as a "servant of God and of the Lord Jesus Christ" (James 1:1). Although his letter is traditionally attributed to James, the brother of Jesus, he doesn't make that claim, which you'd think would have been an important detail for him to include.

James

In James 1:19, he urges everyone to be "swift to hear, slow to speak, slow to wrath." You should control your tongue, he continues, which, although a small part of the body, is one that can turn a "flame into a huge forest fire." But James' consideration of the value of "works" and "faith" makes his letter one of the most interesting and thought-provoking in the New Testament. James 2:15–17: "If a brother or sister be naked, and destitute of daily food, And one of you say unto them, Depart in peace, be ye warmed and filled; notwithstanding ye give them not those things which are needful to the body; what doth it profit? Even so, faith, if it hath not works, is dead, being alone." In other words, what good is faith if you can turn away someone hungry without helping them? James elaborates, saying that "devils also believe" (James 2:19), but that won't save them either.

You'll recall that Paul in Ephesians 2:8–9 said: "For by grace are ye saved through faith; and that not of yourselves: it is the gift of God: not of works, lest any man should boast." Paul's point was that work, in the absence of faith, is useless to enter the Kingdom of God. But if Paul attempts a layup, James is the towering center who blocks the shot and wags his finger at Paul for his futile attempt: James is saying faith is not just demonstrated through good works; faith is *synonymous* with good works.

James continues, urging that class distinctions be minimized and warning the rich of what's to come: "Your riches are corrupted, and your garments are motheaten. Your gold and silver is cankered; and the rust of them shall be a witness against you, and shall eat your flesh as it were fire" (James 5:2–3). (Fun fact: gold doesn't corrode.) James also urges patience: "Be patient therefore, brethren, unto the coming of the Lord. Behold, the husbandman waiteth for the precious fruit of the earth, and hath long patience for it, until he receive the early and latter rain" (James 5:7). In other words: don't worry your pretty little head, the world will end soon enough. This kind of frustration that the apocalypse hadn't occurred likely places the letter toward the end of the first century, when Jesus and his disciples were long gone, yet the earth stubbornly persisted.

1 and 2 Peter

1 Peter and *2 Peter* are traditionally attributed to Apostle Peter but seem to be anonymous and potentially written anywhere from 60–150 CE. 1 Peter speaks of the joy too glorious to define that belongs to believers and compares converts to newborns: "As newborn babes, desire the sincere milk of the word, that ye may grow thereby" (1 Pet. 2:2). Christians should behave with ethical restraint around unbelievers to set a good example. They should respect all, love believers, and "Fear God. Honor the king" (1 Pet. 2:17). This admonition, which is like Jesus' order to "render to Caesar the things that are Caesar's," was probably an advantageous teaching for a religious sect seeking to avoid trouble with Rome. But it can also create mischief. The German Christians who supported Hitler used Bible teachings such these to vindicate their timidity in the face of fascism.

Peter also instructs slaves to honor their masters and women to obey their husbands. Christians should forsake sins and no longer "walk in lasciviousness, lusts, excess of wine, revellings, banquetings, and abominable idolatries" (1 Pet. 4:3). Until Peter shut them down, it sounds like the early converts knew how to party!

2 Peter has a more apocalyptic feel. The Holy Spirit works through prophets; false teachers are to be avoided. God will destroy those who reject Him, just as He spared only Noah from the flood and Lot from the debauchery in Sodom and Gomorrah. The Day of Judgment will come, "But, beloved, be not ignorant of this one thing, that one day is with the Lord as a thousand years and a thousand years as one day. The Lord is not slack concerning his promise, as some men count slackness; but is longsuffering to usward, not willing that any

should perish, but that all should come to repentance" (2 Pet. 3:8–10). You'll recall that in the Synoptic Gospels, Jesus promised to return within the lifetimes of the disciples, yet that didn't happen. Don't be sad, Peter is saying; the world will meet its violent end soon enough. Jesus is just waiting for the right time to set it ablaze.

1, 2, and 3 John

We then move on to the Johannine epistles, specifically *1, 2, and 3 John*. Most scholars believe these works have the same author, but there is no consensus on who it was. They were probably written in Ephesus between 95 and 110 CE. 1 John offers instruction for walking in the light and living as God's children. Proper living means breaking with sin, keeping the commandments, detaching from the world, and guarding against the Antichrist. Living as God's children means breaking with sin, keeping the commandments, loving, and watching out for the Antichrist. I feel that there's a lot of overlap.

This is the most attention the Bible has given to the Antichrist so far. In 1 John 2:18, it seems like there are multiple Antichrists: "Little children, it is the last time: and as ye have heard that antichrist shall come, even now are there many antichrists...." 1 John 2:22 says the Antichrist will reject Christ's divinity: "Who is a liar but he that denieth that Jesus is the Christ? He is antichrist, that denieth the Father and the Son." Given that there are billions of Muslims, Hindus, Buddhists, and atheists, this doesn't narrow the field as much as John might have thought. 1 John 4:3 implies that the Antichrist is an ongoing presence: "And every spirit that confesseth not that Jesus Christ is come in the flesh is not of God: and this is that spirit of antichrist, whereof ye have heard that it should come; and even now already is it in the world." This description of how the Antichrist can be identified seems unhelpfully vague.

2 John 7 also addresses the Antichrist: "For many deceivers are entered into the world, who confess not that Jesus Christ is come in the flesh. This is a deceiver and an antichrist." Again, the Antichrist is linked to deception and denial of Christ's incarnation. 2 John also revisits the power of love: "And now I beseech thee, lady, not as though I wrote a new commandment unto thee, but that which we had from the beginning, that we love one another" (2 John 5).

It's hard to get excited by 3 John. The writer seems to be communicating with a congregate who's not getting along well with someone named Diotrephes. He then says it's best if they just talk in person.

Jude

The final "catholic" letter is *The Letter of Jude*, whose author identifies himself as the brother of James—in other words, Jesus' brother (I think). Unsurprisingly, most scholars believe the letter was written by someone else, likely as late as the early second century. Its purpose seems to be to encourage believers to stay strong in the face of difficult times. False teachers will ultimately be destroyed, just as Sodom was. Christians should be on the lookout for "murmurers, complainers, walking after their own lusts; and their mouth speaketh great swelling words, having men's persons in admiration because of advantage" (Jude 16). In short: keep your eyes on the prize and love God.

REVELATION

Revelation 1-11

Whether watching Hollywood movies like *The Omen*, or reading a book like Stephen King's *The Stand*, you don't have to look hard to see how *The Revelation to John* continues to grip the popular imagination. The book, the final one in the New Testament, is traditionally attributed to John the Apostle, who is also sometimes credited with writing The Gospel of John and the Catholic Epistles (1, 2, and 3 John). However, most scholars doubt that a single person authored all these works, suggesting instead that multiple hands were involved.

Revelation was likely written around 94–96 CE, at the end Emperor Domitian's reign. Its themes—an apocalyptic battle between good and evil, divine judgment, and the promise of a new heaven and earth—can't be separated from the context of Roman oppression and Christian persecution. This is a vision of the long-overdue return of the Son of Man, with fire, fury, and payback. Though Revelation's inclusion in the New

Testament was controversial, it eventually made the cut, except in the Eastern Orthodox canon. Its psychedelic imagery and apocalyptic tone evoke the Old Testament books Ezekiel, Daniel, and Zechariah. It's easy to see why early Christians were divided on whether this fever dream belonged alongside the Sermon on the Mount.

The book opens with John announcing his purpose: "The Revelation of Jesus Christ, which God gave unto him, to shew unto his servants things which must shortly come to pass... who bare record of the word of God, and of the testimony of Jesus Christ, and of all things that he saw" (Rev. 1:1–2). In other words, God gave a vision to Jesus, who passed it to an angel, who passed it to John, who passed it to us. And the big reveal? It's all going to happen "very soon," a promise echoed in the Gospels regarding the return of the Son of Man.

After identifying his location as the island of Patmos (off the coast of modern-day Turkey), John launches into a vivid description of his vision: "I heard behind me a great voice, as of a trumpet... And being turned, I saw seven golden candlesticks; And in the midst...one like unto the Son of man... His head and his hairs were white like wool...and his eyes were as a flame of fire" (Rev. 1:10–14). This imagery borrows heavily from earlier prophetic texts. The golden lampstands recall Zechariah 4:2, and the golden sash (girdle) appears in Daniel 10:5. Nearly every detail in Revelation has some antecedent in the Hebrew Bible, particularly in the prophetic and apocalyptic genres.

Chapters 2 and 3 contain messages to seven churches:

- **Ephesus** – Cannot stand wicked people and "loathes" the Nicolaitans.
- **Smyrna** – "Even if you have to die, stay faithful."
- **Pergamum** – Must repent for eating food sacrificed to idols.
- **Thyatira** – Stop tolerating Jezebels and adulterers.
- **Sardis** – "Wake up...I will come like a thief."

- **Philadelphia** – Promised protection in a time of trial.
- **Laodicea** – Neither hot nor cold; "I will spit you out."

Sardis's "thief" warning echoes Jesus in Matthew 24:43: "If the goodman of the house had known in what watch the thief would come, he would have watched..." Then come the throne room visions, reminiscent of Ezekiel's acid-trip-style prophecy.

In Rev. 4:6–8, John sees: "A sea of glass like unto crystal... four beasts full of eyes... The first was like a lion, the second like a calf, the third had a face like a man, and the fourth was like a flying eagle." These creatures chant (or screech): "Holy, Holy, Holy, Lord God Almighty, which was, and is, and is to come."

Next, a scroll sealed with seven seals appears in the hand of the one on the throne. An angel cries out for someone worthy to open it. Enter: the lamb, with seven horns and seven eyes. The lamb takes the scroll, and all heaven breaks into song.

As the lamb opens the seals, we meet the famous Four Horsemen of the Apocalypse (Rev. 6:1–8):

- **White Horse** – Conquest or false peace: "He went forth conquering."
- **Red Horse** – War: "Power was given...to take peace from the earth."
- **Black Horse** – Economic hardship: "A pair of balances... Hurt not the oil and wine."
- **Pale Horse** – Death: "His name...was Death, and Hell followed with him."

The fifth seal reveals Christian martyrs asking, how much longer until revenge? The sixth seal unleashes cosmic chaos: "A great earthquake...the sun became black...the moon became as blood...the stars fell..." (Rev. 6:12–13).

John then sees four angels at the earth's four corners and 144,000 people; 12,000 from each of the twelve tribes of Israel.

Jehovah's Witnesses later ran with this number, interpreting it as the select group who will reign with Christ in heaven.

When the seventh seal breaks, there is a dramatic pause: "There was silence in heaven about the space of half an hour" (Rev. 8:1). Then come the seven trumpets (Rev. 8–11):

- **First Trumpet** – Hail and fire mixed with blood scorch a third of the earth.
- **Second Trumpet** – A fiery mountain turns a third of the sea to blood.
- **Third Trumpet** – A star named Wormwood poisons a third of the rivers.
- **Fourth Trumpet** – A third of the sun, moon, and stars go dark.
- **Fifth Trumpet** – Locusts from the abyss torture people for five months. Only those without "God's seal" on their foreheads are vulnerable.
- **Sixth Trumpet** – Four angels unleash a massive army that kills a third of humanity. Still, people refuse to repent.
- **Seventh Trumpet** – God's kingdom is declared. The ark appears. Thunder, lightning, earthquakes, and hail follow (Rev. 11:19).

Throughout Revelation, the number seven appears constantly: seven churches, seven seals, seven trumpets, seven eyes. The number symbolizes divine perfection or completeness, a signal that something supernatural is unfolding. Think of it like the color red in *The Sixth Sense*, a visual cue that the spiritual world is bleeding into ours.

Revelation 12-22

We begin Chapter 12 with John's vivid imagery of Archangel Michael battling the dragon, a scene that seems like a precursor to the later Christian legend of St. George slaying the dragon. John describes a woman giving birth to "a man child, who was to rule all nations with a rod of iron" (Rev. 12:5). The devil appears as a red dragon—"that old serpent, called the Devil, and Satan"—with seven heads and ten horns, poised to devour the child. But instead, the baby is whisked away to heaven, and the woman flees into the wilderness.

The dragon ascends to heaven, fights Michael, and is cast back down to earth in defeat. He then pursues the woman, but when he spews water to drown her, the earth miraculously swallows it up. Despite the popular image of Michael slaying the dragon, he doesn't. The dragon is merely banished to earth, where he wages war "on the remnant of her seed."

Next comes a new vision: a beast rises from the sea, with seven heads, ten horns, and features of a leopard, bear, and lion (Rev. 13:2). It serves the dragon, who gives it power and authority. People worship both the beast and the dragon, and the beast is "given a mouth speaking great things and blasphemies," allowed to rule for forty-two months. The number 42 recurs in the Bible: in Matthew 1:17, there are 42 generations from Abraham to Jesus; in 2 Kings 2:23–24, the prophet Elisha summons bears to kill 42 children who mocked his baldness. Is "42" just biblical shorthand for "a bunch?"

Then comes a second beast. It animates statues and brands people with the number 666—on the right hand or forehead. Interestingly, some early manuscripts give the number as 616, but let's be honest: 666 is way punchier. The link between Nero and 666 comes from gematria, a Jewish numerological system assigning numeric values to letters. Many scholars believe Revelation encoded Nero's name as 666: in Hebrew, Neron Kesar (נרון קסר) translates to Nero Caesar (emperor 54 to 68 CE). The numerical value? 666. The alternate 616 reflects a different spelling: Nero Kesar. This interpretation, casting the Beast as Nero, is widely accepted among scholars, though not universally.

The Lamb then appears before the 144,000 now marked with his name on their foreheads. Three angels show up, and the last one announces, "Babylon is fallen, is fallen, that great city" (Rev. 14:8). He's likely not referring to the literal Babylon of the Parthian empire, already a shadow of its former self by 100 CE. More likely, it's a reference to Rome. Angels then begin harvesting humanity like grapes for God's winepress, a metaphor for mass slaughter. What follows is a series of seven plagues:

- **Painful sores** – Afflict those who worship the Beast (Rev. 16:2).
- **Sea turns to blood** – All marine life dies (Rev. 16:3).
- **Rivers and springs turn to blood** – Freshwater is contaminated (Rev. 16:4).
- **Scorching heat** – The sun burns people with fire (Rev. 16:8).
- **Darkness and agony** – The Beast's kingdom is plunged into darkness (Rev. 16:10).
- **Euphrates dries up** – Clearing the way for the Battle of Armageddon (Rev. 16:12).
- **Global earthquake and hailstorm** – The biggest quake in history, followed by 100-pound hailstones (Rev. 16:18–21).

Then one of the angels introduces John to the Whore of Babylon, "arrayed in purple and scarlet" and holding a golden cup. On her forehead is written: "MYSTERY, BABYLON THE GREAT, THE MOTHER OF HARLOTS AND ABOMINATIONS OF THE EARTH" (Rev. 17:5). Either she had an enormous forehead, or the font was tiny.

John explains that the "seven heads are seven hills," an unmistakable reference to Rome's seven hills. He says the woman is "that great city, which reigneth over the kings of the earth" (Rev. 17:18). Again, Rome.

Babylon falls. The faithful are told to flee. Then comes the Battle of Armageddon. A white horse arrives with a Rider whose eyes are like flame, and whose robe is emblazoned with "KING OF KINGS, AND LORD OF LORDS" (Rev. 19:16). An angel "standing in the sun" rallies the heavenly army. On the other side: the Beast and the "false prophet," who had worked signs and wonders. The Rider throws them into a lake of fire, then slaughters their army. An angel chains the dragon, imprisoning him for a thousand years. The souls of the martyrs are resurrected and reign with Christ.

But after the millennium, the Devil is released again. The armies of Gog and Magog (in Ezekiel, Gog is "of the land of Magog," possibly a reference to nomadic tribes from central Asia) are defeated, and Satan is finally thrown into the lake of fire alongside the Beast and the false prophet, where they'll be tormented forever. Next comes the Last Judgment. The dead are raised, and books are opened. Some names are in the Book of Life. Others are tossed into the lake of fire.

Then a new heaven and a new earth appear, and a new Jerusalem descends from heaven. God dwells among the people: "And God shall wipe away all tears from their eyes; and there shall be no more death, neither sorrow, nor crying, neither shall there be any more pain" (Rev. 21:4). This is the verse the minister quotes in *Titanic* as the ship sinks. Note the similarities with Isaiah's vision of a new heaven and new earth. But in Isaiah, people live long (hundred-year) lives, but still die, while in Revelation, they live forever. That's a substantial moving of the eternal goalposts.

The new Jerusalem has a river of life flowing through it, and it is home to God and the Lamb: "...and his servants shall serve him: And they shall see his face, and his name shall be in their foreheads. And there shall be no night there...for the Lord God giveth them light: and they shall reign forever and ever" (Rev. 22:3–5). To summarize: the faithful will die, wait a thousand years, return for Armageddon, get branded on their foreheads, and spend eternity worshiping Christ without ever sleeping.

So ends the Book of Revelation, and the Bible. In Genesis, we were told how it all began: God created heaven and earth, then destroyed it in a flood, then repopulated the planet through Noah. In Revelation, it ends again, this time permanently. God vanquishes the devil, wipes out unbelievers, and builds a final kingdom in the new Jerusalem.

For Revelation to come true, God must deliver on His promise of a sudden, violent upheaval of the world order. Early Christians expected this apocalypse within their lifetime. After all, the Gospels say it would happen before the disciples died. So why was this vision of mass extinction so appealing? Shouldn't good people want a better, more just world for their children, not a scorched-earth reset?

Maybe the harsh realities of first-century Palestine made the fantasy of paradise more tempting. A place with no pain, no death, no mourning—that's a powerful dream if the present feels unbearable.

Fortunately, the prophecy remains unfulfilled. But, as 2 Peter 3:8 reminds us, "One day is with the Lord as a thousand years, and a thousand years as one day." Maybe there's still time. In the meantime, the faithful will wait for an eternity in which they are branded, and never sleep, never love or lose, never have children, never create or discover, and never fall short. They will be eternally obedient, eternally passive. If that's the fate of the virtuous, maybe the lake of sulfur isn't so bad after all.

FINAL THOUGHTS: NEW TESTAMENT

Nature of God

In the Old Testament, God is a tribal warrior-deity, fierce, jealous, and ready to strike down Israel's enemies, but also the Israelites for even petty acts of disobedience. He orders genocide, condones slavery, and dispenses punishment with chilling efficiency. Richard Dawkins famously called this figure "arguably the most unpleasant character in all fiction."

In the New Testament, Jesus appears to represent a dramatic shift. He teaches love, mercy, and compassion. The Sermon on the Mount is perhaps the Bible's most stirring ethical statement. Jesus heals the sick, feeds the hungry, and speaks kindly to society's outcasts. Unlike the sweeping, violent miracles of the Old Testament, Jesus' miracles are intimate actions meant to alleviate human suffering.

Yet the theological break isn't as clear as it seems. Jesus is portrayed not just as a divine messenger but as God Himself in human form. In John 8:58, Jesus says, "Before Abraham was, I am," an unmistakable reference to God's self-identification in Exodus 3:14. And in John 14:9, he states, "Whoever has seen me has seen the Father."

If Jesus is God, then the compassionate healer is also the vengeful destroyer. Can these two portraits be reconciled, or are they fundamentally at odds? The Gospels themselves aren't consistent: in the Synoptics, Jesus and his disciples often seem uncertain about his nature and mission, while in John he speaks with a surer sense of identity and purpose.

Good and Evil

The ethical core of the New Testament is found in Jesus' teachings, especially in the Sermon on the Mount. These teachings emphasize humility, compassion, and reciprocity. They are profoundly appealing, regardless of one's belief in miracles or divinity. When asked what the greatest commandment is (Mark 12:29–31), Jesus replies: Love God and love your neighbor. Notably, he doesn't cite the Ten Commandments.

Yet in Matthew 5:17, Jesus insists he has not come to abolish the Law but to fulfill it. This indicates that the Law's 600+ commandments still apply. If Jesus had wanted to abolish the Law, you would think he'd have said so. Paul, however, is far more revisionary. In Romans 6:14 and Galatians 3:24–25, he declares believers are no longer under the Law but under grace. According to Paul, the Law was a temporary measure, now obsolete. This divergence is stark: Jesus upholds the Law; Paul sets it aside. In Christian history, Paul's view largely prevailed, even when it contradicted Jesus.

The Afterlife

The Old Testament's view of the afterlife is hazy at best. The New Testament offers something more vivid. Jesus speaks of eternal life for believers (John 11:25) and eternal punishment for others (Matthew 25:46). In the parable of the sheep and goats, he describes a final judgment based on acts of compassion.

Paul expands this vision in 1 Corinthians 15, where he describes a bodily resurrection: "the dead will be raised imperishable." Revelation concludes with a dramatic scene of cosmic renewal (Revelation 21:4): "God will wipe away every tear...and death shall be no more."

But even here, the vision is muddled. In the Synoptic Gospels, Jesus suggests people become like angels in heaven, offering few concrete details. Hell, however, is vividly described as a lake of fire for non-believers.

The concept of Hell became the playground for centuries of Christian imagination, spawning ever more elaborate visions of torment for those deemed unworthy. As Mark Twain quipped, we might prefer "Heaven for the climate, Hell for the company."

As Literature

The New Testament contains moments of genuine literary beauty. Paul's "Love Chapter" (1 Corinthians 13) transcends religious boundaries: "Love is patient, love is kind..."

Revelation, while theologically intense, is also a symbolic masterpiece, a wild, apocalyptic vision filled with beasts, seals, bowls of wrath, and a final vision of a new Jerusalem. It reads like political resistance literature; a coded critique of Roman power wrapped in prophetic language.

As Prophecy

Prophecy in the New Testament falls flat. Jesus repeatedly promises the imminent arrival of the Son of Man: "Some standing here...shall not taste of death, till they see the Son of man coming in his kingdom" (Matthew 16:28).

Claims that Jesus fulfilled Old Testament prophecy are often remarkably tenuous. For example, Matthew says Jesus was born in Nazareth to fulfill a prophecy that doesn't exist. He also depicts Jesus entering Jerusalem on two animals, matching a poetic line from Zechariah that referred to a conquering king, not a metaphysical spiritual ruler.

Translation issues exacerbate the confusion. Isaiah 7:14, often cited as predicting the virgin birth, actually uses a word meaning "young woman." Modern translations have corrected this misconception, but the popular myth remains.

Final Reflections

The New Testament offers flashes of brilliance. The Sermon on the Mount and Paul's ode to love are among the most morally resonant texts in the Bible, really in all of literature. But the Gospels contradict each other about Jesus' birth, death, and resurrection. Matthew and Luke offer wildly different nativity stories. The resurrection accounts vary on who visited the tomb, what they saw, and what happened next.

Mark, the earliest Gospel, is the most raw and least adorned with the later theological flourishes found in the others. It omits the virgin birth and, in its original form, ends without a resurrection appearance. Mark shows us a Jesus who acts with urgency, has the power to heal, and often seems unsure of how events will unfold. It also contains peculiar moments other Gospels omit, such as a young naked man fleeing Jesus' arrest. The writers of Matthew and Luke had access to Mark when they wrote their Gospels, yet looked at that detail and said, "no, thanks."

Jesus' following, like many prophetic movements, could have collapsed after his crucifixion. But Paul ensured its survival and expansion. He reinterpreted Jesus' life, shaped Christian doctrine, and opened the faith to non-Jews. By prioritizing belief over good deeds, Paul made conversion easier and more scalable.

Many Christians today, whether they realize it or not, follow Paul more closely than Jesus. His statements on women, the law, and salvation defined Christian orthodoxy, while Jesus' harder teachings, like his rejection of wealth, and his demand for radical love are routinely ignored.

And Jesus himself remains an enigma. Was he a moral teacher, miracle worker, divine incarnation, fraud, or simply a charismatic end-times preacher with delusions of grandeur? What's certain is that he repeatedly foretold the arrival of God's kingdom within the lifetime of his followers. This was no poetic metaphor, it was the beating heart of early Christian hope and expectation. Jesus promised the world would end and it didn't. This wasn't a minor slip; it was a prophetic failure of biblical proportion. If the Gospels are so wrong about their most urgent prediction, it's fair to question everything else they claim about Jesus' nature and actions.

James E. Clark

TIME TO PUT AWAY
CHILDISH THINGS

Religion can offer a profound sense of belonging and purpose for many believers. In the small rural community in southern Indiana where I grew up, people were generally God-fearing, moral, and kind. You could leave your front door unlocked. The politics leaned conservative, but voters often chose Democrats grounded in local values. Churches emphasized Jesus' teachings on charity and humility. If you weren't gay, nonwhite, or otherwise marginalized, it could feel idyllic. That kind of faith—humble, open-hearted, and grounded in ethical conduct—has vanished or is at least vanishing.

In 2024, that same community embraced Donald Trump, a con artist, adulterer, and convicted felon with little understanding of or reverence for Christianity. Nationally, Trump received the votes of some 81% of white evangelicals and 60% of Catholics. While not all of them endorsed every policy, many nonetheless aligned themselves with a figure openly hostile to the ethical teachings at the heart of their religion. Right-wing religious politicians are ascendant in

Congress, the Supreme Court, and most state governments. Laws are rapidly being passed to disenfranchise minorities, trash the environment, limit women's rights, enrich corporations, and downsize or eliminate programs that quite literally feed the hungry and clothe the poor.

Had only atheists voted in 2024, perhaps we would be spared the ongoing erosion of constitutional norms, global leadership, and moral accountability. Combating the rise of Christian nationalism requires a two-pronged approach: top-down and bottom-up. We should advocate for policies and leaders who will uphold constitutional principles and secular governance. But just as importantly, we must work on an interpersonal level, engaging with friends, neighbors, and family members to encourage honest reflection on their beliefs. We should not expect instant renunciations; instead, we can plant seeds of doubt through thoughtful conversation, shared inquiry, and consistent example.

One of the most potent ways to do this is simply to live good, ethical, joyful lives without relying on religion. Demonstrating compassion, purpose, and moral clarity does not depend on belief in a deity; living ethically without faith helps dismantle the false binary between faith and virtue. As Jefferson said, if your belief doesn't pick my pocket or break my leg, believe what you will. But the burden of proof shifts when that belief shapes policy and undermines our shared reality. And in those cases, clear thinking and consistent compassion may be our strongest tools.

Far too often, when believers encounter contradictions, cruelty, or absurdities in the Bible, they don't wrestle with the implications, they turn to apologists. Christian apologists, often scholars or clergy, defend the truth and coherence of biblical teachings using philosophical, historical, and theological arguments. Some are sincere, but many engage less in honest inquiry than in intellectual gymnastics. They begin with the assumption that the Bible must be correct and then twist logic or cherry-pick evidence to make it appear consistent—even when the results defy plain reading, ethics,

301

or historical accuracy. Some contort meanings beyond recognition. Others invent elaborate interpretive frameworks with little connection to the text itself. Whether it's rationalizing God's command for genocide in the Old Testament or explaining away the contradictions in the resurrection accounts, the end goal is less about truth than about preserving belief at any cost.

This is why skeptics need to be especially vigilant. When apologists come armed with confident assertions and intricate theology, it can be disorienting unless you've read the text yourself and are prepared to push back. That doesn't mean engaging in hostile debate, but it does mean refusing to cede ground to those who fail to see the text for what it plainly says.

Some faulty reasoning you might encounter includes:

The Texas Sharpshooter Fallacy

This fallacy occurs when someone clusters together select data points after the fact to support a desired conclusion—like a marksman firing randomly at the side of a barn, then drawing a bullseye around the tightest cluster of bullet holes and claiming perfect accuracy. Apologists employ this technique by highlighting a handful of Old Testament verses that appear to "predict" Jesus' life, while overlooking the hundreds of verses that either contradict that narrative or are clearly unrelated. Rebuttal: The New Testament authors were not impartial observers; they were theological storytellers on a mission. Many "fulfilled" prophecies are pulled wildly out of context, mistranslated, or retrofitted through creative interpretation.

For example, Matthew 2:15 claims Jesus' flight to Egypt fulfills Hosea 11:1, which, in its original context, refers to Israel's exodus, not a future messiah. The key problem here isn't that connections are being made, it's that the "bullseye" is being drawn around the desired outcome, rather than predictions being objectively and consistently validated. In any other field, this would be considered dishonest or disqualifying. In theology, it's too often just referred to as faith.

Special Pleading

When God's actions in the Bible appear morally indefensible, such as endorsing slavery or commanding genocide, apologists often claim that divine morality is simply beyond human comprehension. "God's ways are not our ways," they say, suggesting that we shouldn't hold Him to the same ethical standards we use for anyone else. Rebuttal: If that's the case, then invoking those very same standards to define God as just, loving, or merciful becomes incoherent. You can't appeal to human notions of goodness to defend a being who, by that logic, exists outside them.

Moreover, the visceral discomfort people feel when reading about these acts—slaves being beaten, innocent children killed for their parents' sins—isn't proof of scriptural moral complexity. It's evidence of an evolved human conscience. We recoil not because the Bible taught us justice, but because evolution has wired us for empathy, reciprocity, and fairness.

Strawman Arguments

A common apologist tactic is to paint atheists as morally rudderless, incapable of distinguishing right from wrong without divine commandments. This caricature suggests that without a fear of God, people are prone to nihilism or selfishness. Rebuttal: This is a classic strawman—misrepresenting secular morality to tear it down. In reality, secular ethics are grounded in empathy, reciprocity, and the well-being of others, not threats of punishment or promises of reward.

Consider the concept of the "Golden Rule"—treat others as you'd like to be treated. This principle predates Christianity and appears in nearly every culture and philosophy, from Confucianism to ancient Greek thought to modern humanism. You don't need the Ten Commandments to recognize that lying, stealing, and murder are destructive. These norms evolved because societies that upheld them tended to flourish.

303

Secular people volunteer, give to charity, and care for loved ones not because they fear eternal damnation but because they value life and relationships in the here and now. Research consistently shows that more secular societies, both U.S. states and entire countries, tend to outperform more religious ones on core quality-of-life metrics. Countries like Sweden, the Netherlands, and Norway, with low levels of religiosity, rank near the top in health care, education, gender equity, and overall happiness. Within the United States, the most religious states, such as Mississippi, Alabama, and Louisiana, struggle with higher levels of gun violence, poverty, teen pregnancy, and poor educational outcomes. Conversely, more secular states such as Vermont and Massachusetts fare significantly better.

Philosophical Arguments

These take many forms, including the suggestion that the universe could not exist without a prime mover, that without a "watchmaker" there could be no watch (universe). If a creator was necessary, would that creator also have needed to be created? A watch has a designer, but that doesn't mean a human, full of genetic coding errors also has one: Our bodies seem to be cobbled together rather than miraculously designed. We need to be comfortable with the fact that we don't know exactly how the universe came into being, although it seems like it was simply always present. We don't need "god" to fill in blanks currently unanswered by science.

Appeal to Authority

Apologists will often support a theological or moral argument by citing respected religious figures: *This pastor says...*or *This theologian argues...* The implication is that because someone with clerical status or scholarly credentials made the claim, it must be valid. Rebuttal: Truth isn't determined by titles or robes, but by evidence and reasoning. Expertise can offer insight, but it doesn't exempt an argument from scrutiny.

This fallacy becomes especially dangerous when it shuts down critical inquiry. For example, citing C.S. Lewis to "prove" the divinity of Jesus doesn't settle the matter, it just restates a conclusion with rhetorical flourish. Similarly, quoting William Lane Craig's complex theological defenses doesn't absolve them from rigorous analysis, especially when the logic depends on unverifiable premises. Even quoting the Pope to defend moral views doesn't work unless those views can stand on their own merits.

In every other discipline—medicine, science, law—claims must withstand peer review, experimentation, and logic, regardless of who makes them. A surgeon's opinion on vaccines must be backed by studies, not just status. Likewise, theologians' views on divine justice must be evaluated not by the depth of their faith, but by the strength of their argument.

Equivocation

This fallacy occurs when a word is used with multiple meanings within the same argument, creating the illusion of logic where none exists. In theological debates, terms like "love," "justice," or "goodness" are frequently redefined to excuse actions that would otherwise be considered immoral. Rebuttal: If "love" includes eternal damnation, and "justice" encompasses punishing innocent people or commanding genocide, then those words no longer reflect their commonly understood meanings.

When divine virtues are contorted to justify brutality, they give rise to selective morality. Where certain teachings are sanitized or dismissed, others are enforced with inflexible zeal. Nowhere is this more evident than in how certain biblical passages are treated: not with honest reckoning, but with evasive maneuvering. Christians, like Coach Patches O'Houlihan's misfit team in the movie *Dodgeball: A True Underdog Story*, tend to "**dodge, duck, dip, dive, and dodge**" when confronted

305

with Bible verses they wish to explain away or ignore. Some examples:

- **Slavery:** Exodus 21 lays out rules for owning and disciplining slaves. The New Testament tells slaves to obey their masters with "fear and trembling" (Ephesians 6:5). Far from condemning slavery, Scripture institutionalizes it.

- **Genocide:** In Numbers 21:2–3, the Israelites "utterly destroyed" the Canaanite cities and their inhabitants. In Joshua 6:17-21, during the conquest of Jericho, Joshua carries out the command: "They devoted the city to the Lord and destroyed with the sword every living thing in it, men and women, young and old, cattle, sheep and donkeys." The same god that commands not to kill endorses war crimes.

- **War brides:** In Numbers 31:17–18 God tells Moses how to deal with Midianite prisoners: "Now therefore kill every male among the little ones, and kill every woman that hath known man by lying with him. But all the women children, that have not known a man by lying with him, keep alive for yourselves." Let's not mince words, God is telling Moses to take these virgin girls to be war brides. God could have told Moses to protect the girls, to treat them as their daughters, but instead, he orders his army to commit rape.

- **Divine justice:** God frequently punishes children for their parents' sins. In 2 Samuel 12:14, David's infant son dies for David's transgressions. In Exodus 20:5, God explicitly threatens future generations.

- **Abortion:** The only apparent biblical reference is in Numbers 5, describing a ritual that induces miscarriage in a suspected adulteress—hardly a condemnation. If Jesus had felt strongly about the subject, why didn't he mention it?

- **Homosexuality:** Condemned in Leviticus, never mentioned by Jesus. Also, the hints of David's bisexuality are hard to miss.

- **Divorce:** The Bible is clear that divorce is not sanctioned, and adultery is a grave offense. Leviticus 20:10 states: "If a man commits adultery with the wife of his neighbor, both the adulterer and the adulteress shall surely be put to death." In Matthew 19:3–9, Jesus allows divorce only in cases of sexual immorality and says remarriage after divorce (except in such cases) constitutes adultery. When a modern politician says they want to implement Biblical laws, do they realize what they are signing up for?

- **Migrants:** God commands people to welcome migrants (Matthew 25:35), and Moses repeatedly advocated for strangers, as he had found himself a "stranger in a strange land." Christians are free to denigrate foreigners, but they should not use the Bible to justify their xenophobia.

- **Wealth:** Jesus commanded the wealthy give away their possessions (Luke 18:22) and warned that riches make salvation nearly impossible. This instruction is almost universally ignored by Christianity, particularly by "prosperity gospel" ministers who obscenely flaunt the money they have extracted from the wallets of their often-struggling parishioners.

Individual conversations and intellectual integrity matter, but they aren't enough on their own. To counteract the broader weaponization of faith and the rise of religiously tinted authoritarianism, we must also pursue coordinated political action. This means advocating for structural changes that uphold the separation of church and state while protecting civil rights for everyone, regardless of belief. For example, we should:

- **Evaluate the tax-exempt status for certain churches:** Many religious organizations today function more like businesses than places of worship. They own large real estate holdings, run media networks, and earn big profits, yet still enjoy tax breaks meant for charities. It's time to reconsider tax exemptions for groups that pay clergy millions or operate more like lifestyle brands than nonprofits.

- **End public funding of religious schools:** Public dollars should only be used to support inclusive, science-based education, not private institutions that can legally discriminate, teach dogma, or reject evidence-based learning.

- **Protect LGBTQ+ and reproductive rights federally:** Religious belief is routinely used to justify stripping others of bodily autonomy, identity, and dignity. We need robust national protections to safeguard access to abortion, contraception, gender-affirming care, and marriage equality.

- **Ban government-sponsored prayer:** No public schoolchild or citizen should feel religiously pressured by a government-sanctioned display of piety. Even Jesus warned against performative devotion, saying, "When you pray, do not be like the hypocrites, for they love to pray standing in the synagogues and on the street corners to be seen by others" (Matthew 6:5). True belief needs no spotlight, and the government has no business staging it.

- **Electing qualified political candidates:** We should elect atheists or skeptics to office, both local and national, assuming they are qualified by the Constitution, and we believe they would be capable leaders. Except for President Trump, practically all our presidents in the last 100 years have been Christians, so let's give the secular opposition a chance. It's not impossible for a religious person to be a competent leader, it's just that the temptation to force their mysticism on others can become impossible to suppress. Where are the Thomas Jeffersons of the modern era—imperfect but secular characters who are well-read, accomplished, deeply invested in the American experiment, and cut-throat?

- **Encourage the critical study of religious texts, including the Bible, in public education:** When the Bible is taught as literature or history, not dogma, students gain analytical skills and cultural literacy. They learn how narratives shape civilizations and how to discern myth.

These policies aren't assaults on religion. They're protections against theocratic power. As Isaac Asimov put it, "Properly read, the Bible is the most potent force for atheism ever conceived." When belief is weaponized, when scripture is elevated above law or logic, the antidote is not silence, it's clarity, courage, and action.

If the Bible is truly the product of a perfect, omniscient God, one must ask: *Why does it get so many things wrong?* From its cosmology to its ethics, it reflects a limited and deeply human understanding of the world. It claims Earth existed before stars, that serpents could talk, that diseases came from demons, and a dome covered the earth. These beliefs are not divine; they're Bronze Age guesses, and bad ones at that. A perfect revelation would not contain translation errors, scientific falsehoods, or cultural prejudices of its time. It would astonish us with its prescience. We wouldn't be locked in centuries of debate over its meaning; it would be crystal clear.

This gap between what we'd expect from a divine text and what we find becomes even more glaring when we turn to ancient prophecies and miracles. In Scripture, prophets name kings, foretell wars, and summon plagues. Yet in today's world, the prophetic voice has fallen silent. If divine communication were real, wouldn't it persist? Wouldn't it evolve to speak in our language of evidence, data, and logic?

The same critical lens applies to miracles, especially Christianity's most pivotal one: the resurrection. Paul, in 1 Corinthians 15:19, puts it bluntly: "If in Christ we have hope in this life only, we are of all people most to be pitied." It's a stunning concession. Paul stakes everything on a single, unverifiable, biologically impossible event. This is why the resurrection isn't merely a detail in Christian theology; it's the beam holding the whole roof up.

But even on its own terms, it's shaky. The ancient world was saturated with resurrection myths. Osiris, Dionysus, Mithras were all worshipped for their triumphant return from death. None are historically credible, and the popularity of those legends does nothing to affirm their truth. So, should we believe all resurrection stories? Some of them? Just one? And on what basis: popularity, or the accident of which empire embraced which myth?

Then there's the issue of the failed apocalypse. The Gospels claim Jesus said the "Son of Man" would return before his disciples had died. If the end of days was truly at hand, what was the resurrection for? Wouldn't it be overshadowed by the looming finale? Yet here we are, two thousand years later, staring at a quiet sky while preachers still promise the storm is coming.

Paul was probably right about the resurrection's importance to early believers. But it's unfortunate that he anchored his faith in a supernatural spectacle rather than Jesus' radical vision of compassion, forgiveness, and social justice. Must moral truth be validated by metaphysical fireworks? Were his teachings not compelling enough on their own?

In truth, most believers don't lose faith in one dramatic moment of clarity. Doubt creeps in gradually. Often it begins with a contradiction too large to ignore: a verse that offends morality, a teaching that contradicts experience, a question answered with silence, or the quiet example of someone living a deeply ethical life outside religion. These are the cracks where doubt can make room for a different kind of thinking.

The skeptic's role is not to rip belief from anyone. It's to offer alternatives: clarity instead of fear, accountability instead of blind obedience, inquiry instead of shame. And if someone finds strength, peace, or purpose in their faith—and it harms no one and imposes on no one's rights—then let it be. To be clear, this book does not deny that Christianity has produced good works. Many of Jesus' ethical teachings resonate deeply today. Paul's ode to love in 1 Corinthians is transcendent. And millions of Christians act with selflessness and grace, feeding the hungry, sheltering the vulnerable, and standing with the oppressed.

But those truths coexist with deeper complications. Much of what Jesus is quoted as saying was shaped—or selectively preserved—by followers writing long after his death. Paul, while eloquent at times, also told women to be silent in church and slaves to obey their masters. And many Christians today who act with kindness and courage would surely do so without divine incentive. Faith can also corrupt the actions of otherwise ethical people. As physicist Steven Weinberg noted, "With or without religion, good people can behave well and bad people can do evil—but for good people to do evil, that takes religion."

We shouldn't flinch from acknowledging the Bible's brutality, tribalism, defense of inequality, and sanctification of violence. Yet we can also appreciate its beauty where it appears. The danger is in mistaking it for something it's not: a flawless guide to human morality. The more we tether ethics to inflexible ancient texts, the more we hinder our growth. Using Scripture to govern a modern society is like a surgeon consulting scrolls during open-heart surgery. Unlike the Constitution, which, at least in theory, we can amend to reflect progress, the Bible is frozen in time. It cannot evolve with our expanding understanding of justice, science, or human dignity.

So, here's a final thought experiment: *What if the Bible had never existed?* Yes, we might have lost soaring cathedrals, timeless hymns, and acts of charity done in faith's name. But we might also have avoided the Crusades, the Inquisition, centuries of misogyny, scripture-sanctioned slavery, and the long war against intellectual freedom. Galileo might have been left to gaze at the stars in peace. Darwin might have published without hesitation. The fortunes poured into megachurches might have nourished schools, science, and public health. The halls of Congress might have been unmolested on January 6, 2021.

And maybe we'd come to see something even more profound: that we are all we have. We're not actors in a divine play. We're not the center of the universe. We are a fragile, thinking species adrift on what Carl Sagan called a "pale blue dot"—a lonely speck in a vast cosmic sea, with no one to rescue or condemn us but ourselves.

That realization doesn't diminish us. It elevates us. If there's no script handed down from the clouds, then we are the authors of our own meaning. We are free not to drift in chaos, but to rise with purpose. To build an ethic born not of fear, but of compassion.

As Christopher Hitchens put it, "Human decency is not derived from religion. It precedes it." And maybe that's the point. We don't need heaven to act with conviction, or hell to keep us in check. We just need each other, and the courage to choose what's right, even when no one's watching.

THE LONG ENDING

A SKEPTICAL RESPONSE TO 13 QUESTIONS

Question 1: Did Jesus exist?

It seems highly likely that Jesus was a real person, though the only contemporary references to him are in the Bible. To the broader Roman and Jewish world, he wasn't remarkable enough to be written about during his lifetime. But it seems implausible that his followers would invent him from whole cloth. If Jesus were fictional, why include awkward details like his baptism by John or his betrayal by Judas? Those elements feel like real-world messiness, not idealized myth. Most likely, Jesus was a charismatic Jewish end-times preacher who ran afoul of the Romans and was crucified, just like many other zealots of the time.

Question 2: Are there contradictions in the Bible?

Traditional Christian scholarship often sees the differences among the four Gospels not as contradictions, but as varied lenses through which to appreciate a multifaceted Messiah. As Bernhard Anderson (see For Further Reading) writes: "Each of the Gospel writers presents Jesus to us in his own characteristic way. The greatness of the person could not have been captured in one picture. So we have four portraits, each bringing out its own distinctive facts of the character of Jesus."

That's one way to look at it. Another is to wonder why an all-knowing God would rely on four conflicting accounts with diverging chronologies, incompatible genealogies, and theological agendas. In fact, there are hundreds of contradictions and errors, some amusing, like the differing accounts of how many donkeys Jesus rode into Jerusalem, and others significant. In Matthew, Jesus' family lived in Bethlehem; in Luke, they were from Nazareth. Did Jesus drive out the moneychangers at the start of his ministry (as in John) or at the end (as in the Synoptic Gospels)? Was the sermon

314

delivered on a mount (Matthew) or on a plain (Luke)? Are good works more valuable than faith (James) or is faith more important (Paul)? Is the Mosaic Law to be observed forever (Jesus) or was it temporary (Paul)?

Question 3: Was the Bible pro-slavery?

Yes. Numerous passages in both the Old and New Testaments condone slavery:

- **Exodus 21:2–6** – Hebrew slaves were to be freed after six years unless they chose to remain.
- **Leviticus 25:44–46** – Foreign slaves could be bought and inherited permanently as property.
- **Exodus 21:20–21** – Owners may strike slaves, and as long as they don't die within a day or two, no penalty applies.
- **Ephesians 6:5–8** – Slaves are instructed to obey their masters "as unto Christ."
- **Colossians 3:22** – Slaves are told to obey their masters sincerely.

Some apologists claim, with hazy evidence, that biblical slavery was gentler than slavery in the American South. In both cases, however, slaves were property, subject to sale, inheritance, and harsh punishment. If you take the Bible at face value, God clearly allows humans to own other humans.

Question 4: Isn't the Bible important to teach morality?

Many politicians say so, and there's an ongoing effort to place the Ten Commandments in taxpayer-funded schools. But are the Commandments really that impressive? Four of them are just about God: worship no other gods, don't make graven images, don't take the Lord's name in vain, keep the Sabbath. Five more are basic, universal values: honor your parents, don't murder, commit adultery, steal, or lie. The final one warns against coveting your neighbor's house, wife, servants, ox, or donkey—an odd blend of thought crime and livestock management. Couldn't we all come up with a better list if given ten minutes and a cup of coffee?

Today, slavery is outlawed. Adultery is frowned upon but not criminal. Women are free to marry whom they choose. Sexual assault is punishable by law. Homosexuality is not a crime. Witches are free to practice their (harmless) rites. We can wear polyester and eat shrimp without fear of divine wrath.

In short, modern morality has outpaced Bronze Age ethics. Religion often acts as dead weight on moral progress. Imagine how much further we'd be socially and scientifically without it. And don't underestimate the efforts of Bible literalists to drag us backwards. Do you think science would be objectively taught, LGBTQ+ rights upheld, or women treated equally if Christian nationalists ran the show?

Question 5: Was the Bible anti-gay?

Yes. Leviticus 18:22 says: "Thou shalt not lie with mankind, as with womankind: it is an abomination." Leviticus 20:13 doubles down, prescribing death for the offense. Curiously, lesbianism goes unmentioned, so if you're a female Biblical literalist, you might've found a loophole.

Jesus never directly addressed homosexuality, but he affirmed the law's continuing relevance. In Matthew 5:17–18, he says: "Do not think that I have come to abolish the Law or the Prophets, I am not come to destroy but to fulfill." In other words, we are stuck with Moses' Law forever.

Question 6: Was the Bible "pro-life"?

Modern Christianity is passionately anti-abortion, but the Bible barely mentions it. Indeed, it seems to recognize the difference between a fetus and a fully grown woman, and also to prescribe the administration of the procedure. The clearest reference is Numbers 5:11–31, where a jealous husband can bring his wife to a priest. The priest prepares a potion with holy water, dust, and inked curses, which the woman must drink. If she's guilty of adultery, it induces a miscarriage. If she's innocent, nothing happens. This is many things—bizarre, archaic, misogynistic—but "pro-life" it is not.

In Exodus 21:22–23 a situation is described where a pregnant woman is wounded by an attacker: "If men strive, and hurt a woman with child, so that her fruit depart from her, and yet no mischief follow: he shall be surely punished, according as the woman's husband will lay upon him; and he shall pay as the judges determine. And if any mischief follow, then thou shall give a life for a life." This seems to indicate that if only a fetus is injured or killed, the assailant is to pay a fine; it's only if the woman dies ("mischief follows") that her attacker will be guilty of a capital offense. And Jesus never said a word about abortion.

Question 7: Is the Bible sexist?

Yes. 1 Timothy 2:12 says, "I do not permit a woman to teach or to assume authority over a man; she must be quiet." 1 Corinthians 14:34–35 adds, "Women should remain silent in the churches...they must be in submission." In Genesis 3:16, God tells Eve, "Your desire will be for your husband, and he will rule over you."

Apologists often invoke cultural context, but it's hard to deny that the Bible embeds a profoundly patriarchal worldview. Yes, there are positive female figures like Deborah or Mary, but they are exceptions, not the rule.

Question 8: What is the Bible's Timeline?

The Bible blends myth and history. We know the Earth is about 4.5 billion years old—not 6,000—and that humans in modern form have existed for roughly 200,000 years. The early biblical stories—Creation, the Garden of Eden, Noah's Flood, and the Tower of Babel—are clearly mythological, with no support from archaeology, genetics, or geology. The Exodus story, central to Jewish tradition, likely didn't happen as described, if at all.

As we move into the era of judges and kings, the stories begin to resemble history—but even here, the Bible is not a reliable source. Many figures, like Moses or even Solomon, may be legendary or theological constructs rather than confirmed historical actors. Some events—like the destruction of the northern kingdom of Israel, the Babylonian conquest of Judah, or Cyrus the Great's decree—are historically verified, corroborated by external evidence like archaeological finds, inscriptions, or independent ancient records.

Here's a rough timeline, showing both the traditional biblical chronology and the current scholarly consensus as I understand it, and assembled from a range of sources listed in the "For Further Reading" section.

- **4000 BCE** – Creation, Garden of Eden, Fall of Man (mythical)
- **c. 4000–2000 BCE** – Cain and Abel, the Flood, Tower of Babel (mythical)
- **c. 2000–1500 BCE** – Patriarchs: Abraham, Isaac, Jacob, Joseph (legendary or semi-legendary)
- **c. 1500–1200 BCE** – Moses, Exodus, Red Sea, Ten Commandments (mythical or theological narrative)
- **c. 1200–1025 BCE** – Joshua's conquest, Judges era (legendary; archaeological support lacking)
- **c. 1025–1000 BCE** – Saul, Israel's first king (disputed; minimal evidence)
- **c. 1000–961 BCE** – David (possible historical core)
- **c. 961–922 BCE** – Solomon and the First Temple (temple likely existed; Solomon unverified)
- **922 BCE** – Kingdom splits into Israel (north) and Judah (south) (historically likely)
- **722 BCE** – Fall of Samaria: Assyria destroys Israel (historically verified)
- **701 BCE** – Assyrian siege of Jerusalem under Sennacherib (historically verified)

- **586 BCE** – Babylonian conquest of Jerusalem, destruction of First Temple, exile (historically verified)
- **539 BCE** – Cyrus the Great conquers Babylon; Jews allowed to return (historically verified)
- **516 BCE** – Second Temple completed in Jerusalem (historically verified)
- **332 BCE** – Alexander the Great conquers Judea (historically verified)
- **c. 323–167 BCE** – Hellenistic rule under the Ptolemies and Seleucids (historically verified)
- **167–160 BCE** – Maccabean Revolt against Seleucid Empire (historically verified)
- **140–63 BCE** – Hasmonean Kingdom: Independent Jewish state (historically verified)
- **63 BCE** – Roman general Pompey conquers Judea (historically verified)
- **c. 4 BCE** – Probable birth of Jesus (Herod the Great dies in 4 BCE) (historically plausible)
- **c. 28–33 CE** – Jesus' ministry, crucifixion, and claimed resurrection (ministry and crucifixion widely regarded as historically plausible; resurrection is theological)
- **35–65 CE** – Paul's missionary journeys and letters (historically plausible; letters are earliest Christian texts)
- **64–68 CE** – Execution of Paul under Nero (tradition; plausible but unconfirmed)
- **70 CE** – Destruction of the Second Temple during Jewish revolt (historically verified)
- **c. 65–75 CE** – *Gospel of Mark* written
- **c. 80–90 CE** – *Gospel of Matthew*
- **c. 85–95 CE** – *Gospel of Luke and Acts*
- **c. 90–110 CE** – *Gospel of John*
- **c. 95–100 CE** – *Book of Revelation,* other late epistles

Question 9: What does the Bible say about migrants?

A recurring theme is compassion for the outsider. The Israelites, having once been strangers in Egypt, are repeatedly told to treat foreigners with kindness. This likely arose from the practical concern that travelers in the desert may one day need help themselves.

It's hard to square this ethos with the contempt many modern Christians show toward migrants, especially those who come to work, pay taxes, serve in uniform, and support their families. A nation has every right to enforce its borders, but you shouldn't use the Bible to justify cruelty to migrants.

Question 10: Is God merciful and just?

It sure doesn't seem that way. God often incinerates or slaughters His own people for minor offenses. He punishes David's infant son and his wives for David's sins. If God is loving and omnipotent, why allow children to suffer from terminal diseases? If He can't prevent them, is He truly all-powerful? If He can but chooses not to, is He just?

Question 11: Can science and religion coexist?

Stephen Jay Gould proposed the idea of "non-overlapping magisteria." Science explains the natural world, while religion addresses morality and meaning. But religion has long made claims about how the world works, and science increasingly encroaches on religion's territory. Before the Enlightenment, religious explanations dominated science, history, and ethics. As science advanced, religion has retreated to ever-smaller islands of relevance.

Question 12: Wasn't Bible prophecy fulfilled?

Only when the "prophecy" came after the fact. Daniel describes a goat coming from the West, a clear reference to Alexander the Great. But Daniel was likely written after Alexander's conquest. It's prophecy in hindsight.

The Gospels say the Son of Man would return before the disciples died. He didn't. Writers of the New Testament cherry-picked earlier scriptures to make Jesus seem like a fulfillment of prophecy. For example, Zechariah 9:9 says: "Your king is approaching…humble and riding on a donkey." But the larger passage describes a king bringing political peace and ruling from sea to sea. That didn't happen. Some apologists argue this is "dual prophecy," with hidden, layered meanings. But who decides what the hidden meanings are?

Question 13: What are the Apocrypha, and why don't you cover them in this book?

The Apocrypha are ancient Jewish writings found in the Greek Septuagint and Latin Vulgate, but not in the Hebrew Masoretic Text. These include Tobit, Judith, Wisdom of Solomon, Sirach, and 1 & 2 Maccabees. Catholics and Eastern Orthodox Christians include them in the Bible. Protestants generally don't. During the Reformation, they were rejected because they weren't part of the original Hebrew texts and contained doctrines like purgatory and prayers for the dead. I am limiting my review to the books of the Protestant Bible but might address the Apocrypha separately.

QUOTES

Religion and the Bible

"Religion is regarded by the common people as true, by the wise as false, and by rulers as useful." – Seneca the Younger

"Religion has actually convinced people that there's an invisible man living in the sky." – George Carlin

"Properly read, the Bible is the most potent force for atheism ever conceived." – Isaac Asimov

"Religions are all alike, founded upon fables and mythologies." – Thomas Jefferson

"The God of the Old Testament is arguably the most unpleasant character in all fiction." – Richard Dawkins

"This is the true horror of religion. It allows perfectly decent and sane people to believe by the billions what only lunatics could believe on their own." – Sam Harris

"Religion is such a great thing...it keeps, you know, there's something to be good about. You want to be good; you wanna, it's so important...you want to go to heaven. So, if we don't have heaven, okay, you almost say, 'What's the reason? Why do I have to be good? What difference does it make?" – President Donald J. Trump

"The great unmentionable evil at the center of our culture is monotheism." – Gore Vidal

Reason vs. Faith

"The way to see by Faith is to shut the Eye of Reason." – Benjamin Franklin

"What can be asserted without evidence can be dismissed without evidence." – Christopher Hitchens

"Just because you believe in something does not mean that it is true." – Albert Einstein

"Our ignorance is God; what we know is science." – Edward Gibbon

"While believing strongly, without evidence, is considered a mark of madness or stupidity in any other area of our lives, faith in God still holds immense prestige." – Sam Harris

"Science is not only compatible with spirituality; it is a profound source of spirituality." – Carl Sagan

"The world plainly resembles more an animal or a vegetable than it does a watch or a knitting loom." – David Hume

"The old argument from design in nature...fails now that the law of natural selection has been discovered." – Charles Darwin

"The greatest enemy of knowledge is not ignorance; it is the illusion of knowledge." – Stephen Hawking

"Question with boldness even the existence of a God; because, if there be one, he must more approve of the homage of reason than that of blindfolded fear." – Thomas Jefferson, Letter to Peter Carr

"Give a man a fish and he will eat for a day; teach a man to fish and he will eat for a lifetime; give a man religion and he will die praying for a fish." – Benjamin Disraeli (attributed)

Morality, Human Nature, and Truth

"The so-called Golden Rule is innate in us, or is innate except in the sociopaths who do not care about others, and the psychopaths who take pleasure from cruelty." – Christopher Hitchens

"Is God willing to prevent evil, but not able? Then he is not omnipotent. Is he able, but not willing? Then he is malevolent." – Epicurus

"There is something infantile in the presumption that somebody else has a responsibility to give your life meaning." – Richard Dawkins

"If you can dodge a wrench, you can dodge a ball." – Patches O'Houlihan

Profit, Politics, and Prophecy

"Religion is what keeps the poor from murdering the rich." – Napoleon Bonaparte

"I am a billionaire, because the assignment that the Lord gave me, He said: 'I want you to begin to confess the billion flow.'" – Kenneth Copeland

"Jesus bled and died for us so that we can lay claim to the promise of financial prosperity." – Creflo Dollar

"Again I tell you, it is easier for a camel to go through the eye of a needle than for someone who is rich to enter the kingdom of God." – Matthew 19:24

"First of all, I want to say without question, Trump is going to win the [2020] election." – Pat Robertson

"Watch out for false prophets. They come to you in sheep's clothing, but inwardly they are ferocious wolves." – Matthew 7:15

"A tyrant must put on the appearance of uncommon devotion to religion." – Plato

"With or without religion, good people can behave well and bad people can do evil; but for good people to do evil—that takes religion." – Steven Weinberg

"We must question the story logic of having an all-knowing all-powerful God, who creates faulty Humans, and then blames them for his own mistakes." – Gene Roddenberry

"If God has spoken, why is the world not convinced?" – Percy Bysshe Shelley

"Just in terms of allocation of time resources, religion is not very efficient. There's a lot more I could be doing on a Sunday morning." – Bill Gates

FOR FURTHER READING

Alexander, David, and Pat Alexander, eds. *Eerdmans' Handbook to the Bible*. Grand Rapids, MI: Eerdmans, 1973.

Anderson, Bernhard W. *Understanding the Old Testament*. 4th ed. Englewood Cliffs, NJ: Prentice Hall, 1993.

Armstrong, Karen. *The Bible: A Biography*. New York: Atlantic Monthly Press, 2007.

Armstrong, Karen. *A History of God: The 4,000 Year Quest of Judaism, Christianity, and Islam*. New York: Ballantine Books, 1993.

Brown, Harold O. J. *Heresies: Heresy and Orthodoxy in the History of the Church*. Peabody, MA: Hendrickson Publishers, 1988.

Bruce, F. F. *Paul: Apostle of the Heart Set Free*. Grand Rapids, MI: William B. Eerdmans Publishing, 1977.

Chadwick, Owen. *A History of Christianity*. New York: St. Martin's Press, 1995.

Craig, William Lane. *Reasonable Faith*. YouTube channel. https://www.youtube.com/user/ReasonableFaithOrg.

Deconstruction Zone. YouTube channel. https://www.youtube.com/@Deconstruction_Zone.

Ehrman, Bart D. *Jesus: Apocalyptic Prophet of the New Millennium*. Oxford: Oxford University Press, 1999.

Ehrman, Bart D. *Jesus, Interrupted: Revealing the Hidden Contradictions in the Bible (And Why We Don't Know About Them)*. New York: Harper One, 2009.

Ehrman, Bart D. *The Triumph of Christianity: How a Forbidden Religion Swept the World.* New York: Simon & Schuster, 2018.

Gorelik, Amos. "The Exodus: Does Archaeology Have a Say?" *The Jerusalem Post*, April 14, 2014. https://www.jpost.com/opinion/op-ed-contributors/the-exodus-does-archaeology-have-a-say-348464.

Grimal, Nicholas. *A History of Ancient Egypt.* Oxford: Blackwell, 1988.

Hitchens, Christopher, ed. *The Portable Atheist: Essential Readings for the Nonbeliever.* New York: Hachette Books, 2007.

Josephus, Flavius. *The Complete Works of Josephus.* Grand Rapids, MI: Kregel Publications, 1960.

Maccoby, Hyam. *The Mythmaker: Paul and the Invention of Christianity.* New York: Harper & Row, 1986.

The New Jerusalem Bible. New York: Doubleday, 1985.

Pagels, Elaine. *The Gnostic Gospels.* New York: Random House, 1979.

Perrin, Andrew B., Loren T. Stuckenbruck, Shelby Bennett, and Matthew Hama. *Four Kingdom Motifs before and beyond the Book of Daniel.* Brill, 2021.

Redford, Donald B. *Egypt, Canaan, and Israel in Ancient Times.* Princeton, NJ: Princeton University Press, 1992.

Romm, James, ed. *The Landmark Arrian: The Campaigns of Alexander.* New York: Anchor Books, 2012.

About the Author

James Clark is a military veteran, historian, and former financial executive who brings a lifelong curiosity and sharp analytical lens to questions of belief, culture, and the human condition.

He writes from his home in Northern Virginia, where he lives with Melanie, the love of his life, and their spirited border collie, Nina. Before serving in the U.S. Army, he studied at Indiana University, later earning graduate degrees in Business from Johns Hopkins University and in History from California State University, Fullerton.

Oh, God! My Skeptical Journey Through the Bible is a thoughtful and personal contribution to the ongoing human dialogue about belief, values, and meaning. At its heart is a book-by-book journey through the Bible, approached with skeptical curiosity and measured irreverence that never loses sight of the text's enduring influence.

www.ingramcontent.com/pod-product-compliance
Lightning Source LLC
Chambersburg PA
CBHW060125130626
46556CB00006B/2237